Managing Electronic Records 4th Edition

WILLIAM SAFFADY, PH.D.

ARMA International
Lenexa, Kansas

NEAL–SCHUMAN PUBLISHERS, INC.
New York, London

 An ARMA International Publication

Consulting Editor: Mary L. Ginn, Ph.D.
Composition: Gray Design
Cover Art: Cole Design & Production

Published by

ARMA International
13725 West 109th Street, Suite 101
Lenexa, KS 66215
913.341.3808

Neal-Schuman Publishers, Inc.
100 William St., Suite 2004
New York, NY 10038
212.925.8650

Printed and bound in the United States of America by Lightning Source.

2nd printing, 2012.

The paper used in this publication meets the minimum requirements of American National Standard for Information Sciences–Permanence of Paper for Printed Library Materials, ANSIZ39.48-1992.

ISBN: 978-1-55570-686-9

Contents

Introduction to the Fourth Edition

The amount and variety of recorded information created and maintained in electronic formats has increased dramatically over the past quarter century, and significant continued growth can be expected. Such was the case in 1992, when the first edition of *Managing Electronic Records* was published, and it remains the case today. Given the already widespread and rapidly expanding use of computers, audio recorders, video systems, and other information processing devices, the proliferation of electronic records can only intensify. Historically, records managers in government agencies, corporations, and other organizations directed the majority of their professional efforts toward control of paper documents. Since the late 1980s, however, pressure to address records management problems associated with electronically stored information has been growing. A number of organizations have initiated systematic programs for the storage, retrieval, and control of electronic records. Others can be expected to do so as the growing accumulation of such records demand active professional management. Many records managers view problems posed by electronic records as the most important challenge facing our profession.

The fourth edition of *Managing Electronic Records* provides a comprehensive discussion of records management concepts and methods as they apply to electronic records—that is, to records that contain machine-readable as opposed to human-readable information. It is intended for professional records managers, computer systems professionals, office systems analysts, archivists, administrative system specialists, data center managers, librarians, and others responsible for the creation, maintenance, management, control, and use of electronic records created by computer, audio, and video systems. The treatment is practical rather than theoretical. On completion of this book, the reader should understand:

- The special records management issues and problems associated with electronic records
- The physical and application characteristics of electronic records encountered in offices and other work environments

- Principles and procedures for inventorying electronic records and for determining how long they need to be retained to satisfy legal and operational requirements
- Factors that influence the stability and durability of electronic records
- Methods of protecting vital electronic records against damage and destruction
- Guidelines for the daily management of electronic records as working information resources

Like its predecessors, this edition is organized into seven chapters:

- Chapter 1 defines electronic records and discusses their importance in present and future information systems, their relationship to conventional records, and special issues and concerns associated with their management.
- Chapter 2 presents a detailed survey of the physical and application characteristics of electronic storage media employed by computer, audio, and video systems. It emphasizes magnetic and optical storage media, but it also includes descriptions of solid-state storage as well as obsolete media that may be encountered when inventorying electronic records.
- Chapter 3 discusses file format concepts that records managers must understand in order to effectively deal with computer-processable information. It also includes a discussion of video and audio recording formats.
- Chapters 4 and 5 address the critical issues of inventorying electronic records and preparing retention schedules based on an inventory's findings.
- Chapter 6 discusses vital electronic records.
- Chapter 7 presents guidelines for the storage, care, handling, and labeling of electronic media. It also discusses the role of content management and records management application (RMA) software in organizing, storing, controlling access to, and otherwise managing electronic records.

The first two editions of this book provided a list of books, articles, and other publications for additional reading on specific topics, but those bibliographies were necessarily incomplete and quickly became out of date. Retaining a practice adopted for the third edition, *Appendix A* gives some suggestions for finding additional information about electronic records. Because terminology plays an important role in understanding electronic recordkeeping and communicating records management concepts and requirements to information technology professionals, *Appendix B* provides brief definitions of selected terms and acronyms discussed in the text. Some terms, such as "record" and "archival" are used differently by records managers and information technology specialists. In such situations, this book employs the records management definition. When specific terms are used at meetings or in other situations, definitions should be clarified at the outset to avoid misunderstandings and confusion.

Chapter 1

Concepts and Issues

As their defining characteristic, **electronic records** contain **machine-readable**, as opposed to human-readable, information. Electronic records may contain any type of information. The possibilities include, but are not necessarily limited to, quantitative data of the type contained in databases and spreadsheet files; character-coded text of the type contained in word processing files and e-mail messages; images, including electronic document images as well as video images and computer-generated graphics; and sound, including voice and music recordings. Regardless of content, information contained in electronic records originates as an electronic signal, hence the name. Further, the information is electronically encoded for storage and processing by computers, video devices, audio equipment, or other machines described in this chapter. Coding methods vary. Electronic records created by computers and computer-like devices usually contain digitally-coded information. Video and audio devices have historically relied on **analog coding** methods, although systems that record digitally-encoded video images and audio signals are increasingly available and may ultimately supplant their analog counterparts.[1]

Whenever a coding scheme is employed, electronic records can only be read (retrieved) or otherwise processed by designated machines; for computer records, software is required as well. By contrast, office documents, engineering drawings, and other paper records contain human-readable information; no special equipment or software is required to access such information. Microfilm records likewise contain human-readable information. Although microfilm images are highly miniaturized, their contents are not machine-encoded. Information contained in microfilm images may not be eye-legible, but it is nonetheless human-readable. Once magnified, microfilmed documents require no decoding for reading or printing.

For purposes of this discussion, electronic records, as previously defined, should be distinguished from human-readable paper documents or computer-output-microfilm (COM) images generated from electronic sources. Thus, a business letter created with a word processing program and stored as a computer file is an electronic record; a printed copy of that letter is not. Similarly, a database that contains information about customer orders is an electronic record; a computer-generated list of customer orders printed on paper or microfiche is not. Electronic messages created or received with e-mail programs are electronic records; printed copies of those messages are not. By the same definition, faxes are not considered electronic records unless they are stored electronically rather than printed upon receipt.

Computers of all types and sizes are the most important devices that create, store, and process electronic records, but such records may be produced and maintained by other machines as well. Examples include scientific and medical instruments employed in diagnostic imaging, process engineering, seismology, environmental monitoring, remote sensing, and other applications; flight data recorders, event data recorders, and other unattended data logging equipment; video tape machines and other video recording and playback devices; and voice dictation equipment, telephone answering machines, and other audio recorders.

Electronic records have also been generated by special-purpose business machines that are no longer available. Examples include the electromechanical accounting equipment that automated financial applications during the 1960s and early 1970s, dedicated word processors that were widely utilized in office applications from the late 1960s through the early 1980s, and TWX and telex terminals, which were used through the 1980s for electronic message transmission. Although computer systems have rendered such devices obsolete, electronic records created by them in the past continue to be stored by many businesses, government agencies, and other organizations. Like their newer counterparts, such obsolete electronic records require records management attention if only to ensure that they are evaluated and discarded in a systematic manner.

As discussed more fully in Chapter 2, electronic records may be stored on a variety of media. Magnetic disks and tapes have dominated computer, video, and audio recording since the 1950s. Optical media, which use lasers to record and retrieve information, were introduced in the 1980s. With their high recording densities, they are particularly useful for electronic document imaging, digital video recording, multimedia presentations, and other applications that involve large quantities of machine-readable information. Solid-state storage components, including flash memory cards and USB drives, provide convenient portability for relatively modest quantities of electronic records.

Punched cards and punched paper tapes are the best-known examples of paper-based electronic records. They were utilized widely during the 1950s and 1960s by computer systems and certain pre-computer products, such as tabulating machines, but they are now obsolete media. Occasional attempts to revive the use of paper for machine-readable information have not been successful. Microfilm, which provides compact, stable storage for human-readable document images and computer-generated reports, can also store machine-readable information, but it has never been widely accepted for that purpose. No providers of that type of microfilm were commercially available at the time of the writing of this book. Other forms of electronic records, encountered principally in consumer rather than business applications, include vinyl phonograph records, which have been supplanted by newer technologies, and nonoptical videodisks, which were marketed during the 1980s but are no longer available.

Growth of Electronic Records

Paper has been the most widely utilized recordkeeping medium for centuries. In some work environments paper documents remain the dominant record format in quantity, if not in importance.[2] Given the huge accumulations of older paper records in offices and offsite storage locations, electronic records may not outnumber them for decades. Although computer applications have significantly reduced the creation of certain types of paper records—carbon-interleaved business forms are an obvious example—most industry analysts agree that computerization has actually increased paper, given the high percentage of electronic records that are printed for filing or to produce reference copies. Word processing documents are often printed, for example, as are many e-mail messages, Web pages, spreadsheets, and graphic images. Most databases are principally intended for online access to information, but some database applications generate printed reports or other documents.

A 1999 technology forecast by Price Waterhouse Coopers found that paper consumption increases by 40 percent when an office implements the use of e-mail. Pitney Bowes reported a surge in office printing with a rise of 56 percent between 1996 and 2003 in the five largest international economies. A 2005 report commissioned by the International Union of Forest Research Organizations (IUFRO) concluded that information technology poses a threat to the paper industry. However, it noted that the newsprint sector, which suffers from the immediate availability of online news, has been most deeply affected, while worldwide demand for business papers remains stable.

Nonetheless, e-mail, word processing, and other computer applications have had some impact on the creation and filing of letters, forms, and other paper records. Based on a survey of expert opinions, Pira International, a leading provider of information and research about paper and packaging, listed computer applications among technologies that have a disruptive impact on the paper industry, especially in the United States. According to Research Information Systems Incorporated (RISI), a company that monitors the pulp and paper industry, U.S. sales of business papers per white-collar employee are declining for the first time in history. North American demand for uncoated free-sheet paper, the type used for business records, fell from 15.8 million tons in 1999 to 14.2 million tons in 2004, and a significant risk of further long-term decline exists.[3]

> *For most organizations, electronic records are indispensable information resources for daily operations, as well as long-term planning and decision-making.*

Since the 1970s, computer, video, and audio records created and maintained by corporations, government agencies, and other organizations have increased dramatically in both quantity and importance. In some work environments, these electronic records outnumber paper documents for newly created information. Their business value has similarly increased. For most organizations, electronic records are indispensable information resources for daily operations, as well as long-term planning and decision-making. The growing quantity of electronic records is largely attributable to the proliferation of information processing equipment and software capable of producing such records, which is obviously the case with computer-generated records. Over the past three decades, the number of installed computers of all types and sizes has increased significantly.

The impending demise of mainframe (enterprise-scale) computers has been predicted for more than a decade. However, the number of mainframe computer installations worldwide is variously estimated at 10,000 to upwards of 35,000. The low estimate is limited to IBM zSeries mainframe installations, while the larger number includes legacy mainframes no longer manufactured but remain in use. Mainframes remain the dominant computing devices for many financial and transaction processing applications, some of which date from the 1960s and 1970s. Rather than replacing these mainframe-based legacy programs, many Y2K initiatives repaired and enhanced them, thereby extending their life spans. Some industry analysts estimate that, in large corporations and government agencies, as much as 75 percent of mission-critical electronic information resides on mainframe computers. In recent years, mainframe installations have benefited from a combination of innovative technology, falling hardware prices, lower operating costs, compatibility with popular operating systems, improved networking functionality, and new record-keeping applications, such as **data warehousing** and electronic commerce, that require mainframe-class processing power, reliability, and storage capacity.

In multinational corporations, federal and state government agencies, research universities, and other large organizations, mainframe computers have historically operated as centralized, enterprise-wide information processing resources. That approach to computing dates from the inception of business data processing and was well established by the late 1960s. During the 1970s, however, many mainframe users began complaining about the difficulties of dealing with seemingly unresponsive computer center personnel. They wanted more direct control over computer resources that had become increasingly indispensable to their business operations. Responding to this need, hardware manufacturers introduced smaller computers for departmental installations. Such smaller devices, so-called minicomputers, had been utilized in specialized aerospace and industrial applications since the late 1950s. In the early 1970s, many organizations began using minicomputers to decentralize, or distribute, their computing resources and electronic records. Distributed processing concepts gained popularity quickly. According to a report by the Business Equipment Manufacturers Association cited in the April 1991 issue of *Appliance* magazine, U.S. minicomputer shipments increased from less than 17,000 units per year in the mid-1970s to more than 150,000 units per year by 1990.

Today, minicomputers—now known as *midrange computers*—are installed at millions of sites. IBM has reportedly installed nearly one million iSeries computers and their predecessors, the popular AS/400 processors. Over 3.5 million Unix-based computers, many of them midrange processors, are installed worldwide. This estimate includes 1.75 installations of Sun Microsystems' Solaris version of Unix, many of them implemented on Sun's SPARC servers; one million installations of the AIX operating system running on IBM System p computers or their popular predecessor, the RS/6000; and 500,000 installations of Hewlett-Packard's HP-UX operating system, which runs on HP 9000 processors. Even discontinued midrange computers remain widely installed. As late as 2004, Gartner Group estimated that 400,000 OpenVMS midrange computers remained in use worldwide. Originally developed by Digital Equipment Corporation, OpenVMS processors are now owned by Hewlett-Packard, which no longer accepts orders for new models.

In many medium-size businesses, government agencies, schools, colleges, and other organizations, midrange computers are implemented as enterprise-wide information processing devices. In effect, they function as mainframes for organizations that cannot afford or do not need larger computers. In large corporations and government agencies, however, midrange computers and their associated electronic records are typically decentralized at the department or division level, where they serve multiple users connected by online terminals. In such cases, midrange computers supplement or complement, rather than replace, mainframe installations. They provide another layer of computing and electronic recordkeeping capability in closer physical and organizational proximity to end-users.

The introduction of business-oriented personal computers (PCs) in the mid-1970s, and their rapid and dramatic refinement during the 1980s and 1990s, permitted a further decentralization of computing power at the office or desk level. As cited in the April 17, 2000 issue of *Newsweek*, annual shipments of PCs in the United States increased from 9 million units in 1990 to 43 million units by 1999. The *Computer Industry Almanac* estimated that 600 million personal computers were installed worldwide in 2001. According to the same source, nearly one billion personal computers were in use worldwide at the end of 2006. The United States accounted for 24 percent of that total, followed by Japan, China, Germany, the United Kingdom, France, and South Korea, each of which have at least 30 million PCs installed. According to the US Microcomputer Statistics Committee, a consortium of personal computer vendors, over five million new PCs are purchased monthly in the U.S. alone. Various sources estimate that worldwide shipments of PCs now exceed 250 million units per year, including both office and home installations of desktop and notebook models. This estimate excludes personal digital assistants (PDAs), Web-enabled cell phones, set-top boxes for televisions, and other computer-related information appliances.

Since the mid-1980s, local area networks of increasing size and complexity have been implemented in organizations of all types and sizes. Since the 1990s, the Internet has provided convenient wide-area network linkages of unlimited geographic span. According to www.internetworldstats.com, a Web site that provides Internet usage data for over 230 countries, the Internet had 1.3 billion users, about 20 percent of the world's population, in 2008. In North America, over 70 percent of the population has Internet access. With the advent of client/server technology and concepts, a growing number of information processing applications have moved to networked PCs and servers as an alternative to historically-dominant timeshared installations of centralized mainframes and midrange computers. According to market-research firm IDC, over eight million network servers were shipped in 2007. Installations of data storage peripherals and media, which provide the space necessary to accommodate electronic records, have likewise increased dramatically. Hewlett-Packard alone sold its customers more than 1,200 terabytes (1.2 million gigabytes) of hard disk storage in 2007. According to the Japan Recording Media Industries Association, over 14 billion non-erasable compact discs (CDs) and DVDs were shipped in 2007.

Comparably impressive increases can be cited for computer software and services that generate electronic records. Corporations, government agencies, and other organizations have purchased hundreds of millions of copies of office suites that include word processing, spreadsheet, and database management components. Reports by the Radicati Group, a technology market research firm, estimated 1.2 billion e-mail users worldwide in 2007 and that 183 billion e-mail messages were sent each day in 2006. According to Ferris Research, 780 million business computer users worldwide were using e-mail in 2007, and they sent over 25 billion nonspam e-mail messages in 2006.

By confirming the dramatic proliferation of technology that generates computer-processable information, the statistics cited previously support the business case for systematic management of electronic records; but like many business statistics, they quantify the obvious. Anyone who works in a business, government agency, or other organization knows that computer technology is pervasive and essential as indicated in Figure 1.1.

Dramatic usage growth can also be cited for installations of video equipment, audio recorders, scientific and medical instrumentation, and other machines that create electronic records. The availability, variety, and functionality of video recording devices, for example, have increased dramatically since the early 1980s.

Changes Caused by Technology

Figure 1.1

Work Environment Changes Resulting from Advances in Technology

- **Personal Computers.** Computers outnumber employees in many organizations. Personal computers are commonly seen installed in empty offices formerly occupied by retrenched or retired employees.
- **Software.** Most office documents are produced by word processing software. Conventional typewriters, where they remain in use at all, are reserved for special tasks such as completing business forms or addressing envelopes.
- **Desktop publishing.** Desktop publishing products permit in-house production of newsletters and other highly formatted documents that formerly required professional typesetting and printing services.
- **Financial software.** Accounting, payroll, and other financial applications have been computerized for decades. Even the smallest businesses and government agencies have abandoned manual bookkeeping.
- **Calculators.** Four-function calculators are commonplace, but programmable scientific and business models have been largely supplanted by spreadsheet programs and software for statistical analysis.
- **Databases, document imaging, and content management software.** Significant information is extracted from paper records for entry into computer databases, while document imaging systems and content management software maintain computer-processable file copies.
- **Electronic mail.** A substantial and growing part of each workday is spent reading e-mail.
- **Intranets.** Web pages on corporate intranets are replacing printed forms and procedure manuals.

Businesses, government agencies, and other organizations increasingly use video technology to create visual records of building inspections, laboratory experiments, meetings and conferences, and other activities where full-motion images are required to capture valuable information or occurrences. Video tape recorders, particularly videocassette recorders, are commonplace information storage devices. Video cameras, once encountered only in sophisticated television studios, are compact, easy to operate, and inexpensive. Video recording is routinely used for building surveillance.

The use of word processing software by managerial and professional employees, combined with reorganization of the administrative workforce, has decreased the use of voice dictation equipment. However, voice mail systems and telephone answering machines are widely installed into organizations of all types and sizes. In medical specialties, such as radiology and cardiology, CT scanners, MRI devices, PET scanners, and other computer-controlled instruments that generate electronic records have steadily replaced nondigital diagnostic equipment and methods.

Importance of Electronic Records

In addition to being numerous, electronic records are important information resources, principally because many of them support mission-critical business operations. Corporations, government agencies, and other organizations rely on computers and other electronic technologies to automate their most important activities and store their most valuable information. Since the 1960s, the most significant information has received the highest priority for computerization as organizations seek timely transaction processing, retrieval speed, remote accessibility, and other advantages of automated systems. Reflecting the perceived importance of computer-based information processing, most organizations devote far more personnel and economic resources to the creation and maintenance of electronic records than they do to human-readable paper and microfilm records. Information technology departments are well staffed. By contrast, file rooms, records centers, and microfilming operations are often understaffed, while office filing is usually done by administrative personnel who have many other responsibilities. The U.S. Bureau of Labor Statistics, *Occupational Outlook Handbook, 2008-09 Edition* predicts that employment of file clerks will decline by 41 percent between 2006 and 2016. During the same period, openings for computer support specialists who provide technical assistance to computer users are expected to increase by 13 percent.

As previously noted, financial records have been widely computerized for decades. Accounting and payroll were among the first business operations to be automated. Electronic recordkeeping systems are likewise widely implemented for order fulfillment, invoicing, purchasing, insurance claims payment, loans and investment accounts management, and other transaction processing applications. Personnel records, which contain information about an organization's human resources, are similarly computerized, as are inventory management and property records that contain information about physical assets. Electronic records are also widely utilized to store critical information associated with specific industries or business activities. Examples include experimental and test data maintained by research laboratories, student records maintained by schools and colleges, quality control records maintained by manufacturing facilities, patient records maintained by hospitals and medical clinics, property records maintained by local governments, and drawings, site plans, and other records pertaining to architectural and construction projects.

During the 1960s and 1970s, computerized information systems often stored small amounts of data extracted from source documents for specific purposes such as the preparation of invoices or the posting of credits or debits to specific accounts. Rather than being rendered superfluous by such automated recordkeeping systems, source documents typically retained their utility for reference operations. In many cases, they contained information not included in automated records. Since the early 1980s, however, the breadth and depth of computerized recordkeeping have expanded significantly. Although electronic records may not contain all details from source documents, they are the often first choice for fast, reliable access to essential information about specific matters. Information in a purchasing database, for example, is sufficiently detailed to answer many questions about the terms, conditions, and status of a given procurement transaction. A purchasing file may contain copies of signed purchase orders, technical specifications, competitive solicitations, vendor proposals, product information sheets, and other records, but these documents are only relevant for a subset of information inquiries. Similarly, the information in a human resources database can answer many questions about a given employee's current and previous job titles, salary history, educational background, work performance, and benefits, thereby minimizing the need to consult documents in a personnel file.

Computer-based electronic records often contain more complete information and provide greater functionality than printed copies produced from them. Computer printouts provide a necessarily static and limited view of database records. Online examination of a database may provide additional or more up-to-date information as well as more flexible retrieval functionality. Word processing files may include drafts, backup copies, or alternate versions of documents that are never printed. In some applications, such as the preparation of legal contracts, printed documents may be assembled from prewritten paragraphs stored in multiple word processing files.

Information extracted from source documents may be subject to calculations or other computer processing that generates new content for inclusion in databases, spreadsheet files, or other electronic records. With the proliferation of online information systems and centralized databases accessible from desktop workstations, electronic records increasingly contain unique information that was captured in machine-readable form at its source. Such information may never have existed in paper form, and much of it will never be printed. Web pages, for example, may contain information extracted from paper documents, but their distinctive formats have no printed counterparts. **Electronic data interchange (EDI)** and other electronic commerce initiatives minimize paper records by transmitting computer-processible purchase orders, invoices, and other transaction-oriented information between organizations. E-government initiatives permit online submission of tax returns, building permit applications, zoning variance requests, and other documents that previously required paper forms. Some scientists record results, observations, and other information pertaining to experimental research in electronic laboratory note-books. Such research increasingly relies on machine-readable data generated by scientific or medical instruments. With video recordings, individual visual images can be printed, but the resulting paper copies are often inadequate substitutes for information contained in full-motion recordings. Many voice recordings will never be transcribed due to time and labor constraints. Where audio recordings contain non-verbal information, such as music, transcription is impossible.

Issues and Concerns

As outlined in the preceding section, electronic records—and the technologies that create and maintain them—are increasingly numerous and important information resources in businesses, government agencies, and other organizations. Although designed to address one or more problems encountered in specific information processing applications, electronic records can themselves pose problems that complicate their effective management. These problems are surveyed briefly in this section and examined more fully in subsequent chapters. The problems are not new or unique to this book. The issues and concerns discussed here are widely acknowledged by records managers, as well as by computer systems analysts, office automation specialists, archivists, and others responsible for processing, storing, retrieving, safeguarding or otherwise dealing with electronic records. In particular, significant differences between electronic and nonelectronic records necessitate the modification of certain well-established records management methodologies, many of which were developed for paper-based recordkeeping systems prior to the widespread implementation of computers and other electronic technologies.

Inadequate Controls

Through the mid-1970s, direct access to information processing technology was typically limited to a relatively small percentage of an organization's employees. Many computer applications were implemented in the batch-processing mode, and their operation was closely monitored by well-staffed data processing centers, which assumed full responsibility for program implementation and execution. Computer software was usually custom-developed for specific applications by in-house personnel or contract programmers, a laborious process that greatly increased the implementation time for computer applications and limited the progress of automation. Prewritten software and tools for rapid application development were seldom encountered before the 1980s. Prior to that time, few employees had direct interaction with computing devices.

Timeshared computing was possible in the 1960s, but online terminals were not widely installed in businesses, government agencies, or other organizations until the

1970s. Through the late 1970s, the low capacities of hard drives limited online access to small quantities of computer-processible information. Data communication occurred at such low speeds that remote data entry, interactive information retrieval, file exchanges, and other communication-intensive operations took impracticably long amounts of time to complete. Business-oriented desktop computers had not been developed. The IBM Personal Computer was introduced in 1981, and a version with a hard drive was not available until 1983. In the 1960s and early 1970s, electronic mail systems and local area networks were limited to experimental prototypes. Word processing relied on cumbersome and expensive typewriter-like devices. Document scanners, optical disk drives, and other components of desktop publishing and electronic document imaging systems did not exist. Apart from voice dictation equipment, which was introduced by Thomas Edison in the late nineteenth century, audio and video recording devices were largely relegated to professional applications in studio installations.

> *As with paper and photographic records, an enterprise-wide records management program must assert its authority over, and responsibility for, all electronic media, regardless of their location within the organization.*

Today, of course, much different conditions prevail. Computers and other information processing technologies are considered indispensable, productivity-enhancing tools to be made available to the broadest spectrum of the work force. Many employees have direct, hands-on involvement with information processing hardware and software, but few organizations have implemented formalized controls for the creation, storage, retention, and other management of electronic records associated with such devices. As with paper and photographic records, an enterprise-wide records management program must assert its authority over, and responsibility for, all electronic media, regardless of their location within the organization. In the absence of formalized procedures, end-user computing operations are often performed in a highly discretionary manner. Individual users determine the types of electronic recording media to be employed in specific situations, the names to be used for computer files, backup procedures to be implemented for valuable information, criteria and methods for deleting obsolete records, and other routinely encountered aspects of creating and maintaining electronic records. Many computer users view the electronic records they create and maintain as "personal" files to be stored, discarded, or otherwise managed as they see fit, without regard to broader organizational needs or the relationship of electronic records to reports or other paper documents produced from them.

Information Redundancy

A comparison of electronic and nonelectronic records maintained by a given organization typically reveals considerable redundancy of information in machine-readable and human-readable formats. Many paper documents are produced by word processing software, database management systems, and other computer programs. Such paper records are created from computer-stored information, which they partially or fully replicate. In a word processing installation, for example, a managerial or professional employee may use voice dictation equipment to create an audio recording of a document for subsequent transcription. An administrative employee, using a word processing program, creates a machine-readable version of the document, which is stored in a computer file on a hard drive or some other medium. A paper copy may then be printed for review and mark-up by the document's originator. If revisions are required, the word processing file is retrieved and edited. The new electronic version may replace the old one. Alternatively, it may be stored as a separate computer file, thus permitting a return to the original version at a later time if required. In any case, the revised document will be printed for review and possible further changes. This cycle of revision, recording, and printing is repeated until a satisfactory final version is obtained, at which time the document will exist in multiple versions of varying content and completeness: an audio recording, one or more computer files, and one or more printed copies. As additional complications, backup copies may also be produced of the various computer files, and one or more of the printed copies may subsequently be photocopied, microfilmed, or even scanned.

In some circumstances, such redundancy is both necessary and useful. Different versions of electronic documents and their paper counterparts may need to be retained until the final versions are prepared. The various versions reflect a document's developmental history, but redundant recordkeeping poses both obvious and subtle problems for information management. The former include the increased space consumption—file cabinet and floor space for human-readable records and media space for electronic records—associated with duplicate information; the difficulty of controlling the multiple human-readable and electronic versions of information and of identifying the version required for a given purpose; and the need to establish and coordinate retention periods for all versions.

Other implications of records redundancy are easily overlooked but no less significant. In many countries, for example, electronic records—like their paper and microfilm counterparts—are routinely subject to discovery orders associated with court trials and other legal proceedings. Such discovery orders give the opposing party in a legal action the opportunity to inspect documents or other information pertinent to a given matter. If a business, government agency, or other organization possesses the information in question, it must disclose it. An organization may take great pains to discard specific paper and microfilm records in a timely manner in order to reduce its exposure to discovery actions, only to have the undiscarded electronic counterparts of those records—word processing versions of documents, for example—be subject to subpoena. In government agencies, the same problem applies to records that are subject to freedom-of-information law requests. Retention of obsolete electronic records increases the time and effort required to respond to such requests.

Unstructured Electronic Records

Electronic records are often divided into two categories: structured and unstructured. The phrase "**structured electronic records**" is typically used to describe the contents of computer databases that have a prescribed, repetitive format. An organized, uniform structure is an essential characteristic of computer databases and a key component of dictionary definitions of a database. Thus, the 2006 edition of the *Random House Unabridged Dictionary* defines a database as a "comprehensive collection of related data organized for convenient access," while WordNet, a lexical database developed at Princeton University, defines a database as "an organized collection of related information." According to the *Oxford English Dictionary,* a database is "a structured set of data held in a computer." Similarly, *The Free On-line Dictionary of Computing* defines a database as "one or more large structured sets of persistent data."

A database consists of individual units called "records," which are organized into fields (data elements) with prescribed characteristics. In the parlance of database management, fields contain specific pieces of information, a record is a collection of fields, and a database is a collection of records. Thus, a database associated with a human resources information system may contain one record for each active or former employee of an organization. Each record will include predefined fields for an employee's personal information (such as name, social security number, company address, telephone extension, e-mail address, home address, home phone number, and emergency contact information), employment history (such as appointment and termination dates, current and previous job titles, current and previous salary, and summaries of periodic performance evaluations), special skills (such as education, foreign languages, and professional certifications), and so on. Similarly, a purchasing database may contain one record for each purchase order issued by an organization. Each record will include fields for the purchase order number, purchase requisition number, issuing date, vendor name and other identifiers, descriptions of items and quantities ordered, unit prices, total costs, and so on.

The record structure is determined at the time a database is created. It is based on a detailed analysis of application characteristics and user requirements. Depending on the database, a data dictionary may contain detailed information about the content, format, use, and other characteristics of specific fields. Within a given database, all records have the same fields, although some records may have more or less data in specific fields. Some records may have no data values in certain fields, but those fields are nonetheless present. Thus, records in an organization's human resources database may include a field for termination date, but no value will be entered into that field until an employee retires, resigns, or otherwise leaves the organization.

By contrast, **unstructured electronic records** have no prescribed organization or format. A word processing document or PowerPoint presentation, for example, can contain any type or amount of information in any sequence, subject only to the capabilities and limitations imposed by the software that created it. A digital image can reproduce a document at any resolution with or without compression in black-and-white, grayscale, or color mode, subject only to the capabilities and limitations of the scanner and software that produced the image. Similarly, a digital photograph can depict any scene, in any size or aspect ratio, in black and white or color, and with any visual effects, subject to the capabilities and limitations of the digital camera that generated the photograph. For the most part, video and audio recordings are completely unstructured.

In some cases, however, the distinction between structured and unstructured records is not as clearly drawn. Nominally unstructured records, such as spreadsheets and Web pages, actually have some structure to the extent that their content is formatted according to certain rules. A spreadsheet's rows and columns, for example, can be viewed as variant forms of records and fields, although individual spreadsheet cells may contain unstructured text and appended comments. A Web page constructed with the hypertext markup language (HTML) has a defined structure demarcated by start and end tags and further subdivided into head and body sections, each identified by HTML tags. Most Web pages also have a title bar as well as paragraphs separated by block elements. E-mail messages have unstructured content, but their associated metadata is predefined.[4]

Although they lack the uniformity of database records, spreadsheets, Web pages, and e-mail messages are perhaps more accurately characterized as "semi-structured." In practice, however, they are considered unstructured records, which are typically defined by exclusion as anything except database records.

As discussed in subsequent chapters, systematic management of unstructured electronic records poses significant challenges. Compared to structured electronic records, unstructured records are more numerous and varied. Structured databases are often associated with applications managed by an organization's information technology (IT) department, which determines how they will be stored, accessed, backed up, and archived. By contrast, many unstructured electronic records are created and stored by personal computer users without IT involvement or guidance. They may be saved on local or network storage. They may be organized into folders by the business operations or topics to which they pertain, or they may be comingled with unrelated records and different file types in an unorganized directory or subdirectory. Older database records may be transferred to archive or history files after a given amount of time or when a specific event occurs, but this transfer is rarely done with unstructured electronic records, which may be retained indefinitely or discarded carelessly.

System Dependence

Electronic records, as defined previously, contain machine-readable, analog or digitally-encoded information derived from electronic signals. As described in Chapter 2, such machine-readable information is represented by microscopic alterations in the physical or chemical characteristics of magnetic, optical, or solid-state storage media, which are the visible carriers of electronic records. The electronic records themselves are invisible. As a significant complication, electronic storage media and the information they contain are designed to be recorded and read by specific devices and software. Database records on magnetic tape, for example, must be processed by designated application programs that run under specific operating systems on compatible computers equipped with an appropriate magnetic tape drive. Video and audio recordings are similarly intended for playback by specific devices.

To manage electronic records effectively, records managers must understand the characteristics and capabilities of systems that create and store machine-readable information.

Given this dependent relationship, electronic records cannot be properly understood or evaluated without a thorough knowledge of their associated hardware/software environments. To manage electronic records effectively, records managers must understand the characteristics and capabilities of systems that create and store machine-readable information. Some records managers will consequently require additional training, particularly training in computer technology and automated information processing, which may be obtained through formal courses of study or individual reading. As an additional, potentially significant complication, the future usefulness of electronic records depends on the continued availability of compatible hardware and software. As discussed elsewhere in this book, the future ability to read and process specific electronic records is obviously imperiled by technological advances, which promote product obsolescence and discontinuations.

Media Stability

In many records management applications, the useful life of paper and photographic media equals or exceeds the retention periods for information that such media contain. When processed and stored in a manner specified in national and international standards, silver gelatin microfilm will retain its original information-bearing characteristics for centuries. Diazo, vesicular, and thermally-processed silver microfilms will remain stable for at least 100 years when stored in controlled environments. National and international standards similarly define the characteristics of permanent papers.

With exceptions noted later in this book, the useful lives of magnetic, optical, and solid-state media that store electronic records are generally shorter than those of paper and photographic films. In many cases, the stable life spans of electronic media are shorter than the retention periods for information recorded on such media. Electronic records must consequently be recopied, or migrated, onto new media at predetermined intervals in order to extend their lives for the designated term. This periodic recopying requirement, which has no counterpart in nonelectronic record-keeping systems, complicates the management of electronic records and may prove impractical or impossible to implement in specific situations. Where electronic records must be retained for long periods of time, periodic recopying involves a future commitment of labor and economic resources of uncertain availability.

Transparent Arrangement

In paper filing systems, folders, documents, and other filing units are typically arranged in alphabetic, numeric, or other sequences that can be determined, though not necessarily understood fully, when the records are inventoried or otherwise inspected. Often, an examination of physical file arrangements provides information about the ways in which paper records are referenced or otherwise processed. By contrast, the physical arrangement of electronic records within a given magnetic or optical storage medium may be transparent to users. With magnetic and optical disks, for example, related information is not necessarily stored in contiguous sectors or tracks. Instead, the computer's operating system manages available storage resources, allocating space to specific information on an as-available basis. Unrelated records may consequently be intermixed within sectors of a magnetic or optical disk. Related information may be spread across several platters within a given hard drive, with access provided by directories that contain pointers to the physical locations of specific records. When inventorying electronic records, relating specific data files to their physical storage locations is consequently difficult or impossible. This storage process can pose problems when defining retention periods, purging electronic records, or removing specific media for offline storage.

Remote Access

To access paper or microfilm records, users typically go to the filing areas or other physical locations where the desired records are kept. Such records are customarily removed from their cabinets or other storage containers for reference. Depending on application requirements, they may be taken to another work area for varying periods of time. In networked computer installations, by contrast, electronic records can be accessed from remote workstations and are never physically removed from their original repositories. Such records may be stored at considerable physical distances from prospective users, who never see the physical media on which electronic records are stored and may not be aware of the type of media employed. Some computer storage media are removable from their drives and can be carried, shelved, mailed, or otherwise handled by users in the manner of paper files. However, other media—such as hard drives—are not meant to be handled as physical objects. Although a significant functional advantage in many applications, remote access to computer-stored records poses security problems, including the possibility of intrusion by unauthorized persons and contamination by computer viruses.

General Concerns

Certain widely recognized records management concerns are equally applicable to electronic and nonelectronic records. Issues related to economical storage of recorded information brought records management to prominence as a professional discipline in the 1950s, and they remain important today. Storage space, regardless of record type, is not an infinitely available resource. The proliferation of electronic records requires increasing quantities of storage equipment and media, but the cost of computer storage has been decreasing steadily and significantly and is likely to continue to do so. In 2008, one terabyte of fault-tolerant disk storage could be purchased for about $4,000. (Conventional one-terabyte hard drives could be purchased for a fraction of that amount. However, lacking fault-tolerance, such devices are not suitable for high-performance computing.) Assuming that the cost of hard disk storage falls by 30 percent per year, which is slightly less than the average annual rate of decline in computer storage costs since the early 1990s, one terabyte of fault-tolerant disk storage will cost less than $300 within seven years, a widely encountered retention period for many types of business records. Even when the purchase price is increased to reflect the total cost of ownership,[5] the cost to acquire additional computer storage will soon be lower than the cost of developing and implementing retention guidance for some types of electronic records, which is certainly the case where computer applications must be modified to make them retention-capable.

> *As hardware and software are replaced, an increasing quantity of older records must be transferred to new storage devices or converted to new file formats in order to ensure their future usability.*

However, advocating the indefinite retention of electronic records that lack continuing legal, operational, or scholarly value merely because storage costs are affordable is conceptually problematic. Such a practice would commit an organization to perpetual storage of an increasing quantity of obsolete records with potentially adverse consequences that are not reflected in the total cost of ownership. An organization's storage infrastructure has a significant impact on the optimization of computing resources. Computer hardware and software operate most efficiently within certain storage capacity limits. As those limits are approached or exceeded, data entry, information retrieval, data recovery, and other operations will run more slowly. To address this problem, costly hardware upgrades or archiving solutions may be required. Further, backup operations, especially full backups, will take longer to complete and require more resources as the quantity of stored data increases. Additional magnetic tapes or other backup media must be purchased and, if those media are stored offsite by commercial providers, higher charges will be incurred. Indefinite retention also poses problems for data migration. As hardware and software are replaced, an increasing quantity of older records must be transferred to new storage devices or converted to new file formats in order to ensure their future usability. This requirement will necessarily increase the cost of system replacement.

Even if sufficient space were available to accommodate an organization's electronic records indefinitely, it would not necessarily be advisable to retain them all. With the proliferation of online information systems and centralized databases accessible from desktop workstations, electronic records increasingly contain unique information captured in machine-readable form at its source. As the quantity of electronic records increases, an organization may experience higher costs to comply with discovery orders and, for government agencies, freedom-of-information requests. The burden of protecting personally identifiable information or other confidential records against unauthorized access will also be greater.

Among other general concerns, vital electronic records, like their paper counterparts, are vulnerable to damage or other loss. Magnetic and optical media must be stored and handled in a manner that will safeguard the valuable information they contain. Further, the mere availability of records in electronic form is no guarantee that required information will be conveniently accessible when needed. Electronic records, like their paper counterparts, must be organized for effective retrieval. These concerns are examined in subsequent chapters.

Program Components

Fundamental records management concepts and program components were originally developed for paper documents. However, they are equally applicable to electronic records. Records management is concerned with the systematic control of recorded information. Records management programs should have broad authority over all records, regardless of format or media type. The ISO 15489-1 standard, *Information and Documentation—Records Management, Part 1: General*, defines programmatic requirements for systematic management of recorded information in any format, including computer data, audio recordings, and video recordings.

Electronic records are one of three major types of records maintained by corporations, government agencies, and other organizations. The other two types are human-readable paper documents and photographic records, including microforms. In U.S. government agencies, the definition of records presented in 44 U.S. Code 3301 specifically includes "machine-readable materials, or other documentary materials, regardless of physical form or characteristics." The National Archives of Canada defines records in a virtually identical manner. In the United Kingdom, the Public Records Act of 1958 applies to records that convey information by any means. In Australia, digital data is considered a Commonwealth record under the Archives Act of 1983. Comparable definitions and authority statements have been adopted by other countries, by state and local governments, and by many corporations and other organizations.

Records managers should examine the policy statements or other foundation documents that define the scope of their programs to determine their authority and responsibilities with respect to electronic records. If the foundation documents do not explicitly extend records management authority to electronic records, they should be modified to do so. In the manner described previously, such amendments should define electronic records broadly to encompass any machine-readable media, including audio and video recordings as well as the more obvious computer-processible media. As stated earlier, an enterprise-wide records management program must assert its authority over, and responsibility for, all electronic media, regardless of their location within the organization. Electronic records created by personal computers should be specifically included.

Like its counterpart for human-readable records, a formally established program for the systematic management of electronic records must provide comprehensive coverage of the information life cycle from creation through utilization, destruction, or permanent preservation of such records. Addressing and elaborating on the issues and concerns raised in preceding sections, subsequent chapters describe and discuss various facets of this information life cycle as they apply to electronic records:

- **Media applications.** The systematic management of electronic records begins with records creation and the selection of appropriate records storage media for specific information processing applications. Records managers must develop and implement specifications for the types and characteristics of media to be purchased and utilized for particular electronic records. Those specifications must provide application-oriented guidance based on such factors as the volume of records to be stored, their retention periods, and the nature and frequency of anticipated reference activity.

- **Media characteristics.** To knowledgeably develop guidelines for electronic records, records managers must understand the technical and application characteristics of available electronic storage media and the types of information such media contain. Records managers must be familiar with the storage capacities, recording capabilities, stability, and other characteristics of available magnetic and optical media. They must also understand the types and characteristics of files that contain electronic records, as well as the methodologies and formats used to create such files. Further, records managers must be able to communicate their requirements and concerns to computer systems specialists, computer network managers, and other information professionals.

- **Retention schedules.** The preparation of retention schedules has been a critical component of professional practice since the inception of records management as a specialized information management discipline. Retention schedules establish the essential infrastructure on which many other electronic recordkeeping initiatives are based. They provide an indispensable, formalized foundation for the systematic preservation or destruction of specific electronic records, as well as the conversion of records from one format to another. Records management programs typically devote considerable professional resources to schedule preparation, and many well-established programs have completed retention schedules for the majority of nonelectronic records maintained by their organizations. To be truly complete, however, such schedules must encompass electronic records, including determination of official copies for information that coexists in electronic and nonelectronic formats.

- **Vital records.** The identification and protection of vital records is likewise a longstanding records management responsibility. Briefly defined, **vital records** contain information essential to an organization's mission. Many electronic records support mission-critical applications, and they are properly considered vital records. Chapter 6 surveys the principal components of a vital electronic records program. Such components include a systematic approach to the identification and enumeration of vital records, the analysis of risks to which vital records are exposed, and the development and implementation of appropriate protection methods. In information technology applications, vital records protection is often regarded as a facet of the broader issues of computer security and disaster recovery.

- **Files management.** Records managers are often asked to design filing systems and select equipment and supplies to facilitate the organization and retrieval of paper documents associated with specific applications. Increasingly, these file organization concepts are being applied to the organization of electronic records. Proper care and handling procedures must likewise be implemented for storage and working copies of such removable media as magnetic tapes, diskettes, and optical disk cartridges.

Summary

Electronic records contain machine-readable information generated by computer systems, special-purpose instrumentation, video recorders, audio recorders, and other devices. Such records are commonly stored on magnetic disks, magnetic tapes, and optical disks, although other media have been utilized in the past. Since the 1960s, electronic records created and maintained by corporations, government agencies, and other organizations have increased in both number and importance. The growing volume of electronic records is attributable to the dramatic proliferation of hardware and software capable of generating such records; their importance is derived from their role in mission-critical applications. In most organizations, mission-critical applications receive the highest priority for automation. Electronic records associated with such applications are increasingly viewed as the most valuable and authoritative sources of information pertaining to particular operations or activities. In many cases, they contain information that is not included in paper documents.

Although the number and importance of electronic records are increasing, certain characteristics of those records complicate their effective management. Few organizations, for example, have implemented formalized controls for creation, storage, and retention of electronic records. Personal computer users, in particular, may view electronic records they create as "personal" files to be managed in a discretionary manner. Because they often contain information extracted from source documents and are themselves used to produce paper printouts, electronic records may replicate information contained in other formats. In addition to wasting storage space, such redundant recordkeeping can make controlling and identifying the versions of information appropriate to specific operations difficult. Redundancy also necessitates the coordination of retention periods for electronic records and their nonelectronic counterparts.

As a significant complication, electronic records are entirely dependent on specific hardware devices and/or software configurations for their continued usability. Product obsolescence and discontinuations consequently imperil the future retrieval and processing of electronic records. In addition, the continued readability of electronic records may be affected by the relatively limited stability of magnetic and optical media. In centralized computer installations, electronic records are accessed by remote workstations. Such remote access is unquestionably convenient, but it poses potential security problems. Finally, certain general records management concerns pertaining to storage space, vital records protection, and proper media handling pertain equally to electronic and nonelectronic records.

A formally established program for the systematic management of electronic records must provide comprehensive coverage of the information life cycle from creation through utilization, destruction, or permanent preservation. Records managers must be familiar with the formats, storage capacities, recording capabilities, stability, and other characteristics of electronic media. They must also understand the types and characteristic of files that contain electronic records. The preparation of retention schedules is a critical component in any systematic program to manage electronic records, as is the identification and protection of vital electronic records. Retention recommendations and vital records protection plans must be based on information obtained through a comprehensive inventory of electronic records. Among their other responsibilities, records managers must develop and implement procedures for the organization, care, and handling of storage and working copies of electronic media.

Notes

1 Equating digital records and electronic records or to use those phrases synonymously is not correct. A digital record is one type—admittedly, the most numerous and important type—of electronic record. Analog records are the other type. Thus, it is incorrect to use the phrase "analog records" as a synonym for nonelectronic records, as is sometimes done to differentiate digital images from microfilm images. Digitally-coded records dominate most electronic recordkeeping environments; but even if analog electronic records are entirely replaced by digital records for business purposes, many existing analog video and audio recordings will remain in archival repositories for the foreseeable future, if not permanently.

2 Computer manufacturers, software developers, office automation specialists, and other professionals have predicted that paperless information systems will supplant paper-based recordkeeping, but paper documents and filing cabinets remain an integral component of most business activities. Sales of filing cabinets continue to grow, albeit slowly. According to AKTRIN Furniture Information Center, a market research company that specializes in the furniture industry, sales of filing cabinets increased by 3.2 percent from 1995 to 2005. Similarly, the Business and Institutional Furniture Manufacturers' Association (BIFMA) reported that annual sales of office furniture increased by 7.6 percent to $12.8 billion in 2006. Filing cabinets accounted for 14.6 percent of those sales in 2005, the latest year for which statistics are available. That percentage is the highest since 1995, when filing cabinets accounted for 15.1 percent of office furniture sales.

3 On the other hand, paper consumption in other parts of the world is rising. In China, which is now second only to the U.S. in paper consumption, demand is forecast to increase by 5 percent per year through 2020, at which time China will surpass North America in paper consumption. Poyry, a Finnish research firm that monitors the forest products industry, predicts strong growth in paper consumption in India. Several research studies forecast increased paper consumption in Eastern Europe, where Slovenia is the only country in which paper usage approaches Western European averages.

4 ISO/IEC 11179-1, *Information Technology—Specification and Standardization of Data Elements—Part 1: Framework for the Specification and Standardization of Data Elements* defines **metadata** as "data that defines and describes other data." As applied to e-mail messages and other electronic records, metadata refers to descriptive information that relates to specific electronic records but is not part of the content of the records. Thus, an e-mail message may be accompanied by metadata that includes a system-assigned message number; the identities of the sender and recipients, including recipients of copies and "blind" copies; the date and time of transmission; the transmission route; the date and time of receipt by the addressee; whether the message is a reply to another mes-

sage; whether the message has been forwarded by a recipient; whether the message is encrypted; and the subject. E-mail metadata fields are discussed in RFC 822, *Standard for the Format of ARPA Internet Text Messages*, which was published in August 1982. Metadata concepts are covered by ISO 23081-1, *Information and Documentation—Records Management Processes—Metadata for Records—Part 1: Principles*, and ISO/TS 23081-2, *Information and Documentation—Records Management Processes—Metadata for Records—Part 2: Conceptual and Implementation Issues.*

5 The total cost of ownership (TCO) is a concept introduced by Gartner Group in the late 1980s to account for the true cost of acquiring and using information technology. The TCO encompasses the purchase price of computer components—in this case, computer storage devices and media—plus all direct and indirect costs associated with the use and maintenance of those components. Examples include, but are not limited to, the cost of installation, testing, and deployment; charges for repairs and maintenance contracts; labor costs for operation and technical support; the cost of floor space and utilities; data backup and disaster recovery costs; the cost of migrating data to replacement devices; and administrative overhead costs. For organizations that outsource their computing operations, the TCO includes a reasonable markup for the supplier's profit. Industry analysts agree that the TCO for storage devices is a multiple of the purchase price of the devices themselves, but estimates of that multiple range broadly from 3 to 8. A 2001 Gartner Group report estimated that acquisition costs for storage components account for 20 percent of the TCO, which equates to a TCO multiple of 5.

Storage Media for Electronic Recordkeeping

To knowledgeably evaluate and recommend electronic recordkeeping practices, records managers must be familiar with the physical and functional characteristics of media that store computer, video, and audio information. When inventorying or otherwise examining electronic records, they must be able to recognize various types of storage media and make informed decisions about their suitability for information processing operations, records retention, vital records protection, or other purposes.

As noted in Chapter 1, electronic records may be stored on magnetic, optical, or solid-state media:

- **Magnetic media.** Magnetic recording has dominated computer storage technology since the 1950s. It is also the most widely utilized technology for video and audio recording. Magnetism, one of the earliest known physical phenomena, has been the subject of scientific investigation and practical experimentation since the 16th century. Audio recorders, which utilized steel wires and bands as recording media, were invented in the late nineteenth century. Magnetic tape recorders, developed in the 1930s, were widely available by the 1950s. Prototype video tape recorders were demonstrated in the early 1950s, and operational equipment was in use by the end of that decade. Magnetic disks and tapes for computer applications likewise date from the 1950s.

- **Optical media.** Optical storage products use light, specifically light generated by lasers, to record and/or retrieve machine-readable information. As their principal advantage for electronic recordkeeping, optical storage products offer high recording density and correspondingly high media capacity. This characteristic is particularly important for storage-intensive records management applications such as electronic document imaging. Optical storage media also have longer life spans than their magnetic counterparts, but the resulting advantages for records retention are diminished by hardware dependencies discussed elsewhere in this book. The earliest optical disk products, designed for video recording, date from the late 1970s. Optical disks for computer and audio applications were introduced several years later, but they did not become widely available until the late 1980s.

- **Solid-state storage media.** These media use semiconductor materials rather than magnetic or optical technology. Historically associated with main memory, solid-state media, in the form of flash memory cards and USB flash drives, are increasingly popular as removable storage components in personal computers and peripheral devices such as digital cameras.

The following sections survey the most important magnetic, optical, and solid-state devices and media employed by corporations, government agencies, and other organizations. These media are also outlined in Figure 2.1. The discussion emphasizes characteristics, such as media capacities, that are most significant for electronic recordkeeping. Other characteristics, such as the access times and data transfer rates supported by devices that read and record specific media, are omitted or summarized very briefly. Those characteristics are more important for computer system administrators than for records managers.

The media characteristics described next reflect the state of the art in electronic information storage at the time this chapter was written. Readers are cautioned that some characteristics are likely to change in the future—storage capacities, in particular, are subject to continuing improvements—and that new media formats with dif-

Computer
Storage Media

Figure 2.1

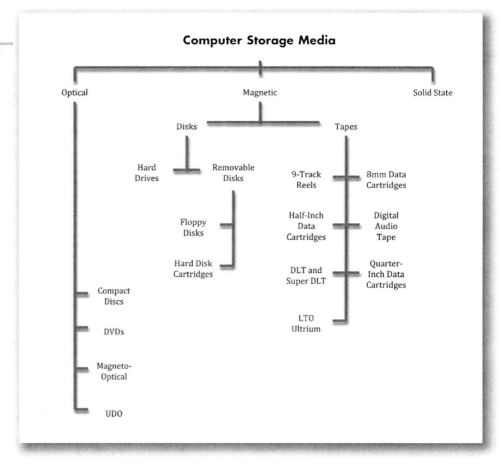

ferent attributes may be developed. Although the following discussion emphasizes the latest models of magnetic, optical, and solid-state storage devices and media, some older configurations and obsolete products are also covered. Records managers cannot ignore storage technologies of the past because discontinued media are often encountered during inventories of electronic records.

Magnetic Media

Magnetic storage media suitable for computer, audio, or video records are composed of a metallic recording layer capable of being magnetized when placed into a magnetic field and of retaining magnetization when the field is removed; a **substrate** or base material, such as an aluminum platter or piece of polyester film, on which the recording material is coated; and a binder, which functions as a carrier for the recording material and bonds it to the substrate. Broadly defined, a magnet is a metal that generates a magnetic field capable of attracting or repelling other metals. The ability to be attracted to or repelled by magnets is a property of all matter. However, the magnetic susceptibility of most substances is too weak to have practical significance, which is the case with most organic compounds and many metals. The magnetic recording materials used in computer applications are characterized by strong, easily detectable magnetization, even in the absence of an external magnetic field.

With iron crystals, for example, atoms are aligned in microscopic regions called "domains." When iron crystals are in an unmagnetized state, their domains are randomly arranged. To record information, an external magnetic field of sufficient strength selectively orients the domains toward a magnet's north or south pole where the attractive forces are strongest. To represent the "one" bits in digitally-coded data, domains may be aligned toward the magnet's north pole, while the "zero" bits are represented by aligning domains toward the magnet's south pole. With computer storage devices, the external magnetic field is generated by an electromagnet called a *read/write head*. When the external field is removed, some magnetism, termed the **remanence**, remains in the recording material. Retrieval is based on detection of this residual magnetism.

Other examples of magnetic recording materials include the gamma form of ferric oxide, cobalt-modified iron oxide, chromium dioxide, pure iron particles, and barium ferrite. These recording materials may be coated on platter-shaped substrates (magnetic disks) or on thin ribbons of polyester (magnetic tapes). Magnetic disks are principally encountered in computer applications. Magnetic tapes are widely utilized for data storage, as well as for audio and video recording.

Hard Disks

A magnetic disk features a platter-shaped substrate coated with a magnetizable recording material. The disk's recording surface is divided into concentric rings or tracks. An electromagnetic read/write head is used for recording and playback. On instructions received from a host computer, a magnetic disk drive positions the read/write head above a designated track while the rotating platter brings the desired disk segment under the electromagnetic mechanism. The individual bits may represent character-coded text, quantitative values, document images, or other computer-processible information. They are usually recorded linearly, sometimes described as longitudinally or horizontally, within each track. Much less commonly, some manufacturers of magnetic disk drives employ perpendicular or vertical recording to increase platter capacity.

Magnetic disk substrates may be rigid (hard disks) or flexible (floppy disks). With the most widely encountered type of hard disk system, one or more platters are built into the drive mechanism that records and reads information. Because the platters cannot be removed, the resulting computer storage device is properly characterized as a fixed, rigid magnetic disk drive. It is popularly described as a *hard disk drive* or, simply, a *hard drive*. The storage device and the recording medium are considered an indivisible unit. In mainframe computer configurations, hard drives are often described as *direct access storage devices* or **DASD** (pronounced "dazdee"). Although hard drives for smaller computers similarly support direct access for recording and retrieval, the DASD designation is rarely applied to them. Removable hard disks and floppy disks combine the direct access characteristics of platter-shaped media with offline storage capabilities for data archiving, backup, data distribution, or other purposes. Historically associated with small computer installations, they have been increasingly supplanted by other storage media.

Since their introduction in the 1950s, hard drives have been the principal storage devices for digitally-coded information and programs that need to be immediately and continuously available to computer users. Intended for active records, hard drives provide convenient online access to electronic records that will be referenced frequently or unpredictably. The earliest hard drives had recording layers composed of iron oxide particles in an epoxy binder. Various other oxide compounds—including barium ferrite, metal particles, and cobalt-modified iron oxide—have also been used as hard disk coatings. Since the 1960s, steady reductions in the size and thickness of recording layers have been accompanied by significant improvements in the recording densities of hard disks. With particulate materials, however, reductions in coating thickness are accompanied by diminished magnetic field strength, as small particles become diluted in nonmagnetic binder materials. Manufacturers of newer high-performance magnetic disks consequently prefer thin metallic films to particulate materials. Composed of iron, nickel, cobalt, or other metals or alloys, such films are coated in a thin, undiluted layer on a hard disk platter. They are durable and offer excellent magnetizable properties.

The principal determinants of hard disk capacity are the number of platters per drive and the areal density within each recording surface. Most hard disk drives contain multiple platters.

The historical development and continuing evolution of hard disk storage can be summarized in four words: smaller, denser, faster, cheaper. Once considered a luxury to be carefully rationed among mission-critical applications, hard drives are increasingly affordable necessities in virtually every computer configuration. The principal determinants of hard disk capacity are the number of platters per drive and the areal density within each recording surface. Most hard disk drives contain multiple platters. Through the early 1990s, for example, full-height hard disk drives for personal computers typically featured 10 platters, while half-height models incorporated a shorter stack of 5 platters. In the mid-1990s, several manufacturers introduced hard disk drives with just two or three platters. Their low heights permit compact equipment designs, an especially important consideration for notebook computers, personal digital assistants, and other mobile computing devices. The number of platters aside, the top and bottom surfaces of individual platters are used for data recording.

With their greater surface areas, large platters can store more information than smaller ones, assuming comparable areal recording densities. Since the 1950s, however, the form factors (diameters) of hard disk platters have decreased steadily, while technological innovations and improved product designs have dramatically enhanced recording densities and storage capacities per platter. The earliest hard drives introduced by IBM in the mid-1950s utilized 24-inch platters. In the decades that followed, they were replaced by mainframe and minicomputer disk drives with 14-inch, 12-inch, and 8-inch platters. Today, high-capacity direct-access storage devices for mainframe and mid-range installations employ multidrive disk arrays with 3.5-inch platters. Hard drives with smaller platters are widely used in personal computers and mobile electronic devices such as personal digital assistants (PDAs) and digital music players. Eventually, they will supplant 3.5-inch hard drives in larger computer configurations. Compared to devices with larger platters, hard drives with small form factors require less floor space, consume less power, and are much less expensive to purchase, install, operate, repair, and replace. They are more reliable, can be scaled to address varied storage requirements, and support faster access times for reading and recording.

The areal recording densities and storage capacities of small platters have improved steadily and significantly in recent years. Multigigabyte models have been commonplace since the mid-1990s, and, with storage capacities doubling at 12-to-18-month intervals, terabyte-level hard drives—once unthinkable in all but the largest mainframe installations—will soon be the norm for personal computers. At the time this chapter was written, terabyte-level storage configurations were widely installed and increasingly affordable.

Multiple hard drives can be configured together as a single logical drive for recording and retrieval purposes. Such hard disk arrays are often supplied in RAID configurations, which incorporate redundant recording and storage procedures for fault-tolerant operation. The **RAID** acronym originally stood for *redundant array of inexpensive disks*, but some vendors now prefer *redundant array of independent disks*. RAID technology spreads and replicates data among multiple drives. Depending on the specific RAID methodology employed, the data may be copied onto multiple disks or split among multiple disks with error correction coding being used to maintain access to recorded information in the event of a hard drive failure. RAID technology can be combined with a "hot spare," a hard drive that can immediately replace a failed drive. The stored data is reconstructed on the spare drive to protect against a second drive failure.

RAID technology is not limited to mainframe, midrange computer, and network server installations. Relatively economical RAID configurations are also available for desktop computers. The much-publicized complexity of newer operating systems and application software, combined with the growing volume and variety of electronic records generated by such programs, have led to dramatically increased storage requirements in small computer installations. Desktop computers now provide storage capacities that would have been unusually high in midrange computer configurations a decade ago.

Removable Hard Disks

As a potentially significant limitation, fixed magnetic disks can become full, necessitating their replacement with higher-capacity models or the purchase of additional hard drives. Alternatively, some electronic records must be deleted or transferred to magnetic tapes or other media for offline storage, thereby freeing space for new information. Hard drives with removable recording media were developed to address this problem. With such devices, a single drive can support an infinite number of disks, any of which can be inserted into the drive as required for recording or retrieval. Hard drives with removable media consequently provide unlimited capacity—provided, of course, that offline storage is acceptable for some electronic records. When greater hard disk capacity is required, users merely purchase additional recording media rather than upgrading or replacing an entire drive.

Among their other advantages for electronic recordkeeping, removable hard disks can be stored in locked cabinets, vaults, or other secure locations to protect sensitive or valuable electronic records against unauthorized access when not in use. Removable hard disks provide a convenient method of transferring electronic records from one computer system to another equipped with compatible drives. They can be used for physical exchange of information and to back up the contents of conventional hard drives. Compared to magnetic tapes, removable hard disks permit faster restoration of electronic records in the event of hard drive failure. Removable hard disks also offer a measure of fault tolerance. If a removable hard disk drive fails, its recording media can be mounted onto an identical device.

In most computer installations, removable hard disk drives have historically served as supplements or complements, rather than replacements, for conventional hard drives.

> *Because removable hard disks must be retrieved from their storage locations and mounted into a drive when required, they are not suitable for electronic records that must be immediately and continuously accessible online.*

Because removable hard disks must be retrieved from their storage locations and mounted into a drive when required, they are not suitable for electronic records that must be immediately and continuously accessible online. Unlike optical disks and certain magnetic tapes, jukebox-type autochangers that provide unattended access to individual media are not available for removable hard disks.

Removable hard disks have a long history. IBM introduced the first magnetic disk drive with removable recording media in 1962. Intended for small mainframe installations that could not afford enough fixed disk capacity to meet their information storage requirements, it featured removable 14-inch disk packs with multiple platters mounted onto a spindle. Similar products were widely encountered in mainframe and midrange computer installations through the early 1980s. When not mounted into their drives, the individual disk packs were stored on shelves under a protective, translucent plastic cover that resembled a hatbox. A variant form of removable hard disk drive, more common in minicomputer installations than mainframe sites, employed 14-inch platters encapsulated in opaque plastic cartridges.

As computer storage media, hard disk packs and 14-inch hard disk cartridges are defunct products. Although drives that accepted hard disk packs and 14-inch cartridges remained available for sale through the late 1980s, new models are not being manufactured. Records managers may occasionally encounter hard disk packs and 14-inch cartridges when inventorying media stored offline by data processing centers. Such media may also be packed into containers transferred to records centers or other offsite storage facilities. In most cases, their contents are not retrievable because compatible drives are not available.

During the 1980s and 1990s, several companies, including SyQuest and Iomega, introduced removable hard disk products for personal computers. These devices separate a drive's read/write head assembly from its platter-shaped recording medium, which is encapsulated in a removable plastic cartridge. Early models offered 5 to 10 megabytes of storage capacity. By the late mid-1990s, cartridge capacities exceeded 100 megabytes. Although technical innovations have continued to increase media capacities, improve hardware performance, and reduce costs, little continuing interest in removable hard disk products exists. The increased affordability of conventional hard drives and the availability of optical disk drives with competitively priced removable media have eroded their market. Removable hard disk cartridges are principally intended for computer-aided design files, desktop publishing files, and other electronic records that do not need to be immediately and continuously available online. Other applications include hard disk backup, digital photography, and recording of music, compressed video, or multimedia programs, all of which are served equally well or better by other storage technologies. Removable hard disk cartridges can also be used to transport information, such as databases or typesetter files, between compatible computer systems or between an in-house computer system and a service bureau, but given the pervasiveness of computer networking, such information is increasingly transmitted electronically rather than transported physically.

As removable media, hard disk cartridges permit offline retention of electronic records, but they are poorly suited to such data archiving. Hard disk cartridge drives and media are proprietary products. Cartridges and drives of different manufacturers are incompatible with one another. Within a given manufacturers' product line, some larger and lower-capacity hard disk cartridges recorded by prior generations of equipment cannot be read by newly-developed drives. Backward-compatibility is not guaranteed, and no safeguards against future discontinuation of specific products are provided. If history is any guide, available products will be replaced by incompatible successors, assuming that removable hard disk technology continues to attract customers.

Floppy Disks

Floppy disks, also known as **diskettes**, are circular pieces of polyester coated with a magnetizable recording layer. Diskette manufacturers have utilized **gamma ferric oxide**, cobalt-modified iron oxides, and barium ferrite, among other recording compounds. Introduced in the early 1970s, floppy disks were initially intended as lower-cost alternatives to hard drives in minicomputer installations. They were subsequently adopted as the principal direct access storage devices for use in dedicated word processors and first-generation personal computers. Through the late 1990s, diskettes remain the most widely encountered examples of removable storage media in personal computer installations, but they have since been supplanted by optical disks and USB flash drives. Once a standard component of every personal computer configuration, floppy disk drives are now relegated to the status of optional storage peripherals, if they are available at all.

Like their rigid counterparts, floppy disks have decreased in size since the 1970s, while their recording densities and storage capacities have risen steadily and significantly. The earliest diskettes measured eight inches in diameter and stored approximately 80 kilobytes of computer-processable data. Within several years, however, improved head designs and thinner magnetic coatings had raised their capacities to megabyte levels, although some products stored considerably less than a megabyte. Eight-inch diskettes were utilized in minicomputer, personal computer, and word processing installations through the early 1980s. They were sometimes described as the "standard" size to distinguish them from 5.25-inch and 3.5-inch diskettes, which came after them. Apart from their external dimensions, however, nothing was standard about eight-inch diskettes. Individual computer systems formatted them for their own purposes, and certain word processors and small business computers required proprietary, preformatted eight-inch diskettes that could be purchased only from designated suppliers.

Eight-inch diskettes are obsolete media. They were ultimately supplanted by 5.25-inch floppy disks, the so-called **minifloppy** variety. Introduced in the mid-to-late 1970s, 5.25-inch floppy disk drives were initially utilized in low-performance personal computer systems intended for educational or consumer markets rather than business applications. Manufacturers of business-oriented computers and word processors continued to favor the 8-inch format until the early 1980s, when IBM selected 5.25-inch floppy disk drives for its personal computer (PC). Business acceptance followed quickly, as 5.25-inch floppy disk drives became standard equipment on IBM-compatible personal computers. The earliest 5.25-inch diskettes were single-sided media with 70 to 120 kilobytes of storage capacity, but they were soon replaced by a double-sided, double-density (DS/DD) format with 360 kilobytes of storage capacity. A double-sided, high-density (DS/HD) 5.25-inch diskette with 1.2 megabytes of recording capacity was introduced in the mid-1980s.

By the mid-1990s, 5.25-inch diskettes had joined their 8-inch counterparts on the list of defunct computer storage media. In personal computer configurations, they were supplanted by 3.5-inch **microfloppy disks**. In their original double-sided, double-density configuration, introduced in the early 1980s, 3.5-inch diskettes could store 720 kilobytes when formatted by the MS-DOS operating system or 800 kilobytes in Macintosh installations, although double-density Macintosh diskettes were also available in a single-sided, 400-megabyte version. Double-sided, high-density (DS/HD) 3.5-inch diskettes, the dominant floppy disk format since the early 1990s, store 1.44 megabytes. The applicable standard is ISO/IEC 9529, *Information Processing Systems—Data Interchange on 90mm (3,5 in) Flexible Disk Cartridges Using Modified Frequency Modulation Recording at 15 916 ftprad on 80 Tracks Each Side.* A double-sided, quad-density (DS/QD) 3.5-inch format, introduced in the late 1980s, could store 2.88 megabytes, but they were rarely encountered.

Smaller diskette formats have not been commercially successful. Early digital cameras used three-inch floppy disks, but they were ultimately replaced by solid-state memory cards. Two-inch floppy disk drives and media with storage capacities up to one megabyte were introduced in the late 1980s and early 1990s by several companies. Principally intended for mobile computing devices and digital photography, two-inch products were not widely adopted.

The megabyte-level storage capacities of high-density and quad-density diskettes were viewed as impressive technical developments in the 1980s. By the end of that decade, however, they limited the usefulness of floppy disk technology for file backup, data archiving, and software distribution. Multimegabyte databases, complex desktop publishing documents, document image collections, multimedia presentations, and other large files could not fit onto a single floppy disk. Personal computer software packages, formerly distributed on one or two diskettes, required a dozen or more in enhanced versions. To address this problem, several manufacturers of computer storage peripherals and media developed higher-capacity 3.5-inch floppy disk drives and media based on innovative recording technologies.

During the late 1980s and early 1990s, several computer storage vendors introduced floppy disk drives and media with 10 to 20 megabytes of recording capacity. These higher-capacity diskette formats attracted intermittent attention but comparatively few customers. Their records management significance is consequently limited. They had so few installations that they are unlikely to turn up in inventories of electronic records. So-called floptical disk drives, developed in the late 1980s, used optically-encoded control information to greatly increase track density when compared to conventional diskettes. Despite their name, floptical media featured a magnetic rather than an optical recording layer. The earliest models offered 21 megabytes of storage capacity per 3.5-inch diskette, but they were not widely adopted. A second-generation floptical disk with 120 megabytes of storage capacity was introduced in 1996. Known as the LS-120 laser servo diskette or, more commonly, the **SuperDisk**, it was intended for PC configurations. A third-generation model doubled the recording capacity to 240 megabytes per diskette, but it had few installations and was eventually discontinued.

The Bernoulli product line, one of the most successful high-capacity diskette technologies, was introduced by Iomega Corporation in 1981. It took its name from a nineteenth century Swiss physicist who formulated a famous fluid-dynamics theorem. Within a Bernoulli drive, spinning motion creates air pressure that lifts a flexible magnetic storage medium toward read/write heads. Because Bernoulli disks are encapsulated in protective plastic cartridges, they are often mistaken for removable hard disks, but they are flexible media. The original Bernoulli drive, called the *Bernoulli Box*, used eight-inch cartridges with 10 or 20 megabytes of storage capacity. They remained available through the late 1980s, but eight-inch Bernoulli drives were eventually supplanted by more compact models that initially provided five megabytes of storage per 5.25-inch cartridge. Successively improved versions increased the capacities of Bernoulli cartridges to 230 megabytes by the mid-1990s when the last drive in the Bernoulli series was introduced.

In late 1994, Iomega announced its Zip drive, the most successful high-capacity floppy disk product. Like the Bernoulli Box, which it ultimately supplanted, the Zip drive employs flexible media encapsulated in protective plastic cartridges. Zip cartridges measure 3.5 inches per side but are thicker than conventional floppy disks. First-generation products, which remained available at the time of this writing, stored 100 megabytes per cartridge. A second-generation version supported a cartridge capacity of 250 megabytes. It remains available along with a 750-megabyte model, but Zip drives and media cannot compete with optical disk products and solid-state memory, which are less expensive and offer higher storage capacities. As the last remaining examples of high-capacity diskette technology, Zip drives and media are end-of-life products.

For those formats that conform to published national and international standards for particular sizes and recording densities, floppy disk technology provides excellent compatibility between the unrecorded diskettes of one manufacturer and the drives of other manufacturers. Once floppy disks are formatted for recording by a particular computer operating system, however, media interchangeability is limited to compatible computer configurations. Addressing this limitation, popular utility programs permit the interchange of 3.5-inch double-density and high-density diskettes formatted for different operating systems. Such programs allow Macintosh computers to load DOS-formatted diskettes, for example. Certain higher-capacity floppy disk products, such as quad-density 3.5-inch drives and SuperDisk drives, were compatible with double-sided, double-density diskettes for reading and/or recording. Other higher-capacity floppy disk drives, such as Iomega's Bernoulli and Zip products, employed proprietary technology. They do not accommodate diskettes in other formats.

Subject to capacity limitations, 3.5-inch diskettes can be used for offline retention of electronic records, but continued availability of compatible hardware to read previously recorded information is a concern. As noted previously, 3.5-inch double-sided, high-density floppy disk drives are no longer standard components in personal computer configurations. As proprietary products, the higher-capacity diskettes are unsuitable for long-term retention of electronic records. Many of these products are obsolete.

Nine-Track Computer Tapes

Broadly defined, a **magnetic tape** is a long strip of polyester film coated with a magnetizable recording material. Magnetizable layers composed of particulate materials, such as gamma ferric oxide, have been utilized since the technology's inception. Newer magnetic tape products utilize chromium dioxide, metal particles, or other media formulations.

Magnetic tape devices and media have a long history in information storage. Audio recording equipment dates from the 1920s. Video recording applications followed in the 1950s. Magnetic tape drives were the principal auxiliary storage devices in early computer installations, but their serial access characteristics rendered them unsuitable for online applications requiring rapid retrieval of information in unpredictable sequences. To access information recorded on a given portion of a magnetic tape, the tape drive must pass through all preceding information. As higher performance magnetic disk technology became more widely available and affordable, magnetic tapes were relegated to batch processing applications, which have been steadily replaced by online systems. Today, computer tapes enjoy a well-established position in electronic recordkeeping. They are the most widely utilized media for backup protection and offline storage of machine-readable data. As such, they complement rather than compete with hard drives. Magnetic tapes are also used for distribution of information and software, particularly in mainframe and midrange computer configurations.

These information management applications are supported by a diverse group of magnetic tape formats, some of which have multiple varieties. Half-inch magnetic tapes wound onto plastic reels have been used for computer storage since the 1950s. The most widely utilized reels measure 10.5 inches in diameter and contain 2,400 feet of tape. Smaller reels (7 inches and 8.5 inches) and different tape lengths (600, 1,200, and 3,600 feet) are available, but they are less commonly encountered. These variations aside, information is recorded and read by a computer peripheral device variously termed a *reel-to-reel tape drive*, a *half-inch reel tape drive*, or a *nine-track tape drive*. The tapes themselves are described as *nine-track tapes* or *nine-track reels* to differentiate them from other half-inch magnetic tapes, which are packaged in cartridges. Across the tape width, the bits that encode individual characters are recorded in nine parallel tracks. Eight of the tracks store data bits that encode characters. The ninth track is reserved for a parity bit that facilitates detection of recording and playback errors.

Individual characters follow one another down the length of nine-track tape. The linear recording density is measured in **bits per inch (bpi)** along the tape's length. Depending on the model, available nine-track magnetic tape drives support linear recording densities of 800, 1,600, or 6,250 bpi. For a 2,400-foot reel of nine-track tape, approximate storage capacities are 20 megabytes at 800 bpi, 40 megabytes at 1,600 bpi, and 160 megabytes at 6,250 bpi. Applicable standards include ISO 962, *Information Processing—Implementation of the 7-bit Coded Character Set and Its 7-bit and 8-bit Extensions on 9-Track 12,7 mm (0.5 in) Magnetic Tape;* ISO/IEC 1863, *Information Processing—9-Track, 12,7 mm (0.5 in) Wide Magnetic Tape for*

Information Interchange Using NRZ1 at 32 ftpmm (800 ftpi)—32 cpmm (800 cpi);
ISO/IEC 3788, *Information Processing—9-Track, 12,7 mm (0.5 in) Wide Magnetic
Tape for Information Interchange Using Phase Encoding at 126 ftpmm (3200 ftpi)—63
cpmm (1600 cpi);* and ISO 5652 *Information Processing—9-Track, 12,7 mm (0.5 in)
Wide Magnetic Tape for Information Interchange—Format and Recording, Using
Group Coding at 246 cpmm (6250 cpi).*

Introduced in 1964, nine-track tape is, in effect, an obsolete computer storage
format. Manufacturers of magnetic tape products have shifted their research and
marketing efforts from half-inch reels to more compact cartridge formats described
next. Technical innovations ceased in the 1970s, and nine-track tapes are no longer
the preferred media for data archiving, data backup, or records retention. In fact, new
nine-track tapes are rarely recorded for any purpose, but nine-track tape drives
remain commercially available to read the hundreds of millions of tapes created in
the past by corporations, government agencies, and other organizations. These tapes
will remain subject to occasional reference, if only to convert their contents to other
media. In particular, legacy data recorded on nine-track tapes must be transferred to
other media when mainframe and midrange computer applications are upgraded or
replaced. This requirement will diminish over time, but it will not be completely
eliminated for many years.

The predecessors of nine-track tape drives employed a seven-track recording
format. Introduced in the early 1950s, such devices have not been manufactured for
almost half a century, but magnetic tapes created by them may be encountered when
inventorying electronic records in computer centers or offsite storage repositories.
Similar in appearance to their nine-track counterparts, seven-track reels featured
recording densities ranging from 100 to 556 bpi. Some older formats for nine-track
magnetic tapes employed recording densities of 200 or 556 bpi. Generally, magnetic
tapes recorded at any density below 800 bpi should be considered obsolete media
that are unreadable by available equipment.

Half-Inch Data Cartridges

Half-inch data cartridges are based on magnetic tape formats developed by IBM
and subsequently adopted by other computer equipment and media manufacturers.
Half-inch data cartridges are principally encountered in mainframe and midrange
computer installations where they offer compact, convenient, higher-capacity alternatives to nine-track magnetic tape drives and media. The first half-inch data cartridge drive, the IBM 3480 Magnetic Tape Cartridge Subsystem, was introduced in
1984. Its chromium-dioxide recording medium is packaged in a plastic cartridge that
measures four inches by five inches by one inch in size. The tape's half-inch width is
divided into two parallel sets of nine tracks each. One set of tracks is recorded from
the beginning to the end of the cartridge, using one-quarter inch of tape width. The
tape is then rewound, and the other set of tracks is recorded from beginning to end.

Most 3480-type data cartridges contain 550 feet of magnetic tape. The nominal
cartridge capacity is 200 megabytes, which is equivalent to five reels of nine-track
magnetic tape recorded at 1,600 bpi or 1.25 reels recorded at 6,250 bpi. Longer tapes,

with storage capacities up to 300 megabytes, are available. Two related data cartridge formats, the 3490 and 3490E, were introduced in 1989 and 1991, respectively. The 3490 format is a version of the 3480 format with data compression capabilities, which can triple cartridge capacity. The 3490E format employs 36-track bidirectional recording and a longer tape than its 3480 and 3490 counterparts. A 3490E data cartridge can store 800 megabytes in the uncompressed recording mode or up to 2.4 gigabytes when compression is employed.

The 3480, 3490, and 3490E data cartridge formats are collectively categorized as 34XX formats. They are covered by various national and international standards, including ISO 9661, *Information Technology—Data Interchange on 12,7 mm Wide Magnetic Tape Cartridges—18 Tracks, 1491 Data Bytes per Millimetre;* ISO/IEC 11559, *Information Technology—Data Interchange on 12,7 mm Wide 18-Track Magnetic Tape Cartridges—Extended Format;* and ISO/IEC 14251, *Information Technology—Data Interchange on 12,7 mm Wide 36-Track Magnetic Tape Cartridges.*

During the 1980s and 1990s, half-inch data cartridges steadily supplanted nine-track reels as the magnetic tape formats of choice for data archiving and backup operations in mainframe and midrange computer installations. Compared to nine-track reels of magnetic tape, half-inch data cartridges require less shelf space for a given quantity of computer-processable information. Their space-saving advantages are particularly significant where large numbers of magnetic tapes must be stored in environmentally-controlled vaults, computer rooms, or other expensive facilities. Replacement of nine-track reels with half-inch data cartridges can expand a vault's capacity, thus avoiding or minimizing costly construction or procurement of additional storage facilities.

For continued utility of information recorded on half-inch data cartridges, manufacturers of 34XX drives have routinely provided backward compatibility with predecessor formats for reading and/or recording. Thus, 3490-type drives can read cartridges recorded in the 3480 format, while 3490E-type drives can read cartridges recorded in the 3480 and 3490 formats.

IBM discontinued its 34XX drives in the late 1990s, although new and refurbished products of other manufacturers were available at the time this chapter was written. The 3590 data cartridge format, the successor to the 34XX format, was introduced in 1995. Developed jointly by IBM and the 3M Company, the 3590 data cartridge is identical to its 34XX counterparts in size, but it contains a metal particle tape designed specifically for high-density recording. A 3590 data cartridge can store 10 or 20 gigabytes of computer-processable information depending on the tape length. When data compression is applied, the cartridge's capacity is tripled. An enhanced version introduced in 1999, can store 40 or 60 gigabytes per cartridge, without data compression or up to 180 gigabytes with compression. For backward compatibility with the many millions of half-inch data cartridges currently in storage, 3590 and 3590E tape drives can read media recorded in the 36-track 3490E format and the 18-track 3480 and 3490 formats.

The 3592 data cartridge, which has replaced the 3590 format, supports uncompressed storage capacities of 60 to 700 gigabytes. Compressed capacities can exceed two terabytes. The 3592 cartridges are available in rewritable and write-once (non-erasable) configurations. The latter are principally intended for financial services applications that require nonerasable media to satisfy retention requirements for certain electronic records as specified in government regulations. The 3592 tape drives are not compatible with 3590 or 34XX data cartridges.

Digital Linear Tape

Digital linear tape (DLT) was introduced in the early 1990s by Digital Equipment Corporation as a higher-capacity alternative to the 34XX formats. In 1994, Digital Equipment sold the DLT technology to Quantum Corporation. Since that time, DLT has established itself as one of the most important data backup formats in midrange computer and network server installations. DLT products are available from many storage peripheral vendors. Like their 34XX and 3590 counterparts, DLT cartridges measure four inches by four inches by one inch in size and contain half-inch tape. The tape's recording layer features a high-density metal particle material.

DLT capacities, which depend on specific equipment and media configurations, have increased steadily and significantly since the technology's introduction. At the time of this writing, the highest capacity DLT cartridges—characterized as *super digital linear tape (SDLT)*—could store 800 gigabytes in an uncompressed format. Cartridge capacity doubles with data compression. Older DLT cartridge formats provided 10 to 40 gigabytes of uncompressed storage capacity, while the first SDLT cartridges could store 110 gigabytes.

Characteristics of unrecorded digital linear tape cartridges are specified in various international standards, including ISO/IEC 13421, *Information Technology—Data Interchange on 12,7 mm, 48-Track Magnetic Tape Cartridges—DLT 1 Format;* ISO/IEC 13962, *Information Technology—Data Interchange on 12,7 mm, 112-Track Magnetic Tape Cartridges—DLT 2 Format;* ISO/IEC 14833, *Information Technology—Data Interchange on 12,7 mm, 128-Track Magnetic Tape Cartridges—DLT 3 Format;* ISO/IEC 15307, *Information Technology—Data Interchange on 12,7 mm, 128-Track Magnetic Tape Cartridges—DLT 4 Format;* ISO/IEC 15896, *Information Technology—Data Interchange on 12,7 mm, 208-Track Magnetic Tape Cartridges—DLT 5 Format;* ISO/IEC 16382, *Information Technology—Data Interchange on 12,7 mm, 208-Track Magnetic Tape Cartridges—DLT 6 Format;* and ISO/IEC 22051, *Information Technology—Data Interchange on 12,7 mm, 448-Track Magnetic Tape Cartridges—SDLT 1 Format.* Higher-capacity DLT and SDLT drives provide backward compatibility with selected lower-capacity DLT and SDLT formats for both reading and recording.

LTO Ultrium

Linear tape-open (LTO) technology is a joint development of IBM, Hewlett-Packard, and Certance, a division of Seagate Technology that was subsequently acquired by Quantum Corporation. Introduced in the late 1990s, it provides high capacity for voluminous data backup requirements in large computer and network server installations. LTO specifications initially involved two different magnetic tape cartridge formats: **Ultrium**, intended for high-capacity storage, and Accelis, designed for fast access to recorded information in tape automation installations. The LTO Accelis format, which employed a different technology than Ultrium, was subsequently discontinued due to low demand. LTO Ultrium format has established itself as one of the most important magnetic tape formats. The applicable standard is ISO/IEC 22050, *Information Technology—Data Interchange on 12,7 mm, 384-Track Magnetic Tape Cartridges—Ultrium-1 Format.*

The LTO Ultrium format features half-inch tape and a single-reel cartridge design. First-generation Ultrium cartridges, known as *LTO-1*, could store up to 100 gigabytes of uncompressed data or twice that amount when compression is utilized. LTO-4, the highest-capacity format available at the time this chapter was written, can store up to 800 gigabytes uncompressed. According to the technology's six-generation migration path, Ultrium cartridges will eventually store up to 3.2 terabytes of uncompressed data or 6.4 terabytes compressed. LTO-5 cartridges, which are scheduled for commercialization in 2009, will store 3.2 terabytes uncompressed.

Quarter-Inch Cartridges

Quarter-inch cartridges (QICs), the most diverse group of magnetic tape products, were introduced in the early 1970s as a lower cost alternative to nine-track magnetic tape reels in small computer installations. They continue to be marketed for hard disk backup, data archiving, and other information storage activities in small-to-midrange computer configurations, including personal computers and network servers. With an installed base of 15 million units by the mid-1990s, QIC drives outnumbered all other magnetic tape devices combined, but they were not widely adopted by desktop computer users, and the network server market ultimately preferred higher-performance tape technologies that offered higher media capacities and automated tape handling devices for unattended backup operations.

Records managers are cautioned that QIC products encompass a variety of formats that were developed at various points in time. Although the earliest quarter-inch cartridge drives and media employed proprietary recording formats, most products introduced in the late 1980s and 1990s complied with specifications developed by Quarter Inch Cartridge Drive Standards Incorporated, an international trade association that ceased operation in 1998. Those specifications were known as *QIC development standards* or **QIC formats**, while compliant quarter-inch cartridge drives and media were described as *QIC products*. Although QIC products replaced older quarter-inch cartridge drives based on proprietary recording formats, records managers may encounter proprietary quarter-inch cartridges when inventorying older electronic records in magnetic tape storage vaults, computer rooms, or other media repositories.

With notable exceptions, quarter-inch cartridges contain magnetic tape that measures one-quarter inch wide. Though described as cartridges, quarter-inch media are actually cassettes that incorporate both a tape supply spool and a take-up spool in a single plastic shell. True cartridges, by contrast, contain only the supply spool; the magnetic tape passes out of the cartridge during use and must be rewound prior to removing the cartridge from its drive. Imprecise descriptive terminology aside, quarter-inch magnetic tape cartridges are available in data cartridge and mini-cartridge configurations. Quarter-inch data cartridges measure 4 inches by 6 inches by 0.625 inch. They are intended for magnetic tape drives in the 5.25-inch form factor. Quarter-inch minicartridges measure two inches by three inches by one-half inch. They are intended for magnetic tape drives in the 3.5-inch form factor. QIC recording formats for data cartridges are identified by the suffix DC, while the suffix MC identifies recording formats for QIC minicartridges.

From their inception, QIC products were designed to back up hard disk drives in one operation with a single recording medium. The media capacities of newly-developed QIC formats consequently approximated prevalent hard drive capacities. Through the mid-1980s, when hard drives stored much less information than they do today, QIC formats for 5.25-inch data cartridges provided less than 200 megabytes of recording capacity, while minicartridge capacities were even lower. As hard drive capacities increased, however, denser QIC formats were developed. Gigabyte-level QIC media were introduced in the early 1990s. Specifications for certain QIC formats permitted data compression, which approximately doubled cartridge capacity.

As a group, data cartridge capacities exceeded their minicartridge counterparts, although the latter, which require smaller drives, were typically preferred by desktop computer users. To achieve higher media capacities, several manufacturers introduced variant QIC technologies that package a wider and/or longer magnetic tape in a minicartridge shell. Although the resulting cartridges did not necessarily contain quarter-inch tape, they were typically categorized as QIC products and were covered by QIC standards. Travan technology, the best-known QIC variant, was introduced in 1994. It was quickly adopted by manufacturers of QIC drives and media. Uncompressed storage capacities range from 400 megabytes per minicartridge for the Travan TR-1 format to 20 gigabytes per minicartridge for the Travan TR-7 format. These amounts double when data compression is applied.

Among other high-capacity QIC variants, the QIC-Wide format was introduced by Sony in 1993. The QIC-EXtra format, also known as the *QIC-EC* or *EC1000 format*, was developed by Gigatek Memory Systems and Verbatim. These QIC formats have been discontinued, but they may be encountered in inventories of electronic records.

Eight-Millimeter Data Cartridges

Several computer storage products are based on technologies adapted from video and audio recording formats described next. The quarter-inch and half-inch magnetic tape drives discussed in preceding sections employ longitudinal recording methods. Their stationary magnetic heads record data in parallel tracks that run the entire length of a tape. By contrast, video and audio tape products employ helical scan technology. They record computer-processable information in narrow tracks positioned at an acute angle with respect to the edges of a tape. As their principal advantage for electronic recordkeeping, helical scan technologies offer higher densities than are possible with longitudinal tape recording. The most widely encountered helical scan formats for computer storage applications are eight-millimeter data cartridges and digital audio tape (DAT).

Eight-millimeter data cartridges are based on eight-millimeter videocassette technology, but they contain a metal particle or evaporated metal tape specifically designed for high-density data recording. The cartridges, which are actually cassettes, measure 3.7 inches by 2.5 inches by 0.6 inch. Sometimes described as *Data8 products* to distinguish them from eight-millimeter video recorders, eight-millimeter data cartridge drives are widely used for backup operations and data archiving in midrange computer and network server installations. Applicable standards include ISO/IEC 11319, *Information Technology—8 mm Wide Magnetic Tape Cartridge for Information Interchange—Helical Scan Recording*, and ISO/IEC 12246, *Information Technology—8 mm Wide Magnetic Tape Cartridge Dual Azimuth Format for Information Interchange—Helical Scan Recording*.

Exabyte Corporation, the first manufacturer of eight-millimeter data cartridge drives, was acquired by Tandberg Data Incorporated in 2006. Exabyte's first-generation eight-millimeter product stored 300 megabytes to 2.5 gigabytes per data cartridge, depending on tape length. Second-generation models offered improved recording techniques and data compression capabilities, which significantly increased media capacity. By the early 1990s, Exabyte's eight-millimeter data cartridges could store 5 gigabytes in the uncompressed recording mode and 10 gigabytes with compression. A longer tape, introduced in the mid-1990s, increased the maximum cartridge capacity to 7 gigabytes uncompressed and 14 gigabytes compressed. In 1996, Exabyte introduced its Mammoth line of eight-millimeter data storage products with 20 gigabytes of uncompressed cartridge capacity. Exabyte's second-generation Mammoth-2 (M2) format provided an uncompressed cartridge capacity of 60 gigabytes. Mammoth format media are covered by ISO/IEC 15757, *Information Technology—Data Interchange on 8 mm Wide Magnetic Tape Cartridge—Helical Scan Recording—DA-2 Format*, and ISO/IEC 18836, *Information Technology—8 mm Wide Magnetic Tape Cartridge for Information Interchange—Helical Scan Recording—Mammoth Tape-2 Format*.

In the late 1990s, Exabyte introduced its line of VXA tape drives, which use packet technology for high reliability and error-free data recovery, even from damaged media. The applicable standard is ISO/IEC 20062, *Information Technology—8 mm Wide Magnetic Tape Cartridge for Information Interchange—Helical Scan Recording—VXA-1 Format*. Uncompressed storage capacities range from 20 gigabytes to 160 gigabytes per eight-millimeter VXA data cartridge. Future VXA products will store up to 640 gigabytes per cartridge.

Sony's **advanced intelligent tape (AIT)** format, which was introduced in 1996, has evolved through five generations. Uncompressed storage capacities range from 20 to 400 gigabytes per eight-millimeter cartridge. Sony's **memory in cassette (MIC)** technology provides an embedded semiconductor chip that provides faster access to data and stores information about a cartridge's history and current status. The AIT format is covered by several standards, including ISO/IEC 15780, *Information Technology—8 mm Wide Magnetic Tape Cartridge—Helical Scan Recording—AIT-1 Format;* ISO/IEC 18809, *Information Technology—8 mm Wide Magnetic Tape Cartridge for Information Interchange—Helical Scan Recording—AIT-1 with MIC Format;* ISO/IEC 18810,

Information Technology—8 mm Wide Magnetic Tape Cartridge for Information Interchange—Helical Scan Recording—AIT-2 with MIC Format; and ISO/IEC 23651, *Information Technology—8 mm Wide Magnetic Tape Cartridge for Information Interchange—Helical Scan Recording—AIT-3 Format.* The next generation AIT cartridge is projected to store 800 gigabytes. Compression doubles the cartridge capacity. Like LTO Ultrium, AIT media are available in rewritable and write-once configurations. The latter are designed to satisfy regulatory compliance requirements for retention of electronic records in the financial services industry.

Sony's super AIT (SAIT) format, introduced in 2003, is a higher-capacity implementation of AIT technology. Featuring a wider tape in a larger cartridge, it is designed to compete with SuperDLT and LTO Ultrium technology. First- and second-generation SAIT cartridges can store 500 and 800 gigabytes, respectively. Uncompressed capacities will ultimately reach four terabytes per cartridge.

As with other computer storage products, new eight-millimeter drives eventually render their predecessors obsolete. Prior to the introduction of VXA technology, Exabyte's new drives offered backward compatibility with selected eight-millimeter data cartridges recorded by earlier models. VXA tape drives cannot read data cartridges recorded by older Exabyte eight-millimeter tape drives, which have been discontinued. Sony's newest AIT drives can read older AIT media, but eight-millimeter data cartridges recorded by AIT and Exabyte drives are not interchangeable.

Digital Audio Tape

As their name implies, **digital audio tape (DAT)** products for computer storage are based on technology originally developed for audio recording. The first DAT systems for computer applications, characterized as *DATA DAT,* were introduced in 1988. Competing industry groups initially proposed different and incompatible data recording methods, but the digital data storage (DDS) format, which was co-developed by Sony and Hewlett-Packard, became the basis for subsequent product development. Specifications for DAT recording formats and media capacities are defined by the DDS/DAT Manufacturers Group, which is comprised of DAT drive and media manufacturers. With lower storage capacities than other magnetic tape technologies, the DDS format is principally intended for small-to-medium-sized businesses, government agencies, and other organizations.

Digital audio tape is 3.81 millimeters wide and features a high-coercivity, metal particle recording material. Tape lengths range from 60 to 170 meters. DAT cartridges, which are actually cassettes, measure 3 inches by 2 inches by 0.4 inch. The original DAT recording format, now termed DDS-1, provided 1.3 gigabytes of storage capacity per 60-meter tape. With 90-meter tape, the cartridge capacity is increased to two gigabytes. A DDS-DC format, introduced in 1992, used data compression, which approximately doubled cartridge capacity. The DDS-2 format was introduced in 1993 as an extension of the DDS-DC format with a higher track density and a longer tape. The DDS-2 storage capacity is four gigabytes per cartridge in the uncompressed mode, or approximately eight gigabytes with data compression. The DDS-3 format, introduced in 1994, provided an uncompressed storage capacity of 12 gigabytes per DAT cartridge. With data compression, the cartridge capacity is 24 gigabytes. The DDS-4 format, introduced in 1997, offers 24 gigabytes of uncompressed cartridge capacity, with data compression raising that amount to 48 gigabytes.

Various standards cover the DDS formats, including ISO/IEC 12247, *Information Technology—3,81 mm Wide Magnetic Tape Cartridge for Information Interchange—Helical Scan Recording—DDS Format Using 60 m and 90 m Length Tapes;* ISO/IEC 11557, *Information Technology—3,81 mm Wide Magnetic Tape Cartridge for Information Interchange—Helical Scan Recording—DDS-DC Format Using 60 m and 90 m Length Tapes;* ISO/IEC 13923, *Information Technology—3,81 mm Wide Magnetic Tape Cartridge for Information Interchange—Helical Scan Recording—DDS-2 Format Using 120 m Length Tape;* ISO/IEC 15521, *Information Technology—3,81 mm Wide Magnetic Tape Cartridge for Information Interchange—Helical Scan Recording—DDS-3 Format Using 125 m Length Tape;* and ISO/IEC 17462, *Information Technology—3,81 mm Wide Magnetic Tape Cartridge for Information Interchange—Helical Scan Recording—DDS-4 Format.*

Although DDS-4 was the last official DDS format, Hewlett-Packard has continued to develop higher-capacity DAT formats. The DAT 72 format, introduced in 2003, provides 36 gigabytes of uncompressed storage capacity (72 gigabytes compressed) on a 170-meter cartridge. The DAT 160 format, introduced in 2007, differs from its predecessors in using an eight-millimeter data cartridge that can store 80 gigabytes uncompressed or 160 gigabytes compressed. Although DAT 160 does not use DDS nomenclature, it is a sixth-generation format. The development path for DAT technology projects an eighth-generation format with an uncompressed storage capacity of 300 gigabytes per cassette.

Depending on the model, a DAT drive provides backward-compatibility with some but not all earlier formats. All DDS drives are backward-compatible with cartridges recorded by their predecessors. Thus, a DDS-4 drive can read cartridges recorded in the lower-capacity DDS-1, DDS-2, and DDS-3 formats with or without compression. DAT 72 drives are backward-compatible with DDS-3 and DDS-4 cartridges. DAT 160 drives can read tapes recorded in the DDS-4 and DAT 72 formats.

Audio Tapes

For many organizations, voice dictation tapes are the oldest category of electronic record. In some businesses and government agencies, voice dictation equipment preceded computer installations by several decades. They were among the first applications of magnetic recording technology. During the 1960s and 1970s, several companies marketed voice dictation systems that utilized magnetic-coated belts, small magnetic disks, and continuous loops of magnetic tape. Such media may be encountered in offsite storage locations and archival repositories, but they are no longer manufactured or sold. Today, voice dictation systems, telephone answering machines, and other office-oriented audio recording products employ magnetic tape cassettes in C-type, microcassette, or minicassette configurations.

C-type cassettes are also described as *standard size* or *Philips-type cassettes.* They measure 3.9 inches by 2.5 inches by 0.5 inch and contain magnetic tape that measures four millimeters wide. Although manufacturers' product designations vary, C-type audio cassettes are typically identified by a code that indicates their recording time in minutes. C-90 cassettes, for example, provide 90 minutes of double-sided recording time (45 minutes per side). C-30 and C-60 are also popular sizes for voice dictation. Other cassette designations range from C-05 to C-120. The longer the recording time, of course, the longer the tape that the cassette contains.

During the 1970s and early 1980s, C-type cassettes were used for data recording by early PCs and word processing systems, automatic send-receive (ASR) computer terminals, point-of-sale terminals, key-to-tape data entry devices, desktop calculators, and some scientific instruments. Cassettes intended for data recording were typically described as *digital* or *data-grade cassettes* to distinguish them from their audio counterparts, which are designed to record analog signals. For the most part, data-oriented cassette recorders were hampered by low media capacities and marginal performance. Other storage devices discussed in this chapter have replaced them in computer installations. Digital cassettes may be encountered when inventorying older electronic records, however. Such media must be viewed as obsolete. Compatible devices are unlikely to be available to read their contents.

As their names suggest, microcassettes and minicassettes are smaller than their C-type counterparts. Audio microcassettes measure 2 inches by 1.25 inches by 0.25 inch. They were originally developed for portable dictation equipment, although they are also used by desktop audio recording devices and transcribers. Audio minicassettes measure approximately three inches by two inches by three-eighths inch. Depending on tape length, they can record 30 or 60 minutes of voice dictation.

Microcassettes and minicassettes are designed to record speech rather than music. C-type audio cassettes may be used for music recording as well as voice dictation. Standards developed by the International Electrotechnical Commission (IEC) specify the magnetic recording media contained in such cassettes. IEC Type I cassettes, widely described as *normal bias cassettes*, contain tape coated with gamma ferric oxide, the same recording material used by nine-track computer tape and some floppy disks. The least expensive Type I cassettes are suitable for voice dictation systems and telephone answering machines where recordable frequencies are limited to a narrow range and high fidelity is rarely required. For music recording, which involves a broader range of audio frequencies, most media manufacturers offer Type I cassettes with improved gamma ferric oxide formulations. IEC Type II and Type IV cassettes are intended exclusively for music recording in applications where high audio quality is an important consideration. Type II cassettes, sometimes described as *high bias cassettes*, contain chromium dioxide tapes. Type IV cassettes contain metal particle tapes. Type II and Type IV cassettes require tape recording equipment compatible with their particular magnetic materials. IEC Type III audio cassettes have been discontinued.

Open-reel magnetic tapes for audio recording are used principally by music studios, although inventories of electronic records may reveal older audio tape reels that contain dictation, interviews, depositions, or other voice recordings. Some government agencies, for example, have produced audio tape recordings of meetings, hearings, and other proceedings for decades. Widths of open-reel tape range from one-quarter inch to two inches. Lengths vary with reel sizes, which may exceed 10 inches in diameter. Several digital audio cassette technologies were developed specifically for music recording. The best-known example, digital audio tape (DAT), utilized digital rather than analog recording techniques to create magnetic tapes with sonic properties similar to those of compact discs (CDs). The **digital compact cassette (DCC)** was introduced by Philips and Matsushita in the early 1990s, but it was discontinued after several years.

Video Tapes

As previously noted, video recording equipment dates from the 1950s. Like their audio counterparts, the earliest studio-oriented video tape recorders utilized open-reel media. Four-head video recorders, typically described as *quadraplex devices*, employed two-inch tape supplied in 2,400-foot lengths. In the 1970s, they were supplanted by helical-scan devices known as *C-format recorders*, which supported a broader range of features than quadraplex technology. C-format devices record video signals on a magnetic tape that measures one inch wide. Individual reels may contain up to three hours of video recording.

U-matic systems, introduced by Sony Corporation in 1971, were the first video recording devices to utilize magnetic tape cassettes. U-matic tape is three-quarters of an inch wide. Recording times range from a few minutes to over one hour per cassette, depending on tape length. U-matic is an obsolete format; however, some businesses, government agencies, and other organizations have large collections of previously recorded U-matic cassettes. For continued utility, such video recordings can be converted to C-format tapes or to one of the cassette formats described next. Video service bureaus offer appropriate conversion capabilities.

Sony introduced the first commercially successful half-inch video cassette recorder, the Betamax, in 1975. Two years later, the Victor Company of Japan (JVC) introduced the VHS video cassette format, which ultimately supplanted its Beta counterpart in business and consumer applications. VHS cassettes measure 7.4 inches by 4 inches by 1 inch. As with the audio cassettes, tape lengths are typically identified by a code that indicates the recording time in minutes when the VHS recorder is operated at the standard play (SP) speed. The most popular length, designated T-120, provides two hours of recording time per cassette at the SP speed, three times that amount at the extended play (EP) speed. Other VHS cassette designations range from T-15 through T-180.

Two versions of the VHS format, Super-VHS (S-VHS) and VHS-compact (VHS-C), have been developed for special situations. The Super-VHS format is intended for applications where image quality is a paramount consideration. S-VHS cassettes are identical to their conventional VHS counterparts in size and appearance, but they contain higher-grade recording materials. A special S-VHS cassette recorder or **camcorder** is required. VHS-C is an implementation of the VHS format designed specifically for use in camcorders. VHS-C cassettes measure approximately 4 inches by 2.5 inches by 0.5 inch. As explained previously, tape lengths are identified by a code that indicates the recording time in minutes at the standard play (SP) speed. TC-20 cassettes, for example, provide 20 minutes of recording time. A VHS-C cassette is inserted into an adapter for playback on a conventional VHS-type video cassette recorder. S-VHS-C, a related format, is a compact implementation of Super-VHS cassette technology. S-VHS-C cassettes are the same size as their VHS-C counterparts.

The Beta format continues to be used by professional video studios and in occasional business applications. Beta-format video cassettes measure 6.1 inches by 3.8 inches by 1 inch deep. As with VHS cassettes, recording capacities vary with tape length and recording speed. Beta video cassettes are identified by a code that indicates the tape length in feet. At the Beta II speed, the recording mode utilized by many prerecorded Beta-format tapes, an L-750 cassette provides three hours of recording time. Other Beta cassette designations range from L-250 to L-830.

The Betacam format, introduced by Sony in 1982, and BetacamSP format, introduced in 1986, use a larger cassette that measures 5.5 inches by 10 inches by 1 inch deep. As high-quality implementations of Beta technology, the Betacam and BetacamSP formats are principally encountered in professional broadcast recording rather than business applications. The same situation occurred with the less successful M videocassette recording format, developed by Matsushita and RCA in the early 1980s, and its higher-quality successor, the M-II format, introduced by Matsushita in 1986. M-II cassettes measure four inches by eight inches by one inch.

Like the VHS-C format, eight-millimeter video cassettes are primarily intended for camcorder applications. The cassettes are identical to their data recording counterparts. Their small size permits the design of very compact, lightweight camcorders. Eight-millimeter tape lengths are identified by a code that indicates the recording time in minutes, ranging from about 15 minutes to two hours per cassette. Eight-millimeter video cassettes employ metal particle recording media. The Hi-8 format is an implementation of eight-millimeter video cassette technology designed specifically for applications where high image quality is required. It is, in effect, the eight-millimeter counterpart of the S-VHS format. Hi-8 cassettes are identical to their conventional eight-millimeter counterparts in size and appearance, but they contain metal-evaporated tape rather than metal particle tape.

The video recording formats and media described previously employ **analog coding,** the historically dominant encoding method in video applications. However, like other information storage technologies, analog video devices are increasingly supplanted by digital recording. Digital video tape technologies date from the mid-1980s. Early examples, such as the D1, D2, and D3 formats, were intended for professional broadcast videotaping. Some digital video tape formats have been adapted for high-capacity data recording. Digital video (DV) cassette formats for business and consumer applications date from the mid-1990s. Conventional DV cassettes measure 3 inches by 5 inches by 0.6 inch deep. **Mini-DV cassettes,** intended for use in digital camcorders, measure 2 inches by 2.2 inches by 0.5 inch deep. DV tape is one-quarter inch wide. Among other digital formats, Digital 8 camcorders utilize the Hi-8 media described previously. D-VHS and Digital-S media are based on VHS and Super-VHS cassettes. Betacam SX and Digital Betacam are digital implementations of the Betacam format.

Types of magnetic media commonly used for computer recordkeeping are listed in Table 2.1. Storage capacity and information management applications are listed for each media.

Obsolete Magnetic Media

> *If information recorded on a given medium has not been retrieved for years or decades, its continuing reference value must be questioned.*

Various magnetic media were utilized by older office machines, video recorders, and other information processing devices that are no longer manufactured or marketed. In the absence of a formal retention program for electronic records, some businesses, government agencies, and other organizations continue to maintain files of obsolete media, even though the equipment required to record and read them is unavailable. Often, such media were shipped to offsite storage locations, or otherwise packed away, when the devices that used them were replaced by new technologies. Examples of obsolete magnetic media that may be encountered during inventories of electronic records are described next. A comprehensive discussion is beyond the scope of this

Magnetic Media
for Computer
Recordkeeping

Table 2.1

Media Type	Storage Capacity	Information Management Applications
Fixed hard disk	multi-GB to multi-TB	Online access to frequently referenced information
Hard disk cartridges	1 GB+	Online access to frequently referenced information; data archiving and backup
Floppy disks	1.44 MB to 750 MB	Data and software distribution, data archiving, and backup
9-track magnetic	40 MB to 180 MB	Data archiving and backup; data and tape reels software distribution
34XX data cartridges	200 MB to 2.4 GB	Data archiving, backup, and distribution
3590 and 3592	10 GB to 2 TB	Data archiving, backup, and distribution data cartridges
Digital Linear Tape (DLT)	10 GB to 800 GB+	Data archiving, backup, and distribution
LTO Ultrium	100 GB to 3 TB+	Data archiving, backup, and distribution
8mm data cartridges	20 GB to 800 GB+	Data archiving, backup, and distribution; video recording
Digital Audio Tape (DAT)	1 GB to 80 GB+	Data archiving, backup, and distribution; audio recording
Quarter-Inch Cartridges (QIC)	40 MB to multi-GB	Data archiving, backup, and distribution

book; for every obsolete medium mentioned here, several dozen additional examples could have been cited. When making retention decisions about obsolete media, records managers should be guided by common sense. If information recorded on a given medium has not been retrieved for years or decades, its continuing reference value must be questioned. If the device required to read the medium no longer exists, the electronic records it contains cannot be retrieved. No business purpose is served by retaining such records. In any case, some obsolete magnetic media have been in storage for many years. Physical or chemical damage, as discussed elsewhere in this book, probably renders them unusable.

The Magnetic Tape/Selectric Typewriter (MT/ST), a word processing system introduced by IBM in the 1960s, stored character-coded text in specially designed magnetic tape cartridges. During the 1970s, the MT/ST was replaced by word processing systems that utilized magnetic-coated tabulating-size cards, popularly described as *mag cards*. As originally developed for the IBM Magnetic Card/Selectric Typewriter (MC/ST), each card could store 5,000 characters, the approximate equivalent of two double-spaced typewritten pages. Magnetic cards utilized by other word processing systems offered higher storage capacities. Through the mid-1970s, magnetic cards competed with magnetic tape cassettes as the dominant media in early word processing installations, but both were eventually supplanted by floppy disks. During the 1960s and early 1970s, some electronic accounting machines utilized paper cards coated with magnetic strips for data recording. Such pre-computer devices and media are no longer manufactured. Small magnetic-coated cards were likewise used by some calculators during the 1970s. Today, credit cards contain a strip of magnetic recording materials, but such media have little records management significance.

Small, removable magnetic disks were employed in the System 6:5, a voice dictation product marketed by IBM during the 1970s. Each disk offered six minutes of audio recording capacity, which is about the time required to dictate a typical business letter. For transcription, individual disks were stacked in cartridges, which had a total playback capacity of five hours. Other dictation equipment, as previously noted, utilized magnetic-coated belts or loops of tape in varying lengths. A typical magnetic belt measured three inches wide and provided up to 20 minutes of audio recording time. Dictation systems that utilized such magnetic belts were discontinued in the mid-1970s.

During the late 1960s and early 1970s, various video recording products were briefly and unsuccessfully marketed under such trade names as Instavision, Cartravision, Betacord, and V-Cord. Remembered only by a small number of embittered customers, they had no impact on records management operations. A quarter-inch video tape format, called the **compact video cassette (CVC)**, was developed by Funai in the early 1980s. Marketed in the United States by Technicolor Audio-Visual, it was not a commercial success. The European V-2000 format, which was utilized in video cassette recorders manufactured by Grundig, was never available in the United States. The eight-track audio cartridge, perhaps the best-known example of a defunct magnetic recording medium, played no role in records management applications.

Optical Disks

As previously defined, optical storage technology uses lasers to record information by selectively altering the light reflectance characteristics of a platter-shaped storage medium. Within an optical storage device, the recorded information is read by a laser and a pickup mechanism that detects variations in reflected light, much as read/write heads sense variations in the alignment of metallic particles within magnetic disks and tapes. To prevent destruction of information, the playback laser operates at lower power or a different wavelength than the laser used for recording.

As their most important characteristic, **optical media** feature high areal recording densities—that is, individual bits that encode machine-readable information are very closely spaced, allowing many bits to be recorded within a given area. The result is high media capacity. When the first optical media were introduced in the early 1980s, they provided gigabyte-level storage at a time when most hard drives and magnetic tapes stored less than 200 megabytes. In recent years, magnetic recording technologies have caught up, but optical media still offer impressive storage capacities.

> *In records management work, optical disks are most closely associated with storage-intensive applications, such as electronic document imaging, but they are suitable for other purposes as well.*

Optical disks in the various formats described next are the most important optical storage media. In records management work, optical disks are most closely associated with storage-intensive applications, such as electronic document imaging, but they are suitable for other purposes as well. Any computer, audio, or video information that can be recorded onto magnetic tapes or magnetic disks can be stored on optical media, and vice versa. In businesses, government agencies, and other organizations, optical media can store huge quantities of character-coded text, computer databases, graphic images, video recordings, and audio signals.

All optical disks are removable media. With the exception of CDs and DVDs, optical disks are encapsulated in protective plastic cartridges that facilitate handling. Consequently, the terms "optical disk," "optical disk cartridge," or simply "optical cartridge" may be used interchangeably. Like magnetic tapes, optical disks are stored offline when not in use and must be inserted into a compatible drive for reading and recording. **Jukebox** units, also known as *optical disk libraries* or **autochangers**, automate this process.

Optical disks are a diverse product group that encompasses several formats with different attributes. At the time of this writing, the most important categories of optical disks were compact discs and DVDs, with **magneto-optical disks** playing a lesser role in some applications. All magnetic media support direct recording. However, optical disks are available in read-only and recordable varieties. **Read-only** optical disks, as their name implies, have no recordable properties. They are limited to playback of prerecorded information generated by a mastering and replication process. **Recordable**

optical disks, by contrast, permit direct recording of machine-readable information. In this respect, they resemble their magnetic counterparts. Recordable optical disks may be write-once or rewritable media. **Write-once optical disks** are sometimes described as *WORM media*; the acronym variously stands for Write Once Read Many or Write Once Read Mostly. Such disks are not erasable. Once information is recorded in a given area of a write-once optical disk, that area cannot be reused. Rewritable optical disks, by contrast, are erasable and reusable. The contents of previously recorded media segments can be deleted or overwritten with new information.

The following sections describe the most important optical disk formats for electronic recordkeeping. Some obsolete formats are also covered. The discussion concludes with a brief description of optical memory cards and optical tapes.

Compact Discs

Compact disc (CD) is the collective designation for a group of interrelated optical storage formats and products that are based on technology developed during the 1970s and 1980s by Sony and Philips. The most widely encountered type of CD is a rigid plastic platter that measures 120 millimeters (4.75 inches) in diameter. The various CD formats are distinguished by the type of information they contain. **Compact disc-digital audio (CD-DA)**, the first and best-known type of optical disk, was introduced in the 1980s as a sonically superior alternative to long-playing phonograph records and audio tape cassettes. Principally a consumer product, it has no records management significance. **Compact disc-read only memory (CD-ROM), compact disc-recordable (CD-R),** and **compact disc-rewritable (CD-RW)** are the compact disc formats for computer-processible information.

As a read-only technology, CD-ROM is essentially a publishing and distribution medium for software, databases, or other computer-processible information. Applicable standards include ISO 9660, *Information Processing—Volume and File Structure of CD-ROM for Information Interchange,* published in 1988, and ISO/IEC 10149, *Information Technology—Data Interchange on Read-Only 120 mm Optical Data Disks (CD-ROM),* issued in 1989 and revised in 1995. Read-only optical disks, as previously defined, contain prerecorded information. They are produced by a mastering and replication process. Computer-generated information, video images, or audio signals to be recorded on a given CD-ROM are organized, edited, and otherwise prepared for submission to a production facility, which produces a master disk from which individual copies are generated by injection molding or some other process. The copies have no recordable properties. They are read by playback devices (CD-ROM drives) that have no recording mechanisms. A 4.75-inch CD-ROM, the most common size, can store about 540 megabytes of computer-processible information. Some product specification sheets cite capacities up to 650 megabytes, but that number represents unformatted capacity. An 80-millimeter (3.2-inch) CD-ROM, which can store about 190 megabytes, is rarely encountered in records management applications.

Compact disc-recordable (CD-R) and compact disc-rewritable (CD-RW) are recordable optical media. CD-R products are write-once optical disks that employ dye polymer recording technology. They feature a transparent polymer that contains an infrared-absorbing dye. Information is recorded by a laser that operates at the dye's absorption wavelength. The laser's energy is converted to heat, which creates pits or bumps in the polymer layer. The pits or bumps typically represent the one bits in digitally-coded data, while zero bits are represented by spaces. CD-RW media, which are erasable, employ phase-change recording technology. With unrecorded media, phase-change compounds exist in either a crystalline or an amorphous state. A laser records information by heating selected areas of the recording layer, inducing a crystalline-to-amorphous or amorphous-to-crystalline transition. Crystalline and amorphous areas have different reflectivity characteristics, which represent the one and zero bits in digitally-coded information.

Competitively priced and available from many suppliers, CD-R and CD-RW drives and media are widely encountered in desktop computer installations where they may be used for data backup, data archiving, or other purposes. Their formatted storage capacities range from 540 megabytes to 660 megabytes, depending on the type of medium selected. When used for digitized audio information, CD-R and CD-RW media provide up to 74 minutes of recording time.

DVD Formats

DVD—which originally stood for *digital video disc* and then *digital versatile disc*—is the replacement technology for CDs, which a DVD physically resembles. Like CDs, DVD media are available in two diameters: 120 millimeters and 80 millimeters. Applicable standards are ISO/IEC 16448, *Information Technology—120 mm DVD—Read-Only Disk*, and ISO/IEC 16449, *Information Technology—80 mm DVD—Read-Only Disk*. DVD specifications were developed in the mid-1990s by a group of cooperating companies. DVD media can store video, audio, or computer-processible information. DVD-video and DVD-audio are consumer formats that have little records management significance. Among the computer formats, DVD-ROM is the higher-capacity read-only successor to CD-ROM. Intended for publication and distribution of large databases, clip art libraries, document image collections, multimedia presentations, or other voluminous information, a single-sided, 120-millimeter DVD-ROM can store up to 4.7 gigabytes.

Recordable DVDs are available in write-once and rewritable formats:

- **DVD-R and DVD+R.** These media are write-once formats with storage capacities of 4.7 gigabytes for single-layer 120-millimeter media and 8.5 gigabytes for dual-layer 120-millimeter media. Each format is licensed by a coalition of computer, optical storage, and electronics companies. DVD-R, which was developed by the DVD Forum in the late 1990s, is covered by ISO/IEC 23912, *Information Technology—80 mm (1,46 Gbytes per side) and 120 mm (4,70 Gbytes per side) DVD Recordable Disk (DVD-R)*, and ISO/IEC 20563, *Information Technology—80 mm (1,23 Gbytes per side) and 120 mm (3,95 Gbytes per side) DVD-Recordable Disk (DVD-R)*, which relates to an older version with somewhat lower storage capacity. DVD+R, developed by the DVD+R Alliance in 2002, is sometimes characterized as a more reliable alternative to DVD-R, but few users are aware of the difference, and most recordable DVD drives can accommodate both formats. DVD+R is covered by ISO/IEC 17344, *Information Technology—Data Interchange on 120 mm and 80 mm Optical Disk Using +R Format—Capacity: 4,7 and 1,46 Gbytes per Side (Recording Speed up to 16X)*, and ISO/IEC 25434, *Information Technology—Data Interchange on 120 mm and 80 mm Optical Disk Using +R DL Format—Capacity: 8,55 and 2,66 Gbytes per Side (Recording Speed 8X)*.

- **DVD-RW and DVD+RW.** These media are the rewritable (erasable) counterparts of DVD-R and DVD+R. The DVD-RW format was developed by the DVD Forum, and the DVD+RW format was developed by the DVD+RW Alliance. The DVD-RW format is covered by ISO/IEC 17342, *Information Technology—80 mm (1,46 Gbytes per side) and 120 mm (4,70 Gbytes per side) DVD Re-recordable Disk (DVD-RW)*. DVD+RW is characterized by its proponents as a more versatile and convenient alternative to DVD-RW, but most recordable DVD drives can read both media. It is covered by ISO/IEC 17341, *Information Technology—Data Interchange on 120 mm and 80 mm Optical Disk Using +RW Format—Capacity: 4,7 and 1,46 Gbytes per Side (Recording Speed Up to 4X)*; ISO/IEC 26925, *Information Technology—Digital Storage Media for Information Interchange—Data Interchange on 120 mm and 80 mm Optical Disk Using +RW HS Format—Capacity: 4,7 and 1,46 Gbytes per Side (Recording Speed 8X)*; and ISO/IEC 29642, *Information Technology—Data Interchange on 120 mm and 80 mm Optical Disk Using +RW DL Format—Capacity: 8,55 and 2,66 Gbytes per Side (Recording Speed 2,4X)*. Compared to write-once DVDs, DVD-RW and DVD+RW media are more expensive.

- **DVD-RAM.** This DVD format was developed in the late 1990s as the first rewritable DVD format. The applicable standards are ISO/IEC 17592, *Information Technology—120 mm (4,7 Gbytes per side) and 80 mm (1,46 Gbytes per side) DVD Rewritable Disk (DVD-RAM)*, and ISO/IEC 17594, *Information Technology—Cases for 120 mm and 80 mm DVD-RAM Disks*. Approved by the DVD Forum, DVD-RAM is principally intended for computer storage rather than video recording. DVD-RAM media are available in single-sided, 120-millimeter configurations with a storage capacity of 4.7 gigabytes and in double-sided, 120-millimeter configurations with a storage capacity of 9.4 gigabytes. DVD-RAM media were originally encapsulated in plastic cartridges, but bare media have supplanted that product configuration.

Increasingly, DVD drives can read DVDs in all formats, with the exception of cartridge-encapsulated DVD-RAM media. DVD drives can also read and record CDs. Several vendors offer optical disk autochangers that co-mingle DVDs and CDs in various formats.

The DVD formats discussed above pre-date the widespread implementation of high-definition television (HDTV) technology. The **Blue-ray disc format** is one of two next-generation DVD formats developed specifically for high-definition video. Developed and licensed by the Blue-ray Disc Association (BDA), a consortium led by

Sony Corporation, Blue-ray technology takes its name from its blue laser mechanism, which permits high-density recording. A dual-layer 120-millimeter Blue-ray DVD can store approximately 50 gigabytes. Experimental prototypes have been developed with capacities exceeding 200 gigabytes.

As DVD-video alternatives, Blue-ray discs (BD-ROM) are read-only media. BD-ROM is the high-capacity counterpart of CD-ROM and DVD-ROM. Recordable Blue-ray media, intended for video and data storage, were introduced in early 2006. BD-R, a write-once medium, and BD-RE, an erasable version, can store up to 27 gigabytes in a single-layer, 120-millimeter configuration or 54 gigabytes in a double-layer, 120-millimeter configuration.

Blue-ray's competitor for pre-recorded video programming, the HD DVD format, was withdrawn in early 2008. HD DVD-R, a recordable version intended for data recording, can store 15 gigabytes on single-layer, 120-millimeter media and 30 gigabytes on double-layer, 120-millimeter media. Given the demise of HD DVD for video programming, the fate of the data recording versions is uncertain.

MO and UDO Disks

Magneto-optical (MO) recording, also known as *thermo-magneto-optical (TMO)* recording, is a hybrid technology. Within a platter-shaped medium, information is stored magnetically but recorded and read by a laser. Magneto-optical disks are actually multilayered magnetic disks. Their glass or plastic substrates are coated with an active recording layer that combines iron with selected other metals. The magneto-optical recording layer is surrounded by additional layers that protect against contaminants and facilitate playback of recorded information. On an unrecorded magneto-optical disk, all particles have the same magnetic orientation. To record information, a highly focused laser beam heats a spot on the disk, causing a loss of the disk's initial magnetic direction. An electromagnet then generates a magnetic field to orient the particles in the desired direction. When read by a laser and pickup mechanism, recorded areas of a magneto-optical disk rotate reflected light in a clockwise or counterclockwise direction to play back the one and zero bits in digitally-coded data.

Magneto-optical disks are encapsulated in plastic cartridges to protect their recording surfaces during media loading, removal, filing, and other handling. The most widely encountered media size is 5.25 inches (130 millimeters). Storage capacities have increased steadily and significantly from 650 megabytes for first-generation products introduced in the late 1980s to 9.1 gigabytes for fifth-generation media introduced in 2001. International standards for 5.25-inch magneto-optical disks were first published in the early 1990s. Since that time, various standards have reflected continuing improvements in magneto-optical recording technology. Examples include ISO/IEC 10089, *Information Technology—130 mm Rewritable Optical Disk Cartridge for Information Interchange*; ISO/IEC 13549, *Information Technology—Data Interchange on 130 mm Optical Disk Cartridges—Capacity: 1,3 Gbytes per Cartridge*; ISO/IEC 13842, *Information Technology—130 mm Optical Disk Cartridges for Information Interchange—Capacity: 2 Gbytes per Cartridge*; ISO/IEC 14517, *Information Technology—130 mm Optical Disk Cartridges for Information*

Interchange—Capacity: 2,6 Gbytes per Cartridge; ISO/IEC 11560, *Information Technology—Information Interchange on 130 mm Optical Disk Cartridge Using the Magneto-Optical Effect, for Write Once, Read Multiple Functionality;* and ISO/IEC 22092, *Information Technology—Data Interchange on 130 mm Magneto-Optical Disk Cartridges—Capacity: 9,1 Gbytes per Cartridge.*

Although newer models have quickly supplanted their predecessors, successive generations of magneto-optical drives have maintained backward-compatibility with older formats for reading previously recorded information. Although 5.25-inch magneto-optical disks are double-sided media, all drives are single-headed devices. Online availability is one-half the disk's storage capacity. Thus, a 5.2-giga-byte magneto-optical disk provides 2.6 gigabytes online. A given magneto-optical cartridge must be ejected, turned over, and reinserted to read from or record onto its opposite side.

The 5.25-inch magneto-optical cartridges are available in write-once and rewritable varieties. Magneto-optical drives can distinguish between write-once and rewritable cartridges and will automatically activate the appropriate recording mode. Smaller magneto-optical disks are available as rewritable media only. The storage capacities of 3.5-inch magneto-optical disks have increased from 128 megabytes for first-generation media introduced in 1990 to 1.3 gigabytes for fourth-generation products introduced 10 years later. The 2.5-inch MiniDisc was introduced by Sony in 1992 as the first magneto-optical disk designed specifically for audio recording. The MD data format, a version for computer-processible information introduced in 1993, was not widely adopted.

Introduced in 2000, the Ultra Density Optical (UDO) format can store up to 30 or 60 gigabytes of data on a double-sided 5.25-inch optical disk cartridge. The applicable standard is ISO/IEC 17345, *Information Technology—Data Interchange on 130 mm Rewritable and Write-Once Read Many Ultra Density Optical (UDO) Disk Cartridges—Capacity: 30 Gbytes per Cartridge (First Generation).* Although sometimes described as *the next generation of magneto-optical recording,* the UDO format uses a combination of blue laser recording and phase-change technology. The technology's development path projects a future doubling of cartridge capacity to 120 GB and again to 240 GB. Available autochangers can store hundreds of UDO cartridges for unattended access to many terabytes of data. Like magneto-optical cartridges, UDO media are available in write-once and rewritable configurations.

Obsolete Optical Disk Formats

Various optical disk formats, introduced during the 1980s and later, have been discontinued or remain in very limited use. Fourteen-inch and 12-inch optical disks were principally encountered in mainframe and minicomputer installations with voluminous storage requirements, where they competed with or supplemented hard drives. They were also used in some digital document imaging installations. Their storage capacities ranged from 2 to 25 gigabytes per optical disk cartridge. Fourteen-inch optical disks were write-once media only. Twelve-inch optical disks were available in write-once and rewritable versions, although the latter were seldom encountered. Eight-inch optical disks were discontinued shortly after their introduction in the 1980s.

A number of vendors introduced 5.25-inch write-once and rewritable optical disks of proprietary design during the mid-1980s and early 1990s, but most of those products were discontinued when magneto-optical technology was introduced in the late 1980s. Their storage capacities ranged from 200 to 650 megabytes. Given their relatively short life cycles—less than five years from introduction to discontinuation in most cases—obsolete optical disk products illustrate the perils of selecting storage media for retention of electronic records.

Introduced in 1978, read-only analog videodisks were the first optical storage products to be successfully commercialized. Originally intended as consumer products, analog videodisks were produced by corporations, government agencies, and other organizations for training and other purposes. In their 12-inch versions, analog videodisks could store 54,000 still-video images or 60 minutes of full-motion television with stereo audio on each of two sides. Eight-inch media could store 24,000 still-video images or 13.5 minutes of full-motion television and stereo audio per side. During the 1980s, several companies developed special production techniques that could store digitally-coded, computer-processable information, including databases and document images, on read-only video disks, but that technology was not commercially successful.

When Sony and Philips introduced the compact disc, they envisioned a variety of formats for different purposes and types of information. Although compact disc technology is widely used for audio and data recording, CD formats for other applications have been less successful and, in some cases, short-lived. Examples include super audio CD (SACD), a higher-fidelity implementation of compact disc-digital audio; CD+G, which combined audio with graphic images; CD-Text, which combined audio and textual information; CD-Video, which combined audio and video information; CD-I, which was intended for multimedia applications; and PhotoCD, which was developed by Eastman Kodak for storage of digital photographs.

Other Optical Media

Optical memory cards, which provide several megabytes of data storage on a wallet-size card, are marketed for healthcare, vehicle registration and warranty management, immigration enforcement, and other applications that require reliable identification cards with modest storage capacity. They are standardized by ISO/IEC 11693, *Identification Cards—Optical Memory Cards—General Characteristics*, and ISO/IEC 11694, *Identification Cards—Optical Memory Cards—Linear Recording Method*. Optical memory cards have limited records management significance. Several optical tape systems with high data storage capacities were demonstrated in the 1990s as high-capacity alternatives to magnetic tape technology, but no optical tape products were commercially available when this chapter was written.

Types of optical media commonly used for computer recordkeeping are listed in Table 2.2. Media size, storage capacity and whether the media is recordable and/or erasable are included for each media.

Optical Disks
for Computer
Recordkeeping

Table 2.2

Media Type	Media Size	Storage Capacity	Recordable?	Erasable?
CD-ROM	4.75 inches	540 MB+	no	no
CD-ROM	3.5 inches	190 MB	no	no
CD-R	4.75 inches	540 MB+	yes	no
CD-RW	4.75 inches	540 MB+	yes	yes
DVD-ROM	4.75 inches	4.7 GB	no	no
DVD-R	4.75 inches	up to 9.4 GB	yes	no
DVD+R	4.75 inches	up to 9.4 GB	yes	no
DVD-RW	4.75 inches	up to 9.4 GB	yes	yes
DVD+RW	4.75 inches	up to 9.4 GB	yes	yes
DVD-RAM	4.75 inches	up to 9.4 GB	yes	yes
BD-ROM	4.75 inches	up to 50 GB	no	no
BD-R	4.75 inches	up to 50 GB	yes	no
BD-RW	4.75 inches	up to 50 GB	yes	yes
Magneto-optical disks	5.25 inches	up to 9.1 GB	yes	yes
Magneto-optical disks	3.5 inches	up to 1.3 GB	yes	yes
Ultra Density Optical	5.25 inches	up to 30 GB	yes	yes

Solid State Storage

Solid-state storage uses semiconductor materials rather than magnetic or optical technology. Solid-state storage devices are sometimes characterized as "solid state drives," although they are not platter-shaped and do not have moving parts. They merely emulate hard drives and other platter-shaped media in selected computer applications.

Unlike conventional random-access memory circuits, solid-state storage relies on nonvolatile flash memory components, which can retain their contents in the absence of electrical power. Solid-state storage may be packaged as memory cards, which are available in many varieties. Examples of this rapidly changing product group include the CompactFlash (CF) card, the memory stick, the MultiMediaCard (MMC), the SmartMedia card, the xD card, the secure digital (SD) card, the miniSD card, and the microSD card. Capacities of all memory card formats have increased steadily since the 1990s and are likely to continue to do so.

> *Although prices of USB drives have declined significantly since their introduction, they are more expensive on a cost-per-megabyte basis than removable magnetic or optical media.*

USB drives combine flash memory components with a USB connector. Highly portable and reasonably durable, they have emerged as convenient alternatives to floppy disks, CDs, and DVDs for physical transportation of information between computers. Available in multigigabyte configurations, USB drives enjoy a capacity advantage over removable disk media. Although prices of USB drives have declined significantly since their introduction, they are more expensive on a cost-per-megabyte basis than removable magnetic or optical media.

Though not actually platter-shaped, so-called solid-state disk drives are intended as high-performance alternatives to magnetic disk drives. Like hard drives, they are built into storage enclosures. The lack of moving parts enhances their operating speed and reduces the risk of mechanical failure when compared to conventional hard drives. Designed to emulate hard drives, solid-state disk drives were initially demonstrated in the late 1970s, but high cost has limited their market to military and industrial installations that require a combination of fast application loading and data access times, compact dimensions, light weight, mechanical reliability, energy efficiency, and shock resistance. At the time this chapter was written, solid-state disk drives were employed in some notebook computers. Compared to comparable devices configured with hard drives, notebook computers equipped with solid-state drives are much more expensive and offer less storage capacity.

Paper-Based Electronic Media

Although electronic records are now stored on magnetic disks, magnetic tapes, or optical disks, various pre-computer and early computer systems relied on paper media. From the 1950s through the 1970s, for example, mainframe and minicomputer installations employed punched card technology for conversion of data and programs to machine-readable form. Data was recorded on such cards by keypunch machines that converted typed characters to predetermined patterns of holes in successive, numbered columns. Typically, the cards are both punched and interpreted; that is, human-readable representations of individual characters are printed at the tops of the columns in which punches are recorded. Punched cards are processed by a card reader, an online peripheral device that detects the pattern of holes punched into successive columns and converts their character content to computer-processible form. Punched cards have also been employed by tabulating machines, sorters, electromechanical accounting machines, programmable calculators, and other pre-computer devices.

Punched cards are obsolete media, but they are of more than historical interest. Hidden away in basements, closets, records centers, or other locations, punched cards are routinely discovered during inventories of electronic records. The most widely encountered examples are tabulating size (3.25 inches by 7.375 inches). They contain 80 columns punched with square holes. Sometimes termed an *IBM card*, it was initially utilized in equipment manufactured by the Tabulating Machine Company, which later became International Business Machines. Versions with as few as 30 columns were employed by the U.S. Census Bureau in the late 19th century. Cards of different sizes and capacities have been utilized by specific computer systems. Remington Rand, for example, introduced a tabulating-size card with 90 columns for use with early UNIVAC computers and certain electromechanical accounting machines. Such cards are easily identified by their round holes. In the late 1960s, IBM introduced a 96-column punched card for use with its System/3 minicomputers. Measuring 3.25 inches by 2.75 inches, it featured three rows of punches representing 32 characters per row.

Punched paper tape, as its name suggests, is a ribbon of paper that uses predetermined patterns of holes and spaces to represent digitally-coded data. The holes are generated by a device called a *paper tape punch* and decoded by a paper tape reader. Five to eight holes, aligned across the width of the tape, are used to represent individual characters. Punched paper tape is one of the oldest electronic recordkeeping media. Its use in telegraphy dates from the 19th century. During the 1960s and early 1970s, punched paper tape was employed by computer terminals, TWX machines, and telex machines for offline preparation of messages or other information to be transmitted to a computer system or through a telecommunications network. Punched paper tape and punched paper belts were also employed as text storage media by some early word processing systems, but they were quickly supplanted by magnetic media. Like punched cards, punched paper tapes that have not been processed for decades may be stored by businesses, government agencies, or other organizations. Originally supplied in 1,000-foot lengths, punched paper tapes in storage typically consist of relatively short strips or rolls.

Summary

Magnetic storage media have dominated electronic recordkeeping for decades and are likely to continue to do so. Magnetic disk drives are the storage devices of choice in high-performance computer applications that require rapid, online access to active electronic records. Magnetic disks themselves are platter-shaped media that may be fixed in or removable from the drives on which information is recorded and retrieved. Fixed magnetic disk drives, popularly described as *hard drives*, are equipped with one or more rigid platters. Their storage capacities have improved steadily and significantly since the 1950s. At the same time, platter sizes have decreased. Mainframes, midrange computers, and network servers increasingly employ high-capacity, multidrive arrays with small platters. Desktop and portable computers are routinely configured with hard drives in capacities formerly associated with large computer installations.

Removable magnetic disk systems provide infinite storage capacity within a given hardware configuration, although some information will necessarily be stored offline at a given moment. Examples of removable magnetic disks include hard disk cartridges and floppy disks. Some removable magnetic disk products have been discontinued over the years. Media produced by such products can no longer be read.

Successfully employed for information storage since the 1920s, magnetic tape is a ribbon or strip of plastic film coated with a magnetic recording material. Utilized for computer, video, and audio recording, magnetic tapes may be packaged on open reels, in cartridges, or in cassettes. In computer applications, magnetic tapes are widely utilized for backup copies, data archiving, and software or data distribution. Reels of nine-track magnetic tape have been employed in mainframe and minicomputer installations since the 1950s. Half-inch data cartridges offer greater storage capacity and more compact dimensions than their nine-track counterparts. Digital linear tape (DLT) and linear tape open (LTO Ultrium) media offer very high storage capacity.

C-type, or Philips-type, magnetic tape cassettes are the dominant magnetic media for audio recording, including voice and music. Microcassettes and minicassettes are used exclusively in voice dictation systems and answering machines. Open-reel audio tape and digital audio tape are principally utilized by professional music studios. The most widely encountered video tape formats feature half-inch magnetic tape packaged in VHS-compatible cassettes, although other cassette formats and open reels of video tape remain in use. Eight-millimeter video tape cassettes have facilitated the development of compact, lightweight camcorders. Newer video storage media employ digital coding rather than the analog coding that has historically dominated video recording.

As an alternative or supplement to magnetic disks and tapes, optical storage systems use lasers to record information by selectively altering the light reflectance properties of specially designed media. As their most significant characteristics for electronic recordkeeping, optical storage media offer high capacity. CDs and DVDs are the most important types of optical storage media. They are available in read-only and recordable varieties. Recordable optical disks are available in write-once and rewritable (erasable) configurations.

Solid-state storage uses semiconductor components. Examples include flash memory cards and USB flash drives. They offer more convenient alternatives to removable magnetic and optical media for physical transportation of information between computers.

Obsolete machine-readable media may be encountered when inventorying electronic records. Examples include magnetic cards, MT/ST tape cartridges, magnetic tape belts, video cassettes in defunct formats, punched cards, and punched paper tape.

Chapter 3

File Formats for Electronic Records

Electronic records generated by computer, video, and audio systems are stored in a manner appropriate to and determined by the hardware and/or software that creates, retrieves, edits, or otherwise processes the recorded information. Following traditional records management practice, a collection of electronic records is termed a **file**. The term may be preceded by an adjective that denotes the physical storage medium on which the information is recorded; hence, the use of such designations as *disk file* and *tape file*. Alternatively, and more meaningfully, a file descriptor may indicate the type of information the file contains and the type of applications it serves. Examples of such designations include a computer file, video file, or audio file. Additional adjectives—such as master, update, temporary, or backup—indicate a file's relationship to other files. Computer files may be further categorized by the type of information they contain. Common examples include text files, spreadsheet files, data files, and image files.

Within each file type, computer-processible information may be recorded in proprietary or nonproprietary formats:

- **Proprietary formats.** As their default operating mode, most computer programs record files in a proprietary format whenever a save command is initiated. When a word processing document created with Microsoft Word is saved, for example, the file format for that version of Word is automatically applied, unless the computer operator selects a different format. Proprietary file formats are sometimes termed *native formats*. They are associated with specific software developers and computer programs.

- **Nonproprietary file formats.** These formats, by contrast, are supported by multiple software developers and computer programs. Nonproprietary formats are sometimes characterized as *neutral formats* or *transfer formats* because they facilitate the exchange of electronic records between computer systems and applications. When imported by a given program, files are usually converted from nonproprietary to proprietary formats for processing or other purposes. Nonproprietary file formats may be based on published specifications prepared by cooperating software developers. Alternatively, a nonproprietary file format may be developed by a single influential software company and adopted by others. In rare instances, nonproprietary file formats have been adopted by standard-setting organizations as national or international standards.

Proprietary and nonproprietary file formats are rarely exclusive options. Many programs support a native file format plus additional proprietary and nonproprietary formats. Further blurring the distinction between the two format categories, files saved in proprietary formats associated with very popular software products can often be imported (read) by competing or complementary products. In effect, popular proprietary formats establish themselves as de facto standard formats. Similarly, a given computer program may be able to export (write) files in the proprietary formats associated with other programs. Where the importing and exporting capabilities of a given computer program are inadequate, various companies offer translator programs or services that can convert files from one format to another.

Whether proprietary or nonproprietary, file formats are usually identified by file name extensions—suffixes that are appended to the name of a given file. A computer's operating system uses the extension to determine which program can open the file. With most computer operating systems, the file name and extension are separated by a period. The extension is typically limited to three or four characters. Common examples include "doc" and "docx," which identify Microsoft Word documents; "xls" and "xlsx," which identify Excel spreadsheets; "pdf," which identifies PDF files; and "ppt," and "pptx," which identify PowerPoint presentations.

A comprehensive survey of proprietary and nonproprietary file formats is beyond the scope of this book. However, the following sections discuss file format concepts and characteristics for the most commonly encountered types of electronic records. This subject is important because file formats have a decisive impact on the future usability of electronic records. **Backward compatibility**—the ability of future computer, audio, and video products to read information recorded in particular formats—is an obvious concern. Most software developers release new versions of, or replacements for, their products at regular intervals. Like the media formats described in Chapter 2, electronic records saved in a particular file format may be rendered unreadable by product modifications and discontinuations. As discussed in Chapter 4, retention designations for electronic records assume backward compatibility with a given file format for the entire retention period, but such compatibility cannot be guaranteed. File formats also play an important role in electronic discovery. As discussed in a later chapter, the Federal Rules of Civil Procedure allow a requesting party to specify the format for production of electronic records in response to a discovery order.

Text Files

Text files are produced by word processing programs, electronic mail systems, desktop publishing and computerized typesetting programs, workgroup software, optical character recognition (OCR) products, and text editors of the type furnished as utility programs with some computer operating systems. As their name suggests, text files contain machine-readable information in character-coded form. Each character is represented by a predetermined sequence of bits, which constitute one byte of computer-processible information. Used in this context, the term *character* denotes a letter of the alphabet, a numeric digit, a punctuation mark, or any other symbol that might be encountered in a typewritten document.

> *Given the increasing globalization of information processing technology, new computer systems and software support multiple languages, including some non-Roman languages.*

The symbolic content of text files is determined by the language in which documents or other textual information is created and the character-generating capabilities of specific computer systems and programs. Given the increasing globalization of information processing technology, new computer systems and software support multiple languages, including some non-Roman languages. Windows-based computers sold in North America, for example, support European character sets, including Cyrillic and Greek. Characters not represented on a keyboard can be generated by specified key-combinations or selected from displayed lists.

Coding Schemes

The bit sequences that represent individual characters are defined by standardized coding schemes that have evolved over several decades:

- **ASCII coding scheme.** The best known and most widely encountered example of a standardized coding scheme is the **American Standard Code for Information Interchange (ASCII)**, which was developed in the early 1960s and has been revised several times over the years. Applicable standards are *ASCII INCITS-4, Information Systems—Coded Character Sets—7-Bit American National Standard Code for Information Interchange (7-Bit ASCII)*, and ISO 646, *ISO 7-Bit Coded Character Set for Information Interchange*. Redundantly termed the *ASCII code*, it uses seven-bit sequences, ranging from 0000000 to 1111111, to represent upper- and lowercase alphabetic characters, numeric digits 0 through 9, punctuation marks, and certain mathematical symbols, as well as control codes and other characters that are not printed. Thus, the seven-bit sequence 1000001 represents the uppercase *A*, the seven-bit sequence 1100001 represents the lowercase *a*, and so on.

- **Seven-bit ASCII.** This coding scheme can encode 128 different characters, which are sufficient for most English-language documents. A typewriter keyboard contains about 95 printable characters, but it is not enough for documents written in other languages that use the Roman alphabet. Such languages include accented characters or other symbols that have no English counterparts. For this reason, 7-bit ASCII is sometimes described as *US-ASCII*. To accommodate a broader range of recorded information, extended versions of the ASCII code use 8 bits, which increases the number of encodable characters to 256. These extended versions can encode accented characters and special symbols. The most widely cited standard is ISO/IEC 8859-1, *8-Bit Single-Byte Coded Graphic Character Sets—Part 1: Latin Alphabet No. 1*, which covers most Western European languages. Other standards in the ISO/IEC 8859 series extend the ASCII code to accommodate Central European, South European, Nordic, and Celtic languages. Over time, new characters, such as the Euro symbol, have been added to extended ASCII coding schemes, but other characters remain excluded. Examples include ligatures, em dashes, and directional quotation marks. ANSI/NISO Z39.47, *Extended Latin Alphabet Coded Character Set for Bibliographic Use*, provides a table of character codes for 35 languages that use the Latin alphabet and 51 Romanized languages.

- **Alphabet.** Most extended versions of ASCII are limited to the Latin (Roman) alphabet. Some standards in the ISO/IEC 8859 series can accommodate Greek, Cyrillic, Hebrew, Arabic, and Thai characters, but they may be interpreted incorrectly by some computer programs, including text retrieval software discussed later in this book. Extended versions of ASCII are incompatible with Chinese, Japanese, Korean, and other Asian languages, which may contain thousands of characters. ANSI/NISO Z39.64, *East Asian Character Code for Bibliographic Use*, addresses this problem by defining a coding structure for Chinese, Japanese, and Korean characters, but Unicode provides a broader approach to computer-processible representation of non-Roman characters. Introduced in the early 1990s as an international replacement for other character coding schemes, Unicode is designed to accommodate every symbol in every written language. It employs the universal character set specified in ISO/IEC 10646, *Information Technology—Universal Multiple-Octet Encoded Character Set (UCS)*, a multipart standard. Unicode began as a 16-bit coding scheme, which could accommodate 65,536 different characters. It has since been expanded to include 32 bits with the potential to encode millions of different characters. The latest versions of Windows and the Macintosh operating system employ Unicode rather than the ASCII coding scheme. Given the increased globalization of the software industry, the number of applications that support Unicode is likely to increase.

- **EBCDIC.** The Extended Binary Coded Decimal Interchange Code (EBCDIC) is an 8-bit character-coding scheme developed by IBM in the 1960s. Used by IBM mainframe and midrange computers, it has limited significance for digital document implementations. With the demise of mainframe-based word processing software and e-mail systems, few applications generate EBCDIC-coded documents.

- **Older character codes.** Older codes—such as the Baudot code, a 5-bit coding scheme used in telex communications, or the binary coded decimal (BCD) code, a 6-bit code used in the 1960s by IBM computers—are no longer encountered.

Word Processing Files

Regardless of the coding scheme employed, text files store information in a relatively unstructured manner. In many word processing applications, for example, a text file contains a single record—the machine-readable equivalent of a typewritten document that contains one or more pages. Alternatively, a text file may contain several or many documents created by word processing programs, electronic mail software, or other systems. Multiple electronic messages may be downloaded to a text file during an online session, for example. In such cases, individual records may be separated by page break commands or other delimiting characters. Their physical sequence within a text file may be based on their order of creation or logical interrelationships. Computer software typically imposes few significant restrictions on the length of text files, size limits imposed on attachments to e-mail messages being a notable exception. File sizes may be limited by available memory or other hardware characteristics, but such constraints are rarely meaningful.

Some text file formats are specific to the computer programs that create them. Word processing programs, for example, record files in proprietary formats. Text files created by such programs combine textual characters with embedded characters that initiate page breaks, paragraph indentations, tabs, underlining, bold printing, italics, superscripts, subscripts, and other formatting features. Although the ASCII code is typically used for both text and control characters, the control characters associated with particular formatting operations are unique to specific programs. Thus, a control character that initiates a page break or underlining with one word processing program may have a completely different meaning, or no meaning at all, with competing products.

As a complicating factor, text file formats may differ among various versions of a given program. Successive releases of a word processing program may not be able to read and edit text files created by all previous versions. Usually, a word processing program can import text files created by one or two previous versions, but it may not be able to export text files in formats compatible with those versions. Software-imposed limitations on backward compatibility pose obvious problems for retrieval of text files created in the past. They are also significant for members of project teams or other work groups who need to exchange documents with other members but have not upgraded to the latest version of a given word processing program. Incompatibility is likewise possible among versions of a given word processing program intended for different types of computers.

To facilitate the exchange of word processing documents and other electronic records, some programs can import and export text files in proprietary formats employed by other programs, including competing products. Some word processing programs, for example, can import and export text files in the proprietary format employed by specific versions of Microsoft Word. Similarly, Microsoft Word can import and export text files in the proprietary format employed by specific versions of WordPerfect. As might be expected, such exchange capabilities emphasize proprietary formats employed by the most popular software packages. At the time this chapter was written, for example, the Microsoft Word format, though properly considered proprietary, had become a de facto standard format for the convenient exchange of documents among many software packages, although determining which version of the Word format is appropriate to be used for that purpose may cause confusion. Not surprisingly, exchange capabilities are seldom provided for proprietary file formats employed by lesser known or discontinued word processing programs. Importation of text files created by such programs must rely on one of the file exchange methods described next.

Exchange of documents in proprietary formats will prove most reliable for text files with straightforward formatting characteristics. The converted files usually retain paragraph markers and indentations, tab settings, page margins, line spacing and justification, headers and footers, and character sizes and styles. Problems can arise, however, when text files include special characters, tabular and multicolumn page formats, mathematical formulas, and embedded graphics. To address this issue, several developers of word processing programs have introduced file formats that promote compatibility among text files created by various competing or complementary products. Eliminating the need for multiple programs that translate to and from specific proprietary representations, they provide a canonical format in which text files can be saved and from which they can be translated:

- **Rich text format (RTF).** Perhaps the best-known example is Microsoft's RTF, which was introduced in the late 1980s for cross-platform exchange of documents. It records text and formatting instructions in a manner that compatible programs can correctly interpret—assuming, of course, that the target program possesses the requisite formatting capabilities. Designed to accurately reproduce the content and appearance of files during translation, the RTF format is supported by Microsoft programs and many competing and complementary products, which can routinely convert documents to and from the RTF format.

- **OpenDocument Format (ODF).** Although it has been widely adopted by software developers, RTF is a proprietary format. By contrast, the OpenDocument Format (ODF) was developed by the Organization for the Advancement of Structured Information Standards (OASIS), a not-for-profit global consortium that promotes open standards for information processing products. The OpenDocument Format is covered by ISO/IEC 26300, *Information Technology— Open Document Format for Office Applications (Open Document) v1.0.* The OpenDocument Format is supported by various office productivity programs, including OpenOffice.org, a free suite of office productivity programs introduced in 2000; StarOffice, a Sun Microsystems product that is based on OpenOffice.org but includes proprietary enhancements; Google Docs, a free Web-based suite of office productivity programs; KOffice, a free office application suite for the KDesktop Environment for Unix workstations; and IBM Lotus Symphony, a free suite of office programs for Windows and Linux computers. Several companies have developed OpenDocument conversion software for use with Microsoft Office programs. The file extension "odt" identifies word processing files saved in the OpenDocument Format.

- **Older text file formats.** Older canonical text file formats, such as IBM's document content architecture (DCA) format, were not widely adopted, and programs that supported them have been discontinued.

Although the file exchange capabilities of a given computer program are inadequate, various utility programs can convert word processing documents and other text files from one proprietary format to another. The most versatile products can accommodate dozens of file formats, often for several computer platforms. Alternatively, computer service bureaus and consulting firms offer file conversion services for unusual situations, including the conversion of text files created by defunct programs and dedicated word processors.

Formats for Compound Documents

Text file formats are intended for alphanumeric information. Strictly defined, they cannot accommodate compound documents that combine text and graphics. Although newer word processing programs routinely support documents with embedded graphics generated by an internal drawing component or exported from other programs, the **portable document format (PDF)** is often a better choice for compound documents with complex formatting characteristics. Developed by Adobe Systems, the PDF format is compatible with character-coded text and graphics, including digitized images, which can be combined within the same page. For character-coded information, PDF preserves fonts, styles, headers, margins, and other page formatting characteristics. PDF files are viewed with the Adobe Acrobat Reader program, which is supplied with most new personal computers or can be downloaded from Internet sites without charge. In 1993, Adobe Systems released the complete PDF specification for use without restrictions.

The PDF format provides excellent functionality for document display, page navigation, printing, and security. Among its advantages, PDF is a cross-platform file format. Software for creating and reading PDF files is available for Windows, Macintosh, and Unix computers, and PDF documents can be reliably interchanged among those platforms. PDF is compatible with distribution of documents via Web sites, e-mail attachments, or computer media such as CDs and DVDs. PDF is standardized by ISO 32000, *Document Management—Portable Document Format—PDF 1.7*. Other ISO standards apply to specialized subsets of PDF. One example is 19005-1, *Document Management—Electronic Document File Format for Long-Term Preservation—Part 1: Use of PDF (PDF/A-1)*. PDF/Archival (PDF/A) is a subset of PDF intended specifically for long-term retention of digital documents.

So-called markup formats provide similar support for compound documents and are compatible with a variety of computer programs. They contain embedded instructions, called *markup codes* or *tags*, which describe various document components such as chapters, titles, headings, paragraphs, lists, and tables. Compatible computer programs interpret the markup instructions and display documents accordingly. Markup codes may be inserted manually or generated by special authoring tools. The syntax and semantics of specific markup codes are defined by sets of rules called **markup languages**. Increasingly, businesses, government agencies, and other organizations utilize markup languages and formats to facilitate the exchange of computer-processable documents.

Some markup languages were developed for specific types of documents. DocBook, for example, is intended for technical documentation. TeX, which was introduced in the 1970s, is particularly useful for formatting complex mathematical formulas. GNU LilyPond is designed for engraving sheet music. Two of the most important and widely publicized markup languages, **hypertext markup language (HTML)** and the **extensible markup language (XML)**, are subsets of the **standard generalized markup language (SGML)**. They are the markup languages used for information on the World Wide Web, as well as on corporate and institutional intranets and extranets. HTML and XML codes are interpreted by Web browsers that display the information as formatted text and graphics. Various software packages support the creation of Web pages with specified content and embedded formatting codes. In addition, some word processing programs can save documents in the HTML format. They automatically insert HTML codes that correspond to specific page, line, and character formats. In addition to text, many Web pages incorporate photographs, illustrations, charts, or other graphics that are stored in one of the formats discussed next.

> *To increase the likelihood of compatibility of computer-processible documents with the broadest range of programs, the safest approach is to store text files with as little formatting as possible.*

Markup languages promote the exchange of computer-processible documents by separating the content and appearance of information. Content is stored as plain text, while the embedded codes specify the appearance of pages. The encoded documents are not formatted. They contain formatting instructions that compatible software interprets. As a complication, however, different versions of a given markup language often incorporate special features and extensions that can pose compatibility problems. Some HTML extensions, for example, are incompatible with certain browsers. To increase the likelihood of compatibility of computer-processible documents with the broadest range of programs, the safest approach is to store text files with as little formatting as possible. That approach is taken by ASCII text files, sometimes described as the *text-only* or *plain text format*.

ASCII Text Files

As their name suggests, ASCII text files use the ASCII code to represent the character content of word processing documents, electronic messages, or other computer-generated text, but they contain little additional information. Most word processing programs and many other software products support the ASCII text file format as an import or export option. The ASCII text file format is typically available with carriage returns at the end of each paragraph or at the end of each line of text. The user selects the desired pattern. In either case, most of the control characters that initiate formatting options are removed when files are saved in the ASCII text format. Consequently, the ASCII text format is sometimes described as the "plain text" format. ASCII text files are identified by the "txt" file extension.

ASCII text files created by one word processing program can usually be imported and edited by others, but the absence of formatting instructions may result in loss of functionality. Paragraph indentations and tabs may be converted to spaces, but line centering, fonts, underlining, italics, and other potentially significant features are not converted. If required, they must be reinserted during document editing.

By transcending proprietary file formats, ASCII text files minimize software dependence and provide some protection against product obsolescence, because computer programs will presumably accommodate the ASCII text format for the foreseeable future. Records managers should consequently consider the ASCII text format, instead of or in addition to, proprietary formats for word processing documents, electronic messages, and other textual information that must be retained for long periods of time. This recommendation is based on the assumption, of course, that special formatting information does not need to be retained for its functional value. As an additional advantage, ASCII text files are accepted as input by text storage and retrieval programs that support online storage and full-text retrieval of documents.

E-mail Messages

E-mail messages consist of an envelope and content. The envelope contains information related to transmission and delivery of the message. The content is the message itself, which consists of character-coded text. The content typically includes header fields that identify the sender, recipient, and subject plus the body of the message. E-mail characteristics are defined in various standards, practices, and recommendations codified by the Internet Engineering Task Force. Examples include RFC 2822, *Internet Message Format*; RFC 2076, *Common Internet Message Headers*; RFC 2045, *Multipurpose Internet Mail Extensions (MIME) Part 1: Format of Internet Message Bodies*; and RFC 2277, *IETF Policy on Character Sets and Languages*.

Low-cost or free e-mail programs, such as Eudora and Pine, use nonproprietary file formats, some of which were developed by academic or government researchers. One example is the mbox format, which stores multiple messages in a single file as plain text. In effect, each user's mailbox is one file. Individual messages are demarcated by a "from" line at the beginning and a blank line at the end. Popular commercial e-mail servers and client software, such as Microsoft Exchange servers with Outlook clients and Lotus Domino servers with Lotus Notes clients, save individual messages as separate files in proprietary formats. The messages, which may consist of plain text or highly formatted content, are stored in databases managed by the e-mail server. Alternatively, some e-mail clients can save e-mail messages on local or network drives apart from the e-mail server. With Microsoft Outlook, for example, messages can be stored in offline folders, which are identified by the ".ost" extension, or in personal files, which are identified by the ".pst" extension. Similarly, Lotus Notes can store e-mail messages on local or network drives as ".nsf" files.

*A **specialized category of e-mail migration software can convert messages to PDF files, digital image formats, or other file formats for electronic discovery, retention, or inclusion in regulatory submissions or other documents.***

E-mail migration software can convert e-mail messages to and from specific formats. Such software is principally intended for organizations that are replacing their e-mail servers and/or clients and want to preserve existing messages in a readable format. This type of conversion is an increasingly important requirement, particularly in organizations with multiple or aging e-mail systems that are due for consolidation or upgrading. The messages to be migrated may be stored on e-mail servers or by e-mail clients on network or local drives. In addition to messages, e-mail migration software can convert address books and calendars maintained by e-mail systems. A specialized category of e-mail migration software can convert messages to PDF files, digital image formats, or other file formats for electronic discovery, retention, or inclusion in regulatory submissions or other documents.

Spreadsheet Files

Text files, as defined above, store alphabetic characters and other symbols encountered in typewritten documents. If text files contain numeric digits, they are simply stored as characters, without regard to the quantities they represent. Spreadsheet files, by contrast, store numbers as quantitative values. They can also store character-coded text, but they differ from text files in their more structured formats.

Spreadsheet files are formatted as tables. They contain information that is stored in cells, which are formed by the intersection of rows and columns in a tabular presentation. Spreadsheet cells may contain quantitative values, formulas, textual information (labels), or even graphics, along with formatting instructions. Taking a widely encountered example, cells in the first column of a budget-planning spreadsheet typically contains labels that identify categories of expenditure such as salaries, fringe benefits, rent, utilities, and so on. Cells in the first row of the spreadsheet contain labels that identify the months of the year or other budgetary periods. Other spreadsheet cells contain dollar amounts associated with specific expenditures for particular budgetary periods. Alternatively, the cells may contain formulas that calculate those dollar amounts. The formulas may include arithmetic operators, predefined mathematical or logical functions, numeric constants, or references to other cells.

Like word processing software, all spreadsheet programs store files in a proprietary format as their default operating mode. These proprietary formats are identified by file extensions. As previously noted, the file extensions ".xls" and "xlsx" identify Microsoft Excel spreadsheets, which are termed *workbooks*. Spreadsheets recorded in proprietary formats associated with Lotus 1-2-3 are identified by file extensions such as ".wk4," ".wk3," ".wk1," and ".wks," depending on the version used to create them. Because proprietary file formats may differ among various versions of a spreadsheet program, backward compatibility is an obvious concern. Successive releases may not be able to read spreadsheet files in proprietary formats associated with all previous versions. Incompatible file formats are likewise possible among versions of a given spreadsheet program intended for different computer platforms.

Some spreadsheet programs can import and export files in proprietary formats employed by other programs, including competing products. As an example, Lotus 1-

2-3 can import files recorded in the proprietary format employed by specific versions of Microsoft Excel. Similarly, Microsoft Excel can import and export text files in the proprietary format employed by specific versions of Lotus 1-2-3. Such file conversions are most reliable for quantitative values and cell labels. Formulas that contain predefined functions or user-defined macros may execute differently in Excel and Lotus 1-2-3.

Several software companies have developed file formats designed specifically for the exchange of spreadsheets among different, otherwise incompatible programs. Examples include the **symbolic link (SYLK) format** introduced by Microsoft for use with its Multiplan spreadsheet program, the predecessor of Excel, and the **data interchange format (DIF)**, which was developed and popularized by VisiCorp, a defunct company that created VisiCalc, the first spreadsheet program developed for microcomputers. Some older spreadsheet files, created by discontinued programs such as SuperCalc or PerfectCalc, may be stored in those formats. If so, they can be loaded for processing by newer programs that import SYLK or DIF files.

Databases

A **database** contains records that are organized into one or more data elements, called **fields**, which store particular categories of information. A database for a human resources application, for example, may contain one record for each employee. Within each record, designated fields may store such information as the employee's name, job title, office location, telephone number, and home address. Field entries may include textual information, quantitative values, or formulas that calculate quantitative values. Within the database, records are sequenced by values contained in a designated field, which is variously described as a *key field*, *sort field*, or *sort key*. Records in a personnel database, for example, may be arranged alphabetically by employee surname, while the records in a vendor information file may be sequenced numerically by vendor number. A secondary sort field differentiates records with identical values in the primary sort field; personnel records for employees with identical names may be sequenced by date of birth, for example.

> *Although flat data files are often adequate for simple applications, more powerful database management programs employ elaborate data structures appropriate to complex information management operations.*

Simple database structures of this type are characteristic of the least expensive data management programs for personal computers. Sometimes described as "flat files," they resemble spreadsheets, a fact reflected by the inclusion of straightforward database capabilities in the most popular spreadsheet programs. Individual records in a database correspond to spreadsheet rows, while fields correspond to the cells within each row. Although flat data files are often adequate for simple applications, more powerful database management programs employ elaborate data structures appropriate to complex information management operations. They generate indexes, tree-like hierarchies, relational tables, and other supporting files that permit rapid access to, and efficient processing of, data records.

Regardless of structure, database files are typically stored in proprietary formats associated with the computer programs that create and process them. Thus, Microsoft Access stores data in its native format, as do Microsoft SQL Server, Oracle, Informix, Sybase, DB2, Lotus Notes, Filemaker, R:BASE, and other database management applications. Customized programming may be necessary to import databases stored in a proprietary format. Some programs, however, include import and export components that permit the exchange of databases with other programs, including competing products. Such file exchange is particularly important when an organization changes database management software, or when a program must process archived data files that were created with discontinued software.

Among the most widely implemented nonproprietary approaches, databases can be imported and exported in the **comma separated values (CSV)** or *comma-delimited format,* an ASCII text format with individual records separated by carriage returns (line feed characters) and the fields within each record separated by commas, tabs, or other delimiting characters. Intended for tabular data, the CSV format can also be used to exchange files between spreadsheet programs or between spreadsheet programs and database management software. As with word processing and spreadsheet files, some programs can import and export data files in formats associated with other programs, including some obsolete programs. As an example, some database management programs for PCs can import and export files in the db2, db3, or db4 formats employed by the once-dominant dBASE product line, although as time passes organizations have less need to do so. With network servers and larger computers, many database products can import files in formats used by Oracle, SQL Server, Lotus Notes, or other widely-installed database management programs.

Image Files

Computer-processible, digitally-coded images are an increasingly common and important type of machine-readable information. They may be created by a wide variety of programs and devices. Possibilities include, but are not limited to:

- Computer-aided design (CAD) programs;
- Computer painting, drawing, and other graphic arts software;
- Software that produce slides, overheads, and other presentation aids;
- Geographical information systems (GIS);
- Desktop publishing programs;
- Spreadsheet programs that include business graphics components;
- Software for statistical and demographic analysis;
- Scanners that generate digitized images from paper documents or microforms;
- Digital cameras; and

- Fax modems and related software.

Depending on the application, computer-processable images may be reproduced in hard copy by printers or plotters, stored for later retrieval as an alternative to paper files, incorporated into Web pages, added to highly-formatted documents by desktop publishing software, transmitted to remote devices over telecommunication facilities, or otherwise processed for specific purposes.

Computer-processable image files may employ vector-based or bit-mapped representation techniques. **Vector-based images** are sometimes characterized as *object-oriented* or *shape-defined representations* because they define computer-processable images as points, lines, circles, or other geometric shapes. In effect, vector-based files contain instructions that allow compatible computer programs to draw the encoded shapes. **Bit-mapped image files,** by contrast, consist of dots, called *pixels*, that represent tonal values. Also known as *raster-based image files,* they are produced by computer painting programs, document scanners, and fax modems. **Digital document imaging systems**, which complement, supplement, or replace paper filing systems and microfilm in many records management applications, employ bit-mapped image representations. Because they utilize different methods of representing images, object-oriented and bit-mapped files are incompatible with one another. Conversion programs exist, but they vary in their ability to reliably produce bit-mapped images from vector-based files, or vice versa.

> *Because image files may need to be referenced for many years, organizations have a strong interest in nonproprietary formats, sometimes described as* metafile formats, *that facilitate the interchange of computer-generated images between different programs and computer platforms.*

Like text files, spreadsheet files, and databases, computer-processable images may be recorded in proprietary or nonproprietary file formats. Proprietary formats are often the default recording mode. As a previously noted complication, proprietary formats employed by previous versions of a given program may not be readable by the latest releases. Similarly, versions of a given program that operate on different computer platforms may generate incompatible image files. Corporations, government agencies, and other organizations are likewise concerned about the future ability to reference images that support mission-critical activities. Because image files may need to be referenced for many years, organizations have a strong interest in nonproprietary formats, sometimes described as **metafile formats**, that facilitate the interchange of computer-generated images between different programs and computer platforms. ISO/IEC 8632, *Information Technology—Computer Graphics—Metafile for the Storage and Transfer of Picture Description Information*, widely known as the **computer graphics metafile (CGM)** standard, defines such a format. The U.S. Department of Defense, the Air Transportation Association, and other organizations have adopted industry-specific application profiles based on ISO/IEC 8632.

One of the most widely adopted nonproprietary formats for bit-mapped images is the **tag image file (TIF) format**, also known as the *tagged image file format* and sometimes abbreviated as TIFF. The TIF format was developed jointly by Microsoft and Aldus Corporation, which was subsequently acquired by Adobe Systems Incorporated. Adobe Systems, which also owns the portable document format (PDF), now publishes and maintains TIF specifications.

TIF is a flexible, multiplatform file format that is well suited to and widely supported by a variety of computer applications, including document imaging, optical character recognition (OCR), desktop publishing, digitization of photographs for electronic manipulation, and PC-based facsimile transmission. A TIF image file includes a header that describes the file's contents, size, and other characteristics. The TIF format is compatible with single- and multi-page documents and with binary, grayscale, and color scanning modes. TIF images can be stored in compressed or uncompressed form. The TIF format is compatible with the **Group 3** and **Group 4** compression algorithms. TIF images can be read by a variety of computer programs, some of which are in the public domain. Plug-ins for Web browsers allow the TIF format to be used in Internet and intranet implementations.

Since the 1990s, the TIF format has become a de facto standard image file format for records management applications, although PDF is an increasingly popular alternative. Some state regulations require the TIF format for digital document imaging systems implemented by government agencies subject to their jurisdiction. With some digital document imaging systems, TIF is the default file format. In other cases, it is an operator-selectable alternative to proprietary formats for importing, storing, and exporting document images. In theory, TIF files created by one computer program can be imported by others. In practice, however, compatibility problems are posed by permissible variations in TIF headers and by different versions of the TIF specification that have developed over time. As a further complication, some image viewer programs support a subset of the TIF specification. They may not be able to display all TIF files.

The **graphics image file (GIF) format**, also known as the *graphical interchange file format*, is a widely utilized image format in Internet and intranet implementations. Developed in the late 1980s by CompuServe and supported by all Web browsers, the GIF format is designed for rapid downloading and browsing of images. Its encoding method displays an approximation of images while complete information is downloaded from a Web server. Designed to enhance the responsiveness of Web pages, this progressive display approach generates low-resolution images that are gradually improved as more detailed information arrives.

The GIF format employs the **Lempel-Ziv-Welch (LZW) algorithm** for image compression. Although no legal restrictions are on the creation or interchange of GIF images, developers of GIF viewers were formerly required to license the LZW compression algorithm, which was patented by Unisys Corporation. To avoid this requirement and address other limitations of the GIF format, the World Wide Web Consortium (W3C) adopted the **portable network graphics (PNG) format** as a GIF replacement. Like GIF, PNG provides cross-platform compatibility, good image compression, and progressive display of images. Compared to GIF, PNG offers improved file compression and better color rendition. Unlike TIF, GIF and PNG are single-image formats. They do not support multiple images per file. This limitation is insignificant for most of the Web pages where the GIF and PNG formats will be used, but it can prove troublesome where digital images are produced by scanning multipage paper documents.

The **JPEG file interchange format (JFIF)** is the file format associated with JPEG compression algorithms, which were developed by the Joint Photographic Experts Group. The JFIF file format and the JPEG compression method are often confused. Many vendors and publications incorrectly describe JPEG as a file format and omit any mention of JFIF, although the combined designation JPEG/JFIF is sometimes used. The confusion is promoted by the use of "jpg" as a file extension for JFIF images. JPEG compression can be used with other file formats, such as TIF, and more commonly PDF. Terminology aside, the JFIF format and JPEG compression method are principally intended for photographs or other continuous tone images. Other examples of file formats for bit-mapped images include BMP, the Windows bitmap image format; PCX, which was developed by Z-Soft for its PC Paintbrush program; PCD, the Photo CD format developed by Eastman Kodak for recording high-quality photographic images onto CDs; PICT, an image format used by some Macintosh graphics programs; RAS, a raster image format developed by Sun Microsystems; and Targa (TGA), which is supported by some computer painting programs.

Every CAD program stores data in proprietary formats, but most CAD products support one or more additional formats—so-called transfer formats—for exchange of information. The drawing (DWG) format is the proprietary vector file format developed by AutoDesk for its popular AutoCAD product line. Given AutoCAD's popularity, the .dwg format is supported by other CAD products, including IntelliCAD from the IntelliCAD Technology Consortium and MicroStation from Bentley Systems, which has its own proprietary DGN format. In addition to DWG, AutoDesk developed the drawing interchange format (DXF) for exchange of CAD files. All versions of the AutoCAD product line can convert DXF files to DWG files and vice versa. Supported by other CAD programs, including such non-CAD programs as Adobe Illustrator and Mathematica, DXF is one of the best-known vector-based image formats, but widespread support for the DWG format by non-Autodesk products has diminished the need for DXF.

Vector-based images have historically been associated with engineering drawings generated by CAD software, although they are also encountered in desktop publishing, geographical information systems (GIS), and other applications. **Encapsulated PostScript (EPS)**, for example, is a vector-based image file format based on the PostScript page description language. Many desktop publishing programs and other graphics software can import and export EPS files. The ".cdr" format is a proprietary vector-based graphic format developed by Corel Corporation for use with its drawing software. Adobe Illustrator Artwork format is designed for single-page vector drawings. Its file extension is ".ai."

Digital map files created by geographic information systems combine geographic information, which indicates the shape and position of specific map features, with display instructions, which describe how a map will be plotted for display or printing.

GIS users must typically import geospatial data from various sources. The DXF CAD format has become popular with some GIS products, but digital map files may include attributes, such as road names or construction dates, for specific geographic features. In this respect, GIS formats differ from CAD formats, which principally contain information about geometric objects but lack attribute data. Most GIS programs employ proprietary spatial data formats that are optimized for efficient storage and processing. The ESRI Shapefile, a well-known example, is identified by the ".shp" and ".shx" file extensions. GIS programs also support transfer formats for importing and distribution of information. Perhaps the best-known example is the Arc Export format, which was developed by ESRI for its popular ArcInfo and ArcView product lines. The Arc Export file extension is "e00." Some GIS programs can also import files in proprietary formats such as the MIF/MID formats used by MapInfo.

The foregoing discussion surveys image file formats that may be encountered in a broad range of organizations and records management environments. Special file formats have been developed for specific subject disciplines or types of information, particularly in scientific fields. The following formats are among the many file format examples that might be cited.

- **Flexible Image Transport System (FITS).** The standard data interchange and storage format for the worldwide astronomy community.

- **Video Image Communication and Retrieval (VICAR).** This format is used for planetary images generated from the Earth and spacecraft by the Jet Propulsion Laboratory.

- **Planetary Data System (PDS).** This format is used for data distributed by the National Aeronautics and Space Administration.

- **Spatial Archive and Interchange Format (SAIF).** A Canadian format for geographic data.

- **Spatial Data Transfer Standard (SDTS).** A U.S. government standard for geologic and other spatial data

- **Digital Line Graph (DLG).** A vector format used by the U.S. Geological Survey for cartographic data.

- **Crystallographic Information File (CIF).** A format intended for crystallographic and other structural science data.

- **Topologically Integrated Geographic Encoding and Referencing (TIGER).** A format used by the U.S. Census Bureau for street maps and other information.

- **Photoshop Document (.psd).** The native format for Adobe's PhotoShop graphics editing software. It is also supported by other Adobe products.

File Compression

To save storage space, computer files can be stored in compressed formats. Such files are sometimes described as "packed," and they may be identified by extensions, such as ".zip" or ".sit," that indicate their compressed status. Compression is widely applied to bit-mapped image files. Most digital document imaging systems marketed for records management applications, for example, store images in compressed formats. If digital document images were not routinely compressed, they would overwhelm available storage capacity in high-volume applications. Compression can also be applied to text, spreadsheet, and data files; the larger the file, the greater the motive for compression. Depending on information characteristics and the method selected, compression can reduce storage requirements dramatically. It also reduces bandwidth requirements when files are transmitted over computer networks.

Available compression methods, or **compression algorithms**, differ in their compression ratios, speed, and suitability for specific types of computer-processible information. In digital document imaging implementations, for example, the most widely employed compression algorithms are based on specifications adopted by the International Telecommunications Union (ITU), formerly known as the Consultative Committee on International Telephony and Telegraphy (CCITT). Termed the Group 3 (G3) and Group 4 (G4) compression algorithms, they take their names from the facsimile transmission standards for which they were originally developed. The **Group 3 algorithm** was popular in the 1980s, but it is no longer used in new digital imaging implementations. It employs one-dimensional compression techniques. The **Group 4 algorithm**, by contrast, uses two-dimensional compression methodologies, which yield higher compression ratios. It is standardized by ITU-T Recommendation T.6, *Facsimile Coding Schemes and Coding Control Functions for Group 4 Facsimile Apparatus,* which was last amended in 1988. In digital document imaging implementations, Group 4 compression is typically applied to TIF images. The resulting combination is sometimes described as *TIF G4,* while uncompressed TIF images are described as *TIF UNC.*

The Group 3 and Group 4 algorithms are intended for **bi-tonal documents** that contain text or line art. The JBIG algorithm developed by the Joint Bi-Level Image Experts Group addresses the same applications. The original JBIG compression algorithm, now known as JBIG1, is standardized by ISO/IEC 11544, *Information Technology—Coded Representation of Picture and Audio Information—Progressive Bi-Level Image Compression*, which was published in 1993. An improved version, known as JBIG2, is standardized by ISO/IEC 14492, *Information Technology—Lossy/Lossless Coding of Bi-Level Images,* which was published in 2001. Developers of the JBIG algorithms claim significant improvements in compression of bi-tonal images when compared to the Group 4 algorithm.

Other compression methodologies have been developed for continuous-tone images generated by document scanners, digital cameras, and other devices. The JPEG compression method is one of the most widely publicized examples. As developed by the Joint Photographic Experts Group, JPEG is actually an interrelated group of algorithms that supports various combinations of image quality and compression. The possibilities range from poor quality images that are greatly compressed to moderately compressed images of higher quality. The original JPEG compression algorithm is standardized by ISO/IEC 10918, *Information Technology—Digital Compression and Coding of Continuous-Tone Still Images,* a multipart specification first published in

1994 with subsequent parts appearing in 1995, 1997, and 1999. JPEG 2000, a successor version, offers very high compression without noticeable quality degradation. It is standardized by ISO/IEC 15444, *Information Technology—JPEG 2000 Image Coding System*, a multipart standard that first appeared in 2000. The JPEG 2000 file extension is ".jp2."

The Lempel-Ziv-Welch (LZW) compression algorithm, introduced in the early 1980s, is suitable for a variety of computer applications, including character-coded text and data files and graphic images. Other popular compression algorithms include PKZip and StuffIt, which are encountered in Windows and Macintosh computer installations, respectively.

Specific compression techniques vary. Some algorithms rely on statistical analysis to reduce symbols to shorter codes. Others substitute short codes for predetermined bit sequences. Still others employ sophisticated mathematical compression schemes. Some compression algorithms are **lossless** (bit-preserving). They achieve compression without omitting any information from computer files. Examples of lossless compression algorithms include Group 4, JBIG, and LZW. By contrast, **lossy compression algorithms** reduce storage requirements by omitting information from computer files. The JPEG compression algorithm, which is normally lossy, draws on studies of human perception to eliminate the least noticeable components of pictorial information. It is intended for images that will be viewed rather than processed by computer software. JPEG 2000 supports both lossy and lossless compression. The MPEG format, which was developed by the Moving Picture Experts Group, employs lossy compression to reduce storage requirements for digitized video images and computer animation. Other digitized video formats, such as QuickTime, may also be implemented with lossy compression. Examples of compressed file formats for digitized audio signals include AIFC, a compressed implementation of the Audio Interchange File Format (AIFF), and MP3, which is the audio compression component of the MPEG format.

> *Compression can reduce file sizes for efficient storage, but it should be used only when necessary.*

Some compression algorithms are based on published specifications; others employ proprietary methods. Compression can reduce file sizes for efficient storage, but it should be used only when necessary. Records managers are cautioned that compressed files can pose significant problems for long-term retention of computer-processible information. In effect, compression introduces an additional layer of software dependency, because future retrieval of compressed information requires access to appropriate decompression programs. Like any software, decompression programs may be discontinued. Further, software modifications over time can pose problems of backward compatibility with files compressed by earlier versions of a given program.

Video Recording Standards

Video recordings, like the video signals generated by television broadcasters and other sources, contain images called *frames* that are composed of very small points of light called *picture elements* or *pixels*. The pixels are arranged in horizontal lines called *scan lines*, which are displayed in an organized pattern called a *raster*. The illusion of moving images is created by slight differences in successively displayed frames.

To ensure compatibility among video signals and devices, the number of scan lines per frame and the frequency of frame changes are specified by television standards. Such standards affect the design and operation of video tape recorders, video cameras, and other devices that generate television signals. Although they are all based on the raster-scanning method of image formation, prevailing television standards differ in the number of scan lines provided per frame and in the frequency with which frames are changed. For standard definition television (SDTV) systems, three different and incompatible television standards are employed by video equipment in various parts of the world. Video recordings produced in one television standard can be played only by devices that adhere to the same standard, which complicates the exchange of video tapes in multinational corporations and other international organizations.

The U.S. standard for television broadcasting was developed in 1941 by the National Television Systems Committee. Termed the *NTSC standard*, it specifies a television frame with 525 scan lines and 30 complete frame changes per second. The NTSC standard has been adopted by Canada, Mexico, Japan, the Caribbean, much of Latin America, Saudi Arabia, and a few other countries. Video cameras, videocassette recorders, DVD players, prerecorded video programming, and other video components sold in those countries conform to the NTSC standard.

The two major European video standards provide more horizontal scan lines and higher quality images than their NTSC counterpart. The United Kingdom, Germany, some other European countries, Australia, New Zealand, and parts of South America, Asia, and Africa adhere to the Phase Alternation Line (PAL) television standard. It provides for 625 scan lines per television frame with 25 complete frame changes per second. France, Russia, and some Middle Eastern countries employ the Sequential Couleur a Memoire (SECAM) television standard, which likewise provides for 625 scan lines per frame and 25 frame changes per second. The SECAM and PAL standards differ, however, in other characteristics, which render them incompatible. Slight differences also exist in national implementations of the SECAM and PAL standards that can pose compatibility problems, even within the same standard.

The three television standards described previously were developed at a time when electronic technologies in general, and video technology in particular, were new and, by current standards, primitive. High-definition television (HDTV) formats take advantage of the significant technological advances that have occurred over the last half-century. The definition, or amount of detail, visible in television images is determined by the number of scan lines that form the image. With 1,000 or more scan lines per frame, HDTV images are noticeably sharper than their NTSC,

PAL, and SECAM counterparts. Prototype HDTV systems were demonstrated in the 1970s, and HDTV broadcasting has been operational in Japan since the 1980s. HDTV-compatible video cameras, video tape recorders, and related equipment have likewise been in use for some time. Like conventional television standards, early Japanese HDTV technology employed analog coding of video images. HDTV broadcasting based on digital rather than analog coding began in the United States in late 1998. HDTV signals are incompatible with television receivers, video cameras, video recorders, and other devices that conform to the NTSC standard, which it is expected to eventually supplant.

HDTV formats support several different resolutions and scanning methods. As defined by the Advanced Television Systems Committee (ATSC), display resolutions range from 1280 (horizontal) by 720 (vertical) pixels to 1,920 (horizontal) by 1,080 (vertical) pixels. In the United States, progressive scanning refreshes the entire displayed image 60 times per second, while interlaced (nonprogressive) scanning refreshes the odd-numbered lines of pixels followed by the even-numbered lines at a combined rate of 30 times per second.

HDTV images contain more information than their standard-definition counterparts. At 1,920 by 1,080 pixels with progressive scanning, one hour of HDTV programming requires over 400 gigabytes of storage. As one of their most important advantages, digitally-coded HDTV signals are compressed to conserve transmission bandwidth and, more pertinent to this discussion, for efficient storage. HDTV compression is based on the **MPEG-2** standard, which was developed by the previously cited Moving Picture Experts Group (MPEG) and approved by the International Standardization Organization (ISO). MPEG is the collective designation for a group of standards for recording digitally-coded audio-visual information in a compressed format. The MPEG format is also used to record video information on DVDs, CDs, and the digital video tape media described in Chapter 2; by digital satellite television systems; and for digital audio recording. The MPEG format is standardized by ISO/IEC 13818, *Information Technology—Generic Coding of Moving Pictures and Associated Audio Information,* which was initially published in 2000.

Audio File Formats

Like video signals, audio information may be recorded on analog or digital media. As described in Chapter 2, voice and music are widely recorded on magnetic tape cassettes and, in some cases, magnetic tape reels. These media store information in an analog-coded format that is supported by audio tape recorders and players. Product compatibility is rarely an issue. Analog-coded voice or music information can be played by any devices that accept specific media such as C-type cassettes or microcassettes.

CDs store digitally-coded audio information in the compact disc-audio (CDA) format, which is supported by CD-ROM and DVD-ROM drives as well as by audio CD and DVD players. As with analog tape recording systems, compatibility of equipment with recorded information is rarely an issue, although some CD-R and CD-RW drives may have problems playing specific CDs. DVD-Audio is a high-capacity, high-quality audio format based on DVD-Video technology. Principally intended for music, DVD-Audio disks can also store a limited amount of video information or graphic still images.

Web pages on the Internet or institutional intranets and extranets increasingly incorporate digitally-coded sound clips that contain voice, music, or other audio information. These sound clips are usually posted to Web pages in the file formats in which they were digitized. Sound clips may be downloaded from Web pages to desktop computers, where they are stored on hard drives, optical disks, or other media. Apart from Web pages, digitized audio information may be incorporated into multimedia presentations, databases, or other electronic records.

> *Whatever file format is employed, appropriate software is required to play digitized audio information.*

As with all electronic records, digitized audio information is distributed and stored in formats determined by computer programs that create the information. These audio file formats differ in their technical characteristics, including file size and audio quality, which affect their suitability for specific applications. Whatever file format is employed, appropriate software is required to play digitized audio information. The required programs are termed *audio players*. In some cases, digitized audio information is compressed for efficient distribution or storage, in which case the audio player must include decompression capabilities. Dozens of compressed and uncompressed formats may be used for computer storage of digitized audio information. Examples include the following:

- **Waveform Audio File (WAV) format.** Developed by Microsoft and IBM for Windows-based computers, which are routinely equipped with appropriate software to play WAV files. Web browsers also incorporate the required audio player. The WAV format stores uncompressed audio files that must be downloaded then opened for playback.

- **Motion Picture Experts Group (MPEG) Audio Layer 3 format.** Better known as the MP3 format, this format is an outgrowth of digital audio technologies developed by Fraunhofer Institut Integrierte Schaultungen (Fraunhofer II-S) in Germany. It is standardized by ISO/IEC 13818-1, *Information Technology—Generic Coding of Moving Pictures and Associated Audio Information—Part 3: Audio.* The MP3 format uses compression algorithms that drastically reduce the size of audio files while retaining a high level of sound quality.

- **Advanced Audio Coding (AAC).** The audio format used by Apple's iPod, ITunes, and iPhone products as well as popular video game platforms. AAC is promoted as a higher performance alternative to MP3. The applicable standard is ISO/IEC 14496-3, *Information Technology—Coding of Audio-Visual Objects—Part 3:Audio.*

- **RealAudio (RA) format.** Created by Real Networks, RA format was introduced in 1995. It is compatible with streaming audio, which is played in real-time from Web servers subject to bandwidth considerations that limit audio fidelity. RealAudio files can also be downloaded for playback. RealVideo is the companion format for streaming video, which is suitable for real-time television transmission.
- **TwinVQ.** Developed in Japan by the NTT Human Interface Laboratories and Yamaha Corporation, it is a file format for compressed audio. Intended for Windows-based computers, it is not as widely encountered as the MP3 format.
- **AU file format.** Developed by Sun Microsystems, AU format is an uncompressed file format used by Unix computers.
- **Audio Interchange File Format (AIFF).** Developed by Apple Computer for Macintosh applications, AIFF is an uncompressed file format that has since been adopted by other companies. The AIFC version supports compression.

Summary

Computer files are customarily categorized by the type of information they contain. Text files, which may be produced by word processing programs, e-mail systems, or other software, contain character-coded information. Historically, the ASCII coding scheme, or one of its supersets, has been used to represent individual characters, but newer applications will increasingly use Unicode, of which ASCII is a subset. Utility programs facilitate the interchange of text files in proprietary formats, some of which are so widely supported that they are considered de facto standards. Alternatively, the ASCII text format provides broad compatibility for file importing and exporting.

Spreadsheet files may contain quantitative values, mathematical formulas, and predefined functions, in addition to textual information. Databases contain records that are organized into fields. Spreadsheet and database formats are typically specific to the programs that created them, but utility programs and ASCII-delimited formats facilitate the interchange of information between different programs.

Computer-processible image files may be vector-based or bit-mapped. The former describes images in terms of geometrical shapes such as points, lines, or circles. Bit-mapped images, by contrast, consist of dots that represent tonal values. Various image file formats have been developed for specific purposes. Commonly implemented formats, such as TIF and GIF, facilitate the exchange of computer-processible images. Image files may be recorded in compressed or uncompressed formats on magnetic or optical media. Compression is the rule in digital document imaging implementations. Other computer files may be compressed to save space or reduce bandwidth requirements during file transfers, but adding a layer of software dependency compression can complicate the long-term retention of computer-processible information.

Television recording standards specify the characteristics of video images and, by implication, the devices that produce and play them. The NTSC standard is employed in North America, much of Latin America, Japan, and some other countries. The PAL television standard is employed in the United Kingdom, Germany, other European countries, and parts of South America, Asia, and Africa. The SECAM standard is employed in France, Russia, and parts of the Middle East. HDTV formats, which record video images in a digital compressed format, are incompatible with existing television standards, which they will ultimately supplant.

Like video signals, audio information may be recorded on analog or digital media. Analog-coded voice or music information can be played by any devices that accept specific media such as C-type cassettes or microcassettes. Digitized audio information is distributed and stored in formats determined by computer programs that create the information. Audio file formats differ in their technical characteristics, including file size and audio quality. Appropriate software is required to play digitized audio information, which may be compressed for efficient distribution or storage.

Chapter 4

Inventorying Electronic Records

Broadly defined, a *records inventory* is a fact-finding survey that identifies and describes the characteristics of records created, received, and maintained by all or part of a corporation, government agency, educational institution, professional services firm, not-for-profit entity, or other organization. The purpose of an inventory is to gather information about the quantity, characteristics, storage conditions, use, and perceived value of an organization's records. Records management is a problem-solving activity. Records management problems cannot be successfully addressed until they are clearly delineated and fully understood. The characteristics of an organization's records cannot be determined by intuition or anecdotal evidence; empirical methods are necessary. Conducting an inventory is the initial step in a scientific approach to systematic control of recorded information. Properly executed, a records inventory provides detailed information about the nature and number of records maintained by a given organization. Whether records are in electronic or nonelectronic form, a thorough inventory is an essential component of an effective records management program.

A records inventory is a means to an end rather than an end in itself. Information collected during the inventory is used to prepare records retention schedules, which, as discussed in the next chapter, indicate the lengths of time that specific types of records are to be kept. As an alternative to inventorying, retention schedules might be based on generic record types that are presumably associated with commonly encountered business activities such as accounting, human resources, engineering, or sales. That approach is based on the assumption, for example, that an accounting office will have ledgers and journals, that an accounts payable department will have invoices and payment records, that a purchasing department will have purchase orders, that a human resources department will have personnel records, that a school district will have student transcripts and course registration records, that an engineering department will have drawings and specifications, that a hospital will have clinical case files, that a legal department will have litigation case files, or that a sales department will have customer order records. As their principal shortcoming, schedules prepared in this manner are characteristically vague and incomplete. They provide highly generalized descriptions that can be difficult to match against the records that an organization possesses, and they necessarily omit records associated with business processes or activities that are unusual or unique to a given organization. Only an inventory based on the empirical methods discussed in this chapter can reliably identify and describe those records.

> *Inventory methodologies for electronic records are similar to, and adapted from, methods for inventorying paper and photographic records, but the distinctive characteristics of electronic records— especially their machine-readable content and dependence on specific configurations of hardware and/or software for continued useful- ness—warrant special consideration.*

A comprehensive inventory, by definition, encompasses records of all types. It must include electronic records as well as human-readable information recorded onto paper or photographic media. In keeping with the scope of this book, however, the following discussion is limited to inventories of electronic records. Inventory strate- gies and procedures for human-readable records have been defined and refined by five decades of records management experience. Well developed and widely accept- ed, they are explained in various records management textbooks and other publica- tions. Inventory methodologies for electronic records are similar to, and adapted from, methods for inventorying paper and photographic records, but the distinctive characteristics of electronic records—especially their machine-readable content and dependence on specific configurations of hardware and/or software for continued usefulness—warrant special consideration. In particular, certain descriptive infor- mation collected during an inventory of electronic records will differ from informa- tion gathered when inventorying human-readable paper or photographic media. Further, inventory techniques for electronic methods differ from those used for non- electronic records.

As with human-readable paper or photographic records, an inventory of elec- tronic records in a given organization consists of the following work steps:

1. Develop an inventory plan.

2. Prepare a survey instrument to collect information about the records covered by the inventory.

3. Conduct the inventory according to plan.

4. Tabulate or otherwise write-up the inventory results, gathering additional infor- mation and performing other follow-up work as necessary.

The following sections explain and discuss these work steps, emphasizing practical considerations for records managers who must plan and conduct inventories of elec- tronic records. Much of the discussion may also apply to human-readable paper and photographic records, but those information resources are outside the scope of this book. As noted next, however, inventories of electronic records may collect information about computer printouts, computer-output microfilm, data entry source documents, or other human-readable records that are related to electronic records. Once an inventory of electronic records is completed, its results must be analyzed. That activity, which leads to the preparation of retention schedules, is considered in Chapter 5.

The Inventory Plan

The purpose of an inventory is to identify and describe records maintained by all or part of an organization. At a minimum, an inventory plan must address the scope of the inventory—the organizational units and types of electronic records to be covered—and the procedures to be used to identify electronic records within a given organization.

As a precondition for developing an effective inventory plan, a records manager must understand the organization's information technology infrastructure. All electronic records are created and maintained by specific hardware components and, in the case of computer records, software. At an early stage in the inventory process, the records manager should create a high-level map that identifies the types of computers installed in specific parts of an organization. The map should also enumerate the applications that run on specific computers. Where applicable, the map should include video and audio recording technologies as well as computers. In a large organization with complex information technology infrastructures, separate maps may be prepared for specific divisions or other business units. Although it is discussed here in the context of inventorying electronic records, a map of an organization's information technology infrastructure can also be useful for e-discovery and disaster recovery initiatives, which are covered in later chapters.

Mapping the IT Infrastructure

Mapping an organization's information technology infrastructure is an essential preparatory step in the inventory process for electronic records. Such a map provides an overview of the hardware and software components that form an organization's electronic recordkeeping environment. The map should cover the following categories of computing resources:

1. **Centralized computers.** These computers are installed in and operated by an organization's information technology (IT) department or equivalently titled business unit. These resources may include mainframes, midrange processors, and network servers. Such computers may run enterprise-wide applications— such as fund accounting, e-mail, or an intranet implementation—that are accessed by many departments. Alternatively, they may run programs utilized by a single department or other business unit.

2. **Decentralized computers.** Decentralized computers, such as departmental servers, may be installed in and operated by individual business units, field

offices, or ancillary enterprises without centralized IT involvement. Such computers typically run specialized applications that are used exclusively by a given business unit. For example,

- In a county government, jail management software may run on a server installed in and operated by the sheriff's office.

- In a hospital, a program that tracks credentials of physicians and other healthcare providers may run on a server installed in and operated by the medical staff office.

- In a school district, a program that manages school bus routes may run on a computer installed in and operated by the transportation office.

- In a pharmaceutical company, molecular modeling software may run on a computer installed in and operated by the research and development division.

- In some organizations, certain departments, field offices, or ancillary enterprises may have their own e-mail servers or intranet implementations operating independently of their centralized counterparts.

3. **Personal computing devices.** These devices include desktop computers and notebook computers, as well as personal digital assistants (PDAs) and similar sub-computing devices.

4. **Hosted computer systems.** These systems are operated for a given organization by an application service provider (ASP) or other external entity.

The infrastructure map does not need to enumerate each and every computer or other information processing device installed in a given organization. Intended as an overview rather than a comprehensive catalog, it should indicate the types of devices associated with specific organizational units and the purpose(s) for which the devices are used. For example, an IT infrastructure map for a town government might identify the following computing resources:

- **A midrange computer such as an IBM iSeries processor.** Installed in and operated by the town's IT department for town-wide administrative applications, such as accounting, or for databases accessed by many departments, or for selected departmental applications such as a property information system.

- **Multiple Windows or Unix servers.** Installed in and operated by the information technology department that run additional town-wide applications, such as e-mail or document imaging, or selected department-specific applications such as collection of property taxes. Some servers may be dedicated to a single application while others support two or more applications.

- **Decentralized Windows or Unix servers.** Installed in and operated by individual town departments for applications that affect just one governmental unit such as social services case management, processing of building permits, public safety, or court calendar management.

- **Personal computers.** PCs include desktop machines and mobile devices used for word processing, spreadsheet processing, small and simple databases, preparation of presentations, and other office applications, including e-mail client software and a Web browser.

- **External computing service.** Hosts the town's Web site on the public Internet.

Similarly, an infrastructure map for a school district's computing resources might include:

- A Unix server installed in and operated by the school district's IT department for district-wide applications such as accounting, human resources, student information, course scheduling, and registration.

- Multiple Windows servers installed in and operated by the IT department that run additional district-wide applications, such as e-mail or the district's intranet, as well as selected department-specific applications such as programs for special education or health services provided by school nurses.

- A server installed in and operated by the school district's transportation department to run scheduling software for school bus routes and fleet management.

- Personal computers, including desktop machines and mobile devices used for word processing, spreadsheet processing, small and simple databases, preparation of presentations, and other office applications, including e-mail client software and a Web browser.

- An external computing service that hosts the school district's Web site on the public Internet.

- An external computing service that hosts Web-based software used by the school district's cafeterias for food service management.

Larger organizations will typically exhibit complex variations of the above patterns. A pharmaceutical company, for example, may have multiple IT departments at corporate headquarters and in individual operating units or subsidiaries. Some large organizations have thousands of Windows servers, including multiple e-mail and file servers. Large departments may operate their own networks with hundreds of servers and desktop computers. An increasing number of companies have outsourced a substantial portion of their centralized computing operations.

Defining the Inventory Scope

The purpose of the inventory is to identify and describe electronic records maintained by all or part of an organization. To accomplish this task in a reasonable amount of time with usable results, an inventory must have a manageable scope, where "scope" denotes the specific parts of an organization and/or the types of records to be included in the inventory.

A comprehensive records management program must encompass all information created, maintained, and used by a business, government agency, or other organization, regardless of the information's physical form or characteristics. Ultimately, inventory initiatives must cover all records, whether electronic or non-electronic (paper and photographic), in every division, department, or other unit of an organization. Enterprise-wide inventories may be feasible in small-to-medium-size work environments—a company, government agency, or other organization with fewer than 50 departments, for example—but ambitious inventory strategies pose significant logistic and analytical complications in large organizations with many business units and complex administrative structures.

Inventorying electronic records is a labor-intensive activity that requires painstaking attention to detail. In large organizations, enterprise-wide inventories that attempt to cover all electronic records in a single initiative can take a long time to complete. Multiyear inventorying projects are not unheard of. Preparation of retention schedules and other tasks that depend on inventory data—and are the rationale for conducting an inventory—will be correspondingly delayed. Further, some information collected during early stages of a lengthy enterprise-wide inventory may become obsolete before the inventory is completed and the findings analyzed. Computer, audio, and video systems that generate electronic records may be modified, replaced, or taken out of service, with a resulting impact on the reference value or other characteristics of electronic records. Departments or other organizational units may merge, expand, or be dissolved. Recordkeeping practices will be affected, and inventory work must be redone.

> *To obtain a satisfactory outcome in a meaningful time frame, a records inventory must have a manageable scope.*

Management can easily lose enthusiasm for inventory projects that fail to show results in a reasonable time frame. Data collection can be accelerated by hiring temporary workers, forming special project teams, or otherwise augmenting a records management program's necessarily limited personnel resources, but data collection is only one part of an inventory initiative. Inventory results must be analyzed by records management staff, an intellectual activity that can rarely be expedited. If useful results are to be obtained, an inventory cannot be rushed. To obtain a satisfactory outcome in a meaningful time frame, a records inventory must have a manageable scope.

For best results, an inventory's scope should be limited initially to a single division or other part of a large organization or to one organizational function that crosses departmental boundaries. In a pharmaceutical company, for example, an inventory of electronic records might begin in the research and development division. When that inventory is completed, the results analyzed, and retention schedules drafted, inventory work can proceed to marketing, manufacturing, and other organizational units. In a university, an inventory might be initially limited to electronic records associated with accounting, human resources, purchasing, and other administrative departments, with academic transcripts, course registration records, financial aid records, health service records, and other student records to follow in a second stage. Alternatively—and, possibly, less successfully—an inventory might be limited to specific types of electronic records such as financial records in a corporation or government agency, case files in a law firm, engineering project records in a manufacturing company, or clinical records in a healthcare facility. Limitations on records type can be combined with organizational limitations. As an example, an inventory might be limited to the research and development division of a pharmaceutical company and, initially, to drug discovery or regulatory records within that division.

Under the best circumstances, inventorying electronic records is a difficult and time-consuming task. Meetings must be scheduled, which can take a surprisingly large amount of time. Information must be collected and analyzed for completeness and usability. Follow-up discussions may be necessary to verify information or clarify specific points. The invisible nature of electronic records complicates matters. Limiting an inventory's scope to a subset of organizational units will make the work more manageable and permit faster completion. Results and benefits will be obtained more quickly, although the results will admittedly impact only a segment of the organization.

Management Support

An inventory of electronic records cannot succeed without top management support and the cooperation of information technology personnel and knowledgeable persons in individual program units[1] that utilize specific computer applications and electronic records. To obtain the required support, the objectives of the inventory and its relationship to the systematic control of electronic records, must be explained to, and appreciated by, appropriate levels of management. To demonstrate its support, an organization's top management should send a directive to all program units that will be affected by an inventory initiative. The directive should announce that an inventory of electronic records has been authorized, and it should solicit the cooperation of program units. Presented as a management memorandum, the directive is typically drafted by the records management staff for top management's signature. At a minimum, the memorandum should:

- Acknowledge the value of electronic records as information resources;

- Emphasize the importance of managing electronic records in a systematic manner;

- Explain, briefly, the role of the records inventory as an essential data gathering activity and the critical first step in the systematic control of the organization's electronic records;

- Indicate when the inventory will begin, who will conduct it, and approximately how long it will take;

- Instruct each program unit to designate a liaison person who will assist the records manager in identifying and understanding electronic records that support their business operations.

Liaison persons, sometimes described as *departmental liaisons* or *departmental coordinators*, are crucial to the success of records inventories and other records management initiatives. Departmental liaisons should be designated for each program unit to be covered by an inventorying initiative. Departmental liaisons will serve as the principal contact persons for all records management activities within their program units. They will assist the records manager in conducting inventories of electronic records and in formulating retention and disposition recommendations. Departmental liaisons should be familiar with the business processes and requirements associated with specific computer applications and electronic records. Where additional program unit employees need to be consulted as subject matter experts, the departmental liaison will identify the appropriate persons and arrange for the records manager to meet with them.

Departmental liaisons play a key role in inventories of both electronic and non-electronic records, but another layer of knowledgeable assistance, not required when inventorying paper files, is typically needed for inventories of electronic records. An inventory will collect information about the business use and technical characteristics of electronic records. Although departmental liaisons are presumably knowledgeable about the purpose and value of electronic records from a business perspective, they may not be able to answer questions about media, file formats, archiving practices, data backup procedures, and other technical matters relating to creation, storage, retention, and protection of specific electronic records. This lack of knowledge is particularly the case for electronic records associated with applications that operate on computers managed by an IT unit or an external hosting service. A departmental liaison may not even know where such computers are located, let alone how specific electronic records are formatted, stored, and protected.

One or more technical liaisons should be designated to address these issues. For applications that operate on computers managed by an organization's IT unit, the technical liaison should be the IT employee who is principally responsible for a given application. For applications that run on departmental servers, the technical liaison should be the departmental employee who manages the application. Some larger departments may have their own IT staffs. For hosted applications, commercial computer service providers have technical support personnel assigned to specific accounts.

Departmental coordinators and technical liaisons play complementary rather than overlapping roles in the inventory process. Departmental coordinators are often unaware of the technical attributes of electronic records, but technical liaisons also may know little about the role of recorded information in specific business operations. Their principal concern is the implementation and operation of hardware and software components for records creation, storage, and protection. To obtain a complete picture of the business use and technical characteristics of specific electronic records, a records manager must obtain information from multiple sources.

Inventory Method

Paper records are customarily inventoried in the program units where they are kept or in other locations, such as offsite storage, to which the records have been transferred. An organization chart is typically used to identify program units that will be visited to identify records and collect information about them. Although that approach can be applied to inventories of electronic records, it is not the best practice. As a potentially significant limitation, inventories conducted at the program unit level may fail to identify electronic records shared by two or more program units. Such records are often associated with enterprise-wide applications that support interdepartmental communications, budget preparation, multidepartmental transaction processing, and such analytical activities as knowledge management, data mining, and decision support. Examples include e-mail, Web pages posted on the public Internet or organizational intranets, digital document repositories created by electronic imaging and content management software, and centralized databases and data warehouses of financial, personnel, customer, product, and other information.

Such applications serve multiple program units, but they are not the property of any single program unit. The records they create and maintain usually reside on mainframes, midrange computers, or network servers operated and administered by a centralized IT department. Program units access these enterprise-wide electronic records, but they are not responsible for storing, protecting, or otherwise managing them. The records are not stored locally. Consequently, they may not be mentioned during program unit inventories and, if they are, a given program unit can address only local uses and retention requirements, which may differ from those of other departments.

> *As the technology-oriented counterpart of an organization chart, the infrastructure map identifies the computers and applications that create and maintain electronic records.*

In some respects, records associated with enterprise-wide applications are the electronic counterparts of centralized files of paper documents or microfilmed records maintained by some organizations. Although the existence of centralized files may be revealed when individual program units are inventoried, program unit personnel may not be able to answer detailed questions about the scope, arrangement, or other characteristics of such files. To obtain this information, records—whether in paper or electronic form—must be inventoried at their centralized locations. To accomplish this task, the IT infrastructure map should be the starting point for an inventory of electronic records. As the technology-oriented counterpart of an organization chart, the infrastructure map identifies the computers and applications that create and maintain electronic records. A technical liaison and one or more knowledgeable departmental coordinators should be identified for each application. As discussed later in this chapter, databases, text files, digital images, or other electronic records associated with specific applications will then be inventoried to collect information about technical attributes and business characteristics that bear on the retention of the records.

The same approach can be applied to electronic records created and/or used by audio and video recording and playback equipment, as well as by data recorders and other specialized instrumentation employed in certain scientific, engineering, and medical applications. As with computer-based information systems, the records manager must first identify the types of devices employed by a given program unit, then determine the electronic records associated with such devices. If a program unit has camcorders or other video recording equipment, for example, the records manager should inquire about videotapes, DVDs, or other media produced by such equipment. Similarly, records managers should inquire about video recordings produced by centralized video departments or video service companies. Given their falling prices and increased ease-of-use, video recording devices are commonplace in organizations of all types and sizes.

As with paper files, inventorying, retention scheduling, and related operations are applied to electronic records at the series level. For purposes of this discussion, a **records series** is a group of logically-related records that supports a specific business or administrative operation. Examples of electronic records series might include:

- A data file of open purchase orders maintained by a purchasing department.
- A collection of CAD files for specific projects undertaken by an engineering organization.
- A database of information about current and former employees maintained by a human resources department.
- A database of academic transcripts for current and former students of an educational institution.
- A database of claims information processed by an insurance company.
- An accounts payable data file maintained by an accounting department.
- A database of building permits, zoning variances, and other property information in a municipal building department.
- A digital repository of regulatory submissions maintained by a pharmaceutical company.
- Stock video footage maintained by the media relations department of a municipal parks department.
- Building surveillance tapes generated by video cameras in a company's office complex.

With some of these records series, the same information may exist in both electronic and nonelectronic formats. Inventorying electronic and nonelectronic records simultaneously may be advisable, particularly in organizations where systematic records management is a new activity and formal records retention schedules are incomplete or nonexistent. Multiformat (integrated) inventories are also recommended for organizations that need to update their retention schedules.

Among its advantages, a multiformat inventory can reduce the number of required site visits and meetings when compared to separate inventories of electronic and nonelectronic records. Multiformat inventories can also provide useful insights into the interrelationship and redundancy of information in various formats. As an example, word processing software may be used to transcribe audio recordings created by voice dictation equipment. The resulting documents may be printed for review and editing. The final versions may be printed for filing or distribution. The electronic draft and final versions may be saved as word processing files on hard drives, with backup copies on magnetic tape or other media. The printed versions may be photocopied multiple times, and the originals or any copies may subsequently be microfilmed or scanned for storage and retrieval.

> *Among its advantages, the integrated approach can simplify the logistics of inventorying by reducing the number of required site visits and meetings when compared to separate inventories of electronic and nonelectronic records.*

If desired, inventories of paper, photographic, and electronic records can be integrated and performed at the same time. If systematic records management is a new activity for a given organization, inventories and retention schedules should cover all types of records. Multiformat inventories are also recommended for organizations that need to update retention schedules that were previously prepared for nonelectronic records. Among its advantages, the integrated approach can simplify the logistics of inventorying by reducing the number of required site visits and meetings when compared to separate inventories of electronic and nonelectronic records.

Integrated inventories can also provide useful insights into the interrelationship and redundancy of information maintained in various formats. Electronic and nonelectronic records series are often related. Related records series are likely the case, for example, with many computer-processible records series, including word processing files from which correspondence and other documents are printed, databases from which paper or computer-output microfilm (COM) reports are generated, and computer-aided design (CAD) files from which engineering drawings are produced. Similarly, audio recordings created by dictation equipment may be transcribed to produce paper copies. Even if electronic and nonelectronic records are not inventoried simultaneously, asking about the existence of electronic counterparts when nonelectronic records are inventoried and asking about nonelectronic versions when electronic records are encountered is always advisable.

To be useful, an inventory of electronic records must collect certain information about the physical and application characteristics of such records. The information will be used to prepare retention schedules for electronic records, as explained in Chapter 5. The effectiveness of an inventory is entirely judged by its suitability for that purpose. Inventories of electronic records must be conducted systematically and efficiently. Inventory procedures must be well planned. A formalized survey instrument will ensure the usefulness, uniformity, and completeness of information collected during the inventory process. The survey instrument, described in detail next, delineates the descriptive data and other items of information that must be collected for each electronic records series.

The survey instrument may be distributed as a questionnaire to liaison persons in individual program units, with completed questionnaires to be returned to the records management unit by a specified date. Alternatively, records management staff can consult with individual program units to conduct physical surveys of electronic records series. In consultation with departmental coordinators and technical liaisons, records managers will personally collect the information required by the survey instrument. The questionnaire and consultative methods are equally applicable to electronic and nonelectronic records. Five decades of records management theory and practice involving inventories of paper files have identified the advantages and limitations of each approach.

The principal advantage of the *questionnaire method* is shorter elapsed time for the information-gathering phase of a records inventory. Shortening this phase is achieved by distributing the inventory workload among departmental coordinators. Multiple program units can consequently be inventoried simultaneously. The *consultative method*, by contrast, relies on the records management staff or, in many cases, a records manager as solo practitioner who must inventory program units sequentially. As its principal shortcoming, the questionnaire method provides limited opportunities for direct interaction between program-unit personnel who conduct the inventory and the records management staff who must prepare retention recommendations based on inventory data. Even under the best circumstances, completing a questionnaire to convey information that is sufficiently clear and detailed to be analyzed by others is difficult. Misinterpretations, discrepancies in calculations, and some marginally useful responses are to be expected. For best results, records management staff should provide orientation sessions for liaison persons, supplemented by detailed written instructions, to explain the questionnaire's purpose and content. The orientation sessions should review the data elements to be collected and provide examples of appropriate responses to specific questions. Records management staff must also be available, in person or by telephone, to answer questions or clarify issues that may arise during the inventorying process.

Although the consultation method takes longer than the questionnaire method and involves a greater commitment of time and resources by the records management unit, it usually yields more accurate, reliable, and immediately usable information about electronic records. It produces more detailed responses and minimizes the potential for misinterpretation. Confusing points can often be clarified during the inventory itself. The consultation method relies on two well-established techniques in information systems analysis: (1) direct observation of electronic recordkeeping practices and (2) interviews with persons who create, maintain, and use electronic records. The records management staff will work directly with departmental coordinators and technical liaisons to identify and describe electronic records associated with specific applications and business operations. Using the formalized survey instrument as a script, the records manager interviews these knowledgeable persons to determine the characteristics of electronic records series maintained by a given program unit. Where more detailed information about specific records series is required, departmental coordinators and technical liaisons can arrange additional interviews with other employees. During interviews, the records manager also has the opportunity to view demonstrations of specific applications and retrieve samples of electronic records for display or printing. Electronic storage media can likewise be examined.

The questionnaire and consultation methods are not mutually exclusive. As a potentially effective combination of the two approaches, records management staff may distribute survey instruments for completion by departmental coordinators and technical liaisons, then conduct site visits and interviews to review, clarify, or expand the responses. In some cases, the questionnaire method is the only practical approach to inventorying electronic records. Due to time or economic constraints, for example, records management staff may be unable to conduct site visits and interviews at field offices, branch locations, international subsidiaries, or other geographically remote program units. If an organization has multiple field offices or branch locations with similar recordkeeping practices, site visits and interviews may be conducted at several of the locations, and the remainder surveyed by the questionnaire method, possibly with telephone interviews to clarify responses.

> *With electronic records, inventories depend less on observation than on informative interaction with a knowledgeable person who can describe the characteristics and use of the records.*

In fact, telephone interviews should be considered as an alternative to questionnaires generally. With sufficient preparation by the records manager and receptive participants, telephone interviews can be effective substitutes for in-person meetings for inventorying many types of electronic records. Given the invisible nature of electronic records, site visits are less important than they are for inventories of paper documents. With electronic records, inventories depend less on observation than on informative interaction with a knowledgeable person who can describe the characteristics and use of the records.

Regardless of the method employed, sufficient time must be allotted to complete the inventory. Although a sense of urgency may stimulate productivity, unrealistic deadlines are not compatible with quality work. If the consultation method is used, site visits and interviews will require at least one-half day per application that generates electronic records, exclusive of preparation, travel time to the interview location, and follow-up work. These tasks can double or triple the time required. Several days and multiple interviews may be required to inventory electronic records associated with complex applications. The list of applications to be surveyed and persons to be interviewed typically expands as an inventory project progresses. As discussed at the end of this chapter, additional time will be required to tabulate or otherwise write up the findings from notes taken during interviews. Follow-up interviews or telephone calls will often be necessary to clarify specific points raised during interviews.

Thus, an inventory of electronic records in a corporation or government agency with 50 computer applications will require at least 100 to 150 working days, exclusive of the time required to analyze inventory results and draft retention schedules as discussed in the next chapter. That estimate may be optimistic. As previously noted, scheduling interviews can be a time-consuming, frustrating process. Persons who are most knowledgeable about electronic records are often very busy and may be reluctant or unable to commit time to a project in which they are not directly involved. Canceled interviews are inevitable and must be rescheduled. Follow-up requirements are unpredictable and can prove time-consuming. Additional interviews may be required to fully understand the characteristics and business value of some electronic records. Inventories that combine electronic and nonelectronic records will take longer to complete.

Even when the questionnaire method is used, inventorying electronic records is a time-consuming process. Some responses will be late. Repeated telephone calls may be necessary to obtain the completed questionnaires. Responses prepared by departmental coordinators and technical liaisons must be reviewed and, where necessary, clarified by records management staff. Systematic, thorough inventories cannot be rushed. Top management must understand that time spent obtaining reliable, detailed information about electronic records will facilitate the preparation of appropriate retention recommendations, the identification of vital electronic records, and other records management activities that depend on accurate, complete inventory data.

The Survey Instrument

Electronic records are typically inventoried at the series level, where a records series is a collection of logically related records that support one or more operations performed by an organization. The identification of electronic records is complicated by the fact that such records, as previously noted, are invisible. They may be maintained on magnetic tapes, optical disks, or other removable media described in Chapter 2; but many are stored out of view, on nonremovable hard drives. Major electronic records series are associated with important technology initiatives and business processes. Typically notable for both their quantity and significance for essential operations, they are readily identifiable. Records managers may have to work harder when preparing the IT infrastructure map and during interviews to identify and collect information about minor electronic records series, which are less important and usually less voluminous. No matter how diligent the inventory procedures, some minor series may be overlooked.

As discussed in the preceding section, a survey instrument specifies the descriptive data and other items of information to be collected for each electronic records series covered by the inventory initiative. Depending on the inventory method employed, the survey instrument may be formatted as a questionnaire. Alternatively, it may simply be a checklist of questions to be asked by records management staff—that is, a script to be used when interviewing departmental coordinators, technical liaisons, and other knowledgeable persons. A sample checklist is provided in Figure 4.1.

Regardless of approach, the following discussion lists and explains the types of information to be collected about each series during an inventory of electronic records. Typically, an inventory begins with general information about the scope, purpose, and quantity of an electronic records series. Other information describes

---

Checklist for Inventorying Electronic Records Series

❑ Series title
❑ Summary description
❑ Copy type(s)
    ❑ Storage copy
    ❑ Working copy
    ❑ Security copy
❑ File type
❑ Dates covered
❑ Arrangement
❑ Quantity
    ❑ Item count
    ❑ Bytes
    ❑ Recording time
❑ Estimated growth
❑ Physical storage requirements
❑ Storage location(s)

❑ Media characteristics
    ❑ Type and size of medium
    ❑ Brand and model
    ❑ Recording format
    ❑ Special features
❑ Media manufacturing date
❑ Hardware environment
❑ Software environment
    ❑ Systems software
    ❑ Application software
❑ Reference activity
❑ Retention requirements
❑ Relationship to human-readable records
❑ Supporting files
❑ Vital record status

---

the physical and technical characteristics of electronic media, their storage locations, and reference requirements for electronic records series.

Series Title

The series title is the name by which an electronic records series is known to those who maintain and use it. The title will identify the electronic records series in retention schedules, reports, and other documents prepared from inventory data. Consequently, it should be as descriptive as possible. At a minimum, the title must clearly distinguish a given electronic records series from others. Examples of acceptably descriptive series titles for electronic records include "Human Resources Database" for a database of information about an organization's current and former employees; "Student Health Database" for a database of health records maintained by a school's health services unit; "Technical Reports Catalog," for a data file of bibliographic citations pertaining to research reports created by a pharmaceutical laboratory; "Construction Cost Estimates," for spreadsheet files pertaining to projects undertaken by a construction company; "Standard Contract Clauses," for word processing files that contain clauses to be incorporated into contracts prepared by the contract management unit of a government agency; "Building Site Inspections," for videotapes that provide visual records of field inspections undertaken by a municipal building department; and "Liability Case Depositions," for audio recordings of legal depositions maintained by a law firm.

Summary Description

A brief (approximately one paragraph) description of the contents of the electronic records series should summarize its business purpose, scope, and contents. As an example, the following description might apply to a student health database maintained by a school district's health services department:

> Contains personal and health information for each student enrolled in the school district. One database record per student. Each record contains the student's name, address, parent or guardian contact, grade, teacher, immunizations, physical examinations and screenings, medical conditions, health alerts, doctor's orders for medications, and reports of visits to and treatment received from school nurses.

Similarly, the following description summarizes the essential characteristics of a fundraising database maintained by the membership and development department of a not-for-profit organization:

> Contains information about donors, including previous and prospective donors. One database record per donor. Each record contains the donor's name, address, telephone number, e-mail address, occupation, previous giving history, and reports of interactions. Staff enters notes of telephone conversations or other contacts with prospective donors.

With some records series, such as the previous "Construction Cost Estimates" example, the title describes the contents, but additional details can clarify the business purpose and scope of such a series. The additional details might indicate the specific construction projects for which costs are estimated, the types of estimates provided, the circumstances under which the estimates are prepared, or the series' relationship to other records series maintained in the program unit or elsewhere in the organization. Similarly, a brief descriptive paragraph for the "Building Site Inspections" series of videotapes might indicate the specific buildings covered by the videotaped inspection reports and describe the circumstances under which the videotapes were created. In every case, a statement of purpose should indicate the electronic records series' relationship to the program unit's mission, administrative activities, or business operations.

Copies / Backup Practices

An electronic records series may be a unique accumulation of information or one of several copies. In the latter case, which is more likely where appropriate backup procedures are implemented, the type of copy should be indicated. A given electronic records series may be a storage copy, a working copy, or a security copy kept offsite.

Backup practices must be identified for each records series. As explained in a later chapter, computer files may be backed up incrementally or fully at predetermined intervals. The type and frequency of backup operations for a given records series should be determined.

Multiple copies of electronic records series should be separately identified, and their intended purposes should be reflected in their series titles. For example, a descriptive title, such as "General Ledger—Full Backup," could be used for a security copy of an electronic records series recorded on magnetic tape, while a title, such as "General Ledger—Year-End Archival," might denote a copy that contains older, inactive electronic records intended for long-term storage.

File Type

Electronic records series are usually categorized by file type, where a file broadly denotes a collection of electronic information. Electronic file types, as explained in Chapter 3, include computer files, video files, and audio files. Electronic files may be further categorized by the type of information they contain and by the format in which the information is recorded. Examples of descriptive categories for computer-processible information include text files, spreadsheet files, databases, or image files. For each category, further subdivision provides additional description. Text files, for example, might be categorized as ASCII text, ASCII text with line breaks, or native word processing formats. Image files might be categorized as TIF, GIF, PDF, or proprietary formats. Video recordings may be described by the television standard employed. Audio recordings may be categorized as music or spoken word.

Dates Covered

During inventories, records managers must determine the inclusive (beginning and ending) dates for information contained in each electronic records series. Compared to paper documents and microfilm maintained by a given program unit, electronic records series will usually have more recent beginning dates. Computer-processible records series rarely predate the mid-1960s for information generated by mainframe computers, the mid-1970s for information generated by midrange computers, and the mid-1980s for information generated by personal computers. In most organizations, video recordings date from the mid-1980s, when videocassette recorders and portable video cameras became widely available and affordable. Often, audio recordings are the oldest types of electronic records maintained by an organization. Voice dictation equipment has been used in office applications since the early twentieth century.

Regardless of type, electronic records series that support ongoing business operations will have open ending dates because new records continue to be created and stored. Closed electronic records series are typically characterized by obsolete media, defunct systems, or discontinued business operations. When a given computer application is replaced, the data may not be migrated to a successor application. Such legacy data constitutes a closed series. It may continue to be accessed by its originating application, which will need to remain in service for that purpose, but no new information will be added to it. When a school district replaces its student information system, for example, it will not necessarily migrate data for students who have graduated or left the district. Yet, that data may need to be retrieved when former students request transcripts or return to the school district. To address this requirement, the school district may continue to operate the older application as long it is able to do so or until the retention periods for the records expire. With longer retention periods, keeping legacy applications in service is, of course, more difficult.

Arrangement

The arrangement is the physical sequence of electronic records within a series. It denotes both the sequencing of information within a given medium—the arrangement of records within a magnetic tape, for example—and the sequencing of individual media within a collection—the arrangement of multiple tapes in relation to one another. Arrangement concepts are borrowed from paper filing systems, where alphabetic, numeric, or other arrangements are easily identified and reflect users' reference requirements. In paper filing systems, documents are usually arranged by their principal retrieval parameter. If patient records are requested by patient name, for example, they are filed in that sequence. Similarly, legal files retrieved by case number are filed by that identifier.

Arrangement concepts are applicable to some electronic records, particularly audio and video recordings. In a series of videotaped building inspections, for example, there may be one tape per inspection, and the tapes may be arranged by building number or project number. Similarly, dictated correspondence and other office documents may be arranged chronologically within a series of audiotapes. In an oral history collection, interviews may be recorded on separate audiotapes, which are arranged alphabetically by the name of the interviewee.

Arrangements are more difficult to determine and less meaningful when inventorying computer records series. Electronic records stored on a hard drive, for example, are invisible; records sequences cannot be determined by observation, as they can with paper files. Further, the arrangement of word processing documents, spreadsheet files, database records, digital images, or other information within a hard drive is usually beyond the user's control. A computer's operating system uses directories, tables, and indexes to determine where electronic records will be stored, often on a space available basis. Files are recorded in clusters that are not necessarily contiguous. When a file is retrieved, the operating system reassembles it from scattered clusters. Users are unaware of the physical sequence in which information is recorded within a given hard drive.

Within magnetic tapes, information is often recorded in the sequence in which it will be processed. Back-up tapes usually mirror the sequence of the media they copy, although incremental backups contain only information that has changed since the last backup operation. For removable computer media—such as magnetic tapes and optical disks—arrangement is often synonymous with the shelving sequence in offline storage. Such media may be arranged on shelves by control number, application, originating department, date, or other parameters.

Quantity

For each records series, the inventory must collect information about the quantity of electronic records and the locations and conditions in which the records are stored. The quantity of a given electronic records series should be expressed in one or more measures appropriate to the type of records being inventoried. For computer back-up copies, video recording, and audio recordings, quantity is easily measured by the number of tapes or other media that a given records series occupies. For video and audio records, quantity may also be measured by recording time in minutes or hours.

If an electronic records series does not fill a given medium, the percentage occupied should be indicated. If other records series are stored on the same medium, they should be described briefly. For word processing documents, e-mail, databases, digital images, or other computer-processable records series, quantity is customarily measured in bytes or multiples thereof (megabytes, gigabytes, terabytes, etc.). Thus, the total collection of an organization's e-mail in active inboxes may be calculated at 2.5 terabytes, while a large collection of digital images may total 10 terabytes. These measures may be supplemented by an item count in the case of magnetic tapes or other removable media.

Estimated Growth

Anticipated annual growth rates for a given electronic records series are most easily and conveniently determined when the series is subdivided by year or other chronological periods.

Information about the annual growth of electronic records is essential for planning future storage requirements. When presented to management in an appropriately alarmist manner, growth estimates can also encourage a sense of urgency about records retention initiatives. Unless the operations they support are discontinued, the quantity of electronic records created and maintained by a corporation, government agency, academic institution, professional services firm, or other organization will increase over time. Anticipated annual growth rates for a given electronic records series are most easily and conveniently determined when the series is subdivided by year or other chronological periods. In such cases, the number of media, byte totals, or other quantity measures can be compared for different years.

Where a given records series is not subdivided by year, annual growth must be estimated in other ways such as relating the growth of records to some measurable factor. As with paper documents, the creation of electronic records is typically linked to events or transactions such as the receipt of new orders by a sales department, the issuance of new policies or receipt of new claims by an insurance company, the acceptance of new clients by a social services agency, the hiring of new employees by a manufacturing company, or the initiation of new projects by an engineering organization. If it is determined that such events or transactions are increasing at a specific annual rate, it follows that electronic records associated with such transactions will grow at a corresponding rate. Thus, if a database record is created each time an order is received from a customer and if new orders are increasing by 10 percent per year, the number of database records pertaining to customer orders should also increase by 10 percent. If 15,000 order records were created this year, 16,500 order records will be created next year. Similarly, if the number of building permits issued by a municipality is increasing by 15 percent per year, the number of database records maintained by the municipality's permit processing application should increase by 15 percent.

Where the foregoing methods are inapplicable, dates for database entries, word processing documents, video recordings, or other items from one or more segments of an electronic records series can be tabulated and the totals compared. As an aid to such tabulations, media directories, described in a later chapter, often indicate creation dates for specific files.

Physical Storage Requirements

Physical storage requirements are meaningful only for electronic records series stored on removable media. Quantity estimates, measured in linear feet occupied by magnetic tapes or optical disks, provide useful information about the amount of shelf space required by a given electronic records series. Such measurements alert the records manager to potential storage space problems posed by voluminous electronic records series. Some organizations, for example, have huge collections of backup tapes in storage.

The approximate number of linear feet occupied by commonly encountered types of media discussed in Chapter 2 can be calculated from the following measurements:

- **Nine-track magnetic tape reels:** one linear inch per reel, 12 reels per linear foot.
- **Half-inch magnetic tape cartridges:** one linear inch per cartridge, 12 cartridges per linear foot.
- **Digital linear tape (DLT) and LTO Ultrium cartridges:** one linear inch per cartridge, 12 cartridges per linear foot.
- **Eight-millimeter data cartridges:** 0.75 linear inch per cartridge, 16 cartridges per linear foot.
- **Digital audio tape (DAT) cartridges:** 0.5 linear inch per cartridge, 24 cartridges per linear foot.
- **QIC magnetic tape cartridges:** 1.5 linear inches per QIC data cartridge, eight cartridges per linear foot; one linear inch per QIC minicartridge, 12 cartridges per linear foot.
- **Diskettes, 3.5 inch:** 0.14 linear inch per diskette, 85 diskettes per linear foot.
- **Audiotape cassettes:** 0.75 linear inch per boxed cassette, 16 cassettes per linear foot.
- **VHS videotape cassettes:** one linear inch per cassette, 12 cassettes per linear foot; 1.25 linear inches per cassette in a plastic box, 9 cassettes per linear foot.
- **Mini DV digital videotape cassettes:** 0.5 linear inch per cassette, 24 cassettes per linear foot.
- **Optical disk cartridges, 5.25-inch:** 0.75 linear inches per cartridge, 16 cartridges per linear foot.
- **CDs and DVDs:** 0.5 linear inch per CD or DVD in plastic box, 24 CDs or DVDs per linear foot.

Storage Location(s)

Depending on the circumstances in which they are created and used, electronic records series may be housed in an office, a computing facility, an offsite warehouse, or another location. Records from a given series may be stored on different types of media and in multiple locations; active records may be kept on a hard drive, for example, while older records are transferred to magnetic tape for offsite storage. An inventory should indicate all storage locations for each electronic records series and for all copies of a given series, including backup copies. If storage facilities have special security or environmental attributes, whether suitable or unsuitable, they should be noted.

Media Characteristics

The inventory must include a detailed description of the physical and technical characteristics of the media on which particular electronic records series are stored. As discussed in Chapter 2, magnetic disks, magnetic tapes, and optical disks are the most important media for electronic records, but punched cards, paper tape, or other obsolete media may also be encountered, particularly when inventorying offsite storage locations.

The description of physical and technical characteristics should include the type and size of medium (820-meter LTO Ultrium cartridge, 4.75-inch DVD-R, 3.5-inch diskette, etc.), the brand and model (the manufacturers' product designation such as Imation Super DLT II cartridge or Maxell DVM-60 digital video cartridge), the recording format (such as double-sided, high-density for 3.5-inch diskettes or 9.4 gigabytes for double-sided DVD-R media), and any special attributes or enhancements (such as backcoating) that may affect performance. This information will be used to evaluate the likely future viability and reliability of media on which electronic records are stored.

Media Manufacturing Date

The stability of magnetic and optical media is measured from the media manufacturing date, not the date when information was recorded.

Information about media stability and hardware or software dependencies is necessary to estimate the remaining service lives of specific media that contain electronic records. As discussed elsewhere in this book, magnetic and optical media are subject to time-dependent degradation that will ultimately affect their utility for recording and retrieval of information. If the remaining stable life of a given medium is shorter than the retention period for the electronic records that the medium contains, the records must eventually be recopied onto new media. The stability of magnetic and optical media is measured from the media manufacturing date, not the date when information was recorded.

Unfortunately, media manufacturing dates can be difficult to determine. Occasionally, manufacturing dates are printed on media packaging or shipping documents. If the manufacturing date is not indicated, the procurement date or the date when the medium was first put into service is often a satisfactory substitute. Presumably, the media in question were recently manufactured when purchased or initially used. As discussed later in this book, including the manufacturing date, or an estimate thereof, when preparing media labels is useful.

Hardware Environment

Electronic records depend on specific hardware components for reference or other uses. An inventory must consequently include a list and description of all equipment required to retrieve or otherwise process a given electronic records series. In some cases, a generic hardware description will suffice. Examples of acceptable generic descriptions include: "a Macintosh computer system with a DVD-R drive," "a video cassette recorder with Super-VHS playback capabilities," or "an audio cassette deck with Type IV tape compatibility." Some electronic records can only be utilized with specific equipment, however. This requirement is the case with certain computer-processable electronic records that require specific brands and/or models of computers and storage peripherals. Hard disk cartridges and high-capacity diskettes, for example, require proprietary storage peripherals. Further, inventories may encounter older electronic records that require discontinued equipment such as nonstandard 5.25-inch write-once optical disk drives or U-Matic videocassette players. Electronic records may also require computer configurations or storage peripherals that an organization has replaced with different models.

Software Environment

Computer-processable electronic records are intended for use with specific programs. The inventory must include a list, with brief descriptions, of all computer programs required to reference or otherwise process electronic records. The list must include systems software (operating systems, compilers, interpreters, and utility programs), as well as application software (word processing programs, spreadsheet programs, database management systems, document imaging programs, etc.). Program names and version numbers must be provided because electronic records created by one version of a given computer program may not be compatible with other versions. For custom-developed software, the programming language should be determined and a brief developmental history obtained. For prewritten software packages, the publisher or procurement source should be indicated. As with hardware components, some organizations may maintain electronic records that require obsolete software components such as discontinued software packages or custom-developed programs that have been removed from service.

As a potential complication discussed in Chapter 3, some computer applications employ compression algorithms to reduce storage requirements for data, text, or image files. Such algorithms can have an impact on the future utility of electronic records because compressed information must be decompressed by compatible programs for reference or other processing. When inventorying compressed records, specific compression algorithms and software requirements should be determined. Although it reduces storage costs, compression adds another layer of software dependency to the management of electronic records. To minimize future problems, compression should be used sparingly for electronic records intended for long-term storage. With some computer-processible information, such as document images or multimedia presentations, compression is necessary for efficient storage, which is rarely the case with word processing documents, database records, or other character-coded information.

Reference Activity

Reference activity means the frequency with which a given records series is consulted for operational or other purposes. Analysis of reference activity should consider the business processes or operations that an electronic records series supports, the method and frequency of reference, the departments or other organizational units that use the records, and access privileges or restrictions associated with specific users and/or business operations.

> *For electronic records series, as with most information, the value of information usually diminishes over time.*

This information is best obtained by interviewing representative users of an electronic records series. The departmental coordinator, as described earlier in this chapter, is a good starting point, but additional users may need to be consulted to ensure that all viewpoints are represented. Ideally, a knowledgeable user will be able to make a reasonable estimate of the number of times that all or part of a given records series is consulted per month, year, or other time period. For electronic records series, as with most information, the value of information usually diminishes over time. During interviews with knowledgeable users, the records manager should determine the point in time when reference activity begins to decline and, where applicable, the point in time when all or part of a given electronic records series is no longer needed. Accounts payable records, for example, may be consulted frequently to answer questions about unpaid invoices, but reference activity typically falls off significantly after payment is made. Similarly, a high school counselor will frequently consult a student information system to determine grades, courses taken, and other information about currently enrolled students, but the need for this information will decline sharply after students graduate.

The records manager should also determine the users' speed expectations when retrieving information from specific electronic records series because such requirements will dictate the devices and media to be used for records storage. Three levels of retrieval requirements can be distinguished:

1. **Online.** Certain information processing applications require that electronic records be immediately and continuously available to support important and urgent business operations. Such records are consulted frequently and, more often than not, unpredictably. To satisfy such reference requirements, electronic records are stored on hard drives for online access in fractions of a second. Less commonly, they may be recorded onto optical disks housed in autochangers.

2. **Offline.** Removable electronic media, such as magnetic tapes and optical disks, may be stored on-premises in desktop trays, cabinets, shelving units, or other containers until required for specific information processing operations. Retrieval times with offline media may be measured in minutes or fractions of an hour. Manual intervention is required for media retrieval, mounting, and reshelving.

3. **Offsite.** Removable magnetic and optical media can be stored in records centers, warehouses, or other offsite locations. Offsite storage is best suited to inactive electronic records or to security copies. Depending on the offsite storage location, retrieval times may be measured in hours or days.

Sensitivity

Many electronic records contain personally identifiable information, trade secrets, business plans, competitive intelligence, or other sensitive or confidential information that requires special handling. These records must be identified during the inventory, and access restrictions, including any restrictions imposed by privacy legislation, must be fully understood.

Retention Requirements

A records inventory is a means to an end, rather than an end in itself. Its principal purpose is to provide the information necessary to prepare retention schedules for electronic records covered by the inventory. As discussed in the next chapter, many retention recommendations rely on the perceived requirements of program units that create, maintain, and use electronic records. Such requirements are typically based on operational experience with specific electronic records series. Knowledgeable persons in a program unit may contend, for example, that a specific electronic records series be retained for seven years because it has consulted records from that series that were seven years old. During the inventory, records managers must ask about a program unit's operational retention requirements. Records managers should also identify events—such as the end of a fiscal year, expiration of a contract, or completion of a project—that may cause electronic records within a given series to become less active and, ultimately, inactive.

The records manager must also ask about a program unit's existing retention practices for specific records series. In the absence of systematically developed retention schedules, some program units formulate their own retention guidelines. In such situations, the time period must be determined and appropriateness of existing retention practices evaluated. In particular, the records manager must ask about the program unit's reason for adopting the existing retention practice.

Relationship to Nonelectronic Records

The same records may exist in multiple formats. Many electronic records are related to, and often duplicate, human-readable information recorded onto paper or microfilm. In most word processing applications, for example, paper file copies are printed from computer-processable files. E-mail may be printed for reference or filing. Databases are used to print paper reports that provide a "snapshot" of database records at a particular point in time or for a particular set of variables. Whenever paper or microfilm records are encountered during an inventory, the records manager should inquire about any electronic records with identical or similar contents. Whenever electronic records are encountered, records managers should inquire about corresponding paper and microfilm records.

Supporting Files

The inventory should include a brief description of any electronic or other files that support the creation, maintenance, or use of a given electronic records series. As an example, some databases and other computer files rely on indexes that contain pointers to specified field values. Such indexes are essential to effective and efficient processing of database records or other information. Similarly, collections of document images are typically supported by a computer database that serves as an index to the images. If the database is discarded or damaged, image retrieval will prove difficult or impossible.

Vital Record Status

As discussed more fully in a later chapter, vital records contain information essential to an organization's mission-critical operations. To eliminate the need for a separate survey of vital records, identifying potentially vital records during a records inventory is useful.

Inventory Followup

As previously explained, inventory information will be used to prepare retention recommendations for specific electronic records series. Responses to questions contained in the survey instrument must be both accurate in content and correctly interpreted by the records manager. If the questionnaire method is utilized, the records manager should review the responses with liaison persons or others responsible for completing the questionnaire in each program unit. To avoid misunderstanding that can lead to inappropriate retention recommendations, the records manager's interpretation of major points should be confirmed by the program unit. Clarification should always be requested for vague or incomplete responses.

If the consultative method is used, the records manager should prepare a written summary of information obtained during each interview with departmental coordinators or other knowledgeable persons. The summary can be written as if it were the minutes of a meeting. The written summary should be submitted to the interviewee to review for correctness and completeness. The interviewee should be instructed to make comments, additions, corrections, clarifications, or modifications as needed. Such follow-up work steps will necessarily increase the time required to complete inventories of electronic records, but they are highly advisable. The time and effort required to conduct thorough inventories of electronic records and accurate interview summaries will be repaid in appropriate retention recommendations less likely to require time-consuming negotiation and revision.

Summary

The purpose of a records inventory is to gather information about the number and characteristics of an organization's electronic records. Conducting a thorough inventory is the critical initial step in a systematic approach to retention of electronic records.

Electronic records are inventoried at the series level, where a series is defined as a group of logically-related records that support one or more business operations. Adapting a technique that is widely utilized for paper documents, electronic records are often inventoried on a program unit basis. As a potential shortcoming, such inventories may fail to identify electronic recordkeeping systems shared by multiple program units. To address this problem, electronic records may be inventoried by identifying and analyzing the automated information systems with which they are associated.

To demonstrate its support for records management initiatives, an organization's top management should send a directive to all program units. The directive should announce that an inventory of electronic records has been authorized and solicit the cooperation of individual program units. Liaison persons, to be designated by each program unit, will serve as principal points of contact for inventorying and related records management activities.

To formalize working procedures, a specially designed survey instrument must be developed to collect information about specific characteristics of electronic records. The survey instrument may be distributed as a questionnaire to program unit liaisons. Alternatively, it can be used as an interview guide by records management staff who will determine records characteristics in consultation with liaison persons or other program unit personnel. The questionnaire method typically shortens the completion time required for a records inventory, but misinterpretations, discrepancies, and some marginally useful responses can be expected. The consultation method, which relies on interviews and observation, can minimize these problems, but it is often more time-consuming.

Regardless of approach, the survey instrument should collect information about the title and purpose of each electronic records series, the physical and technical characteristics of the media on which the series is recorded, the locations where such media are stored, the types of hardware and software with which the media must be utilized, the current volume and anticipated growth of records contained in a given series, the records' reference characteristics and retention requirements, and the relationship of particular electronic records series to other machine-readable and human-readable information created, maintained, and used by the organization. Because the information gathered during an inventory of electronic records will ultimately be used to formulate retention recommendations, accuracy is critical. To avoid misinterpretations, information obtained through consultations or questionnaires should be carefully reviewed with liaison persons or other program unit representatives.

Notes

1 For purposes of this discussion, a program unit is broadly defined as a division, department, section, or other administrative unit of a business, government agency, professional services firm, academic institution, or other organization. As a generic designation, *program unit* avoids confusion associated with differing hierarchical relationships among administrative units. In some organizations, departments are subordinate to divisions; in other cases, the reverse is true. A department may be divided into offices, branches, or sections; alternatively, a section, branch, or office may be the highest level in an organization's administrative hierarchy. Program units are typically distinguished by their specific missions and responsibilities, which are presumably related to and supported by the records they create or maintain. Some program units may be large departments with hundreds of employees and huge quantities of electronic and nonelectronic records; others may be small offices staffed by one or two persons who maintain a few paper files and a small quantity of electronic records.

Chapter 5

Retention Schedules for Electronic Records

As explained in Chapter 4, a records inventory is a means to an end. Its principal purpose is to obtain information required to formulate retention schedules for an organization's records. Broadly defined, a **records retention schedule**—variously described as a *records retention and disposition schedule* or, simply, a *records disposition schedule*—is a list of records series maintained by all or part of an organization, together with the period of time that each series is to be kept. Some retention schedules also include information about the reasons records are kept for specified time periods, as well as instructions regarding the locations and conditions under which records are to be retained. Retention schedules may be maintained as paper copies or computer files. In the latter case, they may be printed for reference purposes, although corporations, government agencies, and other organizations are increasingly posting Web-based versions of retention schedules on intranets as more convenient alternatives to printed copies, which can be time-consuming to distribute and difficult to update.

Retention schedules may be enterprise-wide or program-specific in scope. An enterprise-wide retention schedule, sometimes described as a *master schedule*, specifies retention periods for designated records series, regardless of the particular program units where the series are maintained. Master retention schedules are sometimes characterized as *functional schedules* because they categorize records series by the business functions to which they pertain rather than the business units where the records are maintained. Examples of functional categories include administrative records, financial records, human resources records, legal records, procurement and supply records, product development records, manufacturing records, and sales and marketing records. An organization may issue separate master schedules for specific functional categories. Separate master schedules is the approach taken, for example, by the National Archives and Records Administration (NARA), which has issued separate retention schedules for several dozen categories of records commonly held by U.S. government agencies. Alternatively, a single master schedule may provide retention guidance for an entire organization.

By definition, a master schedule provides one set of retention guidelines for all program units in an organization. A given program unit will maintain a subset of the records series enumerated in the master schedule. A program-specific retention schedule, by contrast, is limited to those records series actually held by a specific department, office, or other program unit. Sometimes described as activity-oriented or departmental retention schedules, program-specific retention schedules are custom-prepared for each program unit within an organization.

As their principal advantage, program-specific retention schedules are highly prescriptive. They list only those records series that a given program unit maintains, with unequivocal retention designations for each. Each program unit has direct input into the determination of retention periods. Because program-specific retention schedules are tailored to the requirements of individual program units, they are easy to understand and may include detailed implementation instructions. Functional schedules, by contrast, may be difficult for individual program units to interpret. To determine retention requirements, a program unit must first locate its records series among the many listed in the functional schedule. In some cases, program units identify records series by different titles than those listed in the functional schedule, which necessarily lists each records series under a single name in a single functional group. An exact match is further complicated by slight variations in the scope and content of records series maintained by different program units. Offsetting these potential problems, proponents of functional retention schedules claim that they promote consistent retention practices across organizational units, can be prepared more quickly than program-specific schedules, and are easier to update when organizational changes occur. Program-specific schedules can be difficult to update, given the increasing incidence of reorganizations, mergers, divestitures, and other changes that realign or eliminate departments.

Master schedules provide retention guidance for records held by multiple program units. The retention designations are based upon input from some, but not necessarily all, program units that maintain a given records series. Presumably, the retention designations reflect the longest retention requirements for the listed series. For records that exist in multiple copies, however, a program unit may want to discard its copies of a given records series before the generalized retention period has elapsed. To address this requirement, a general schedule may designate an office of record that is responsible for retaining specific records series for the entire time period designated in the schedule. Other program units can discard their copies of that series when local need has expired, but they must not retain them longer than the designated retention period.

An organization may issue general retention guidelines for its commonly held or enterprise-wide records series, and prepare customized program-specific schedules for electronic records that are unique to particular departments, offices, or other program units.

General and program-specific schedules are not mutually exclusive options. They can, and often do, coexist in a given organization. Both types are equally applicable to electronic and nonelectronic records. General schedules can prove particularly useful for commonly encountered types of electronic records, such as e-mail or draft versions of word processing documents, or for enterprise-wide information resources referenced by many program units. Examples of the latter include centralized databases, data warehouses, and Web pages on organizational intranets or the public Internet. An organization may issue general retention guidelines for its commonly held or enterprise-wide records series, and prepare customized program-specific schedules for electronic records that are unique to particular departments, offices, or other program units. In the U.S. government, the National Archives and Records Administration has issued a general schedule for commonly encountered types of electronic records, including e-mail, electronic records used solely to update other records, electronic records created to test the performance of computer systems or to monitor system usage, electronic versions of paper records designated as official copies or scheduled for disposal, and data compilations aggregated or extracted from other electronic records. U.S. government agencies must prepare schedules for electronic records not covered by the general schedule and submit those schedules to the National Archives and Records Administration for approval.

Whether they are enterprise-wide or program-specific in scope, retention schedules must cover all records, regardless of format, that are maintained by a corporation, government agency, professional services firm, academic institution, not-for-profit entity, or other organization. Retention guidance for electronic and nonelectronic records can be integrated into a single schedule or covered by separate schedules. Integrated schedules are particularly recommended for organizations that have no formalized retention schedules. In that case, electronic and nonelectronic records can be inventoried and scheduled in the same initiative. The integrated approach is likewise suitable where existing schedules for nonelectronic records require updating, additions, or other revisions. Organizations that have acceptable schedules for nonelectronic records may prefer to issue separate schedules for electronic records. Alternatively, an organization's existing schedules can be modified to incorporate electronic records series without altering retention designations for nonelectronic records.

With respect to content, a retention schedule must list electronic records series and indicate the period of time that each series is to be retained. Other useful information includes the physical storage media to be used, the location(s) where the records are to be stored, the date and method of records destruction where applicable, and storage or records transfer instructions if destruction is not authorized. If this information is not contained in a retention schedule itself, a separate operating procedure or other supporting documentation must provide it.

A retention schedule may specify more than one physical storage medium and location for an electronic records series. As an example, computerized customer order records maintained by a mainframe or midrange computer may be stored on a hard drive to support frequent inquiries during the period of order fulfillment and for a brief amount of time thereafter. As orders are processed and shipments completed, however, certain records will be referenced less frequently. Those records may then be transferred to magnetic tapes or other removable media for offline storage. This approach to information management is sometimes described as **data archiving**. The removable media may initially be retained in office locations and then transferred to offsite storage after a specified period of time. As used in this context, data archiving denotes the transfer of information from online to offline media, presumably for more economical storage. It does not imply permanent preservation, as is the case with so-called archival records. Records subject to data archiving may ultimately be discarded.

Retention Concepts

The preparation of retention schedules is a defining characteristic of records management work and a fundamental aspect of professional practice. Retention schedules are the core component in a systematic program to manage electronic records. They provide a foundation upon which other records management activities discussed in this book are based. Electronic records, like their nonelectronic counterparts, are the property of the corporation, government agency, academic institution, professional services firm, or other organization that creates and maintains them. By preparing retention schedules, an organization acknowledges that systematic disposition of its electronic records is a critical information management activity to be governed by formalized operating procedures rather than at the discretion of individual employees.

Benefits of Retention Schedules

The business benefits of formalized retention schedules for paper records have been widely acknowledged for over half a century. With slight variations, those benefits apply to electronic records as well. When properly formulated, implemented, and enforced, retention schedules will:

- Ensure the availability and utility of specific electronic records series for appropriate periods of time, allowing such records to be referenced or reprocessed, as required, in the future;

- Ensure compliance with recordkeeping requirements specified in legal statutes and government regulations;

- Ensure that electronic records deemed relevant for litigation, government investigations, or other legal proceedings will be preserved until the matters to which they pertain are resolved;

- Prevent the unauthorized or arbitrary destruction of electronic records, thereby avoiding potential legal problems associated with such actions;

- Identify electronic records with long-term business or scholarly value;

- Prevent the unwarranted accumulation of obsolete electronic records, thereby eliminating the possibility that such records will be mistakenly used for decision-making, transaction processing, or other purposes;

- Make the most effective use of available storage devices and media for electronic records by identifying records series appropriate to online and offline storage;

- Minimize storage requirements by destroying (deleting or discarding) electronic records no longer needed;

- Release hard drives, magnetic tapes, rewritable optical disks, and other recording media for reuse, thereby minimizing expenditures for new media.

Given dramatic declines in the cost of computer storage, the cost of developing and implementing retention guidance for electronic records may exceed the cost of simply buying additional storage, as needed, to store future accumulations of electronic records.

No one disputes the importance of complying with recordkeeping requirements, preserving evidence, ensuring that electronic records will be available to support an organization's business operations, identifying electronic records with long-term business or scholarly value, and preventing the inadvertent use of obsolete electronic records. Since the late twentieth century, however, questions have been raised about the importance of minimizing storage requirements as a justification for electronic records retention. Given dramatic declines in the cost of computer storage, the cost of developing and implementing retention guidance for electronic records may exceed the cost of simply buying additional storage, as needed, to store future accumulations of electronic records.

Expanding upon a calculation presented in Chapter 1, a terabyte of hard disk storage in a fault-tolerant, high-performance network configuration with RAID 10 functionality could be purchased for about $4,000 in 2008. Multiplying this amount by a factor of 5 to allow for implementation, backup, and charges incurred over the service life of a given storage device, $20,000 is a more accurate estimate of the total cost of ownership for one terabyte of computer storage. Even then, however, the cost of computer storage compares favorably with the cost to store an equivalent quantity of paper records. One terabyte can store approximately 20 million digital images of letter-size pages. That quantity of paper records would occupy about 1,600 four-drawer file cabinets, which will cost almost half a million dollars to purchase. These cabinets will occupy about 15,000 square feet of office space, at a cost that will range upward from $300,000 per year, depending on location. If stored offsite, 20 million pages of paper records will occupy about 16,000 cubic-foot containers. Even at a very competitive annual charge of $1.50 per cubic foot per year, the cost of offsite storage will exceed the total cost of ownership for one terabyte of computer storage in less than one year.

Indisputably, the destruction of obsolete electronic records will reduce an organization's storage requirements and costs. To accomplish this destruction, however, computer applications must be modified to permit the identification and purging of electronic records with elapsed retention periods. From a cost-justification perspective, the cost of programming labor to make, test, and deploy the required modifications must not exceed the savings in storage costs that will result from implementation of a retention methodology. With programming costs ranging from $100 to $250 per hour, including labor, supervision, computer resources, and administrative overhead, this objective may be attainable now, although with difficulty, but it will be harder to realize in the future. Since the 1990s, the cost of hard disk storage has fallen by over 30 percent per year. If that trend continues, benefits associated with the systematic destruction of electronic records will become less and less significant as time passes. Five years from now, the total cost of ownership for one terabyte of computer storage will be less than $4,500. Within 10 years, the total cost of ownership will fall below $1,000, at which point the cost of merely discussing retention guidelines for one-terabyte of electronic records will likely exceed the cost of actually retaining such records.

The above calculations suggest that preservation rather than destruction should be the key concern of electronic records retention initiatives. Further, for economy of storage, organizations should prefer electronic records over paper documents as official copies for retention purposes whenever possible. This course of action will become more advisable as time passes. As the per-terabyte cost of hard drives continues to decline, the gap between computer and paper storage costs will widen. Although computer storage costs benefit from technological innovations, paper storage costs, which depend on labor costs, real estate costs, and other nontechnological factors, will likely increase over time.

Criteria for Retention Decisions

Retention concepts developed over the last 50 years for paper documents are applicable to electronic records. A comprehensive inventory, as described in Chapter 4, will identify the electronic records series to be included in retention schedules. The inventory provides information about a records series' relationship to specific business functions. The inventory survey instrument, as previously outlined, solicits descriptions of the physical characteristics of electronic storage media, the types and quantity of records for each electronic records series, the ways in which electronic records are organized, the business operations for which the records are consulted, and the relationship between a given electronic records series and other electronic and nonelectronic records. The records manager, in consultation with persons who are knowledgeable about the characteristics and use of the records, will use the inventory information, supplemented in some cases by additional research, to determine appropriate retention periods for specific electronic records series.

A retention period places a value on an electronic records series. The value is an estimate of the series' future usefulness or lack thereof. Because retention periods are estimates, uncertainty and the risk of an inappropriate retention decision are unavoidable, but a careful analysis of retention requirements, based on an understanding of a given records series' purpose and characteristics, will increase the likelihood of a satisfactory determination.

Retention decisions are principally based on the content and purpose of records rather than their format, although format considerations can prove significant in circumstances discussed later in this chapter. Like their nonelectronic counterparts, retention periods for electronic records are determined by legal, operational (administrative), and historical/scholarly (research) criteria:

- **Legal criteria.** These criteria may be defined by laws or government regulations that mandate the retention of records for specific periods of time. A broader group of legal considerations is concerned with the admissibility of electronic records as evidence in trials and other legal proceedings. Some records managers consider fiscal and tax-oriented retention criteria, which are concerned with the management and expenditure of public or corporate funds, to be distinct from legal parameters. Many fiscal and tax retention criteria, however, are embodied in laws and regulations. For purposes of this discussion, they are considered a subset of legal criteria.

- **Operational criteria.** These criteria are based on the continued need for specific records series to support an organization's mission, the public interest (in the case of government records), or the owners' interest (for records of public or privately held companies, including sole proprietorships and partnerships). Such criteria are concerned with the availability of electronic records for long-term administrative consistency and continuity, as well as for the day-to-day operations of individual program units. Operational criteria are the most important considerations when determining retention periods for many, if not most, electronic records. This statement does not denigrate the importance of legal criteria. It merely recognizes that many records are not subject to legally-mandated recordkeeping requirements and have no evidentiary significance or that operational retention requirements are often longer than legal retention requirements for a given records series.

- **Historical/Scholarly criteria.** Legal and operational significance aside, electronic records maintained by corporations, government agencies, academic institutions, professional services firms, not-for-profit entities, and other organizations may contain information of interest to historians, political scientists, sociologists, economists, demographers, public policy analysts, or other scholars. Some electronic records are also of interest to genealogists, private investigators, market trends analysts, and others who are not necessarily scholars but are nonetheless involved in research. Research-oriented retention criteria are sometimes characterized as secondary value to distinguish them from the primary business purposes for which electronic records were created.

This chapter discusses legal and operational criteria for retention of electronic records. (As noted previously, legal criteria include fiscal and tax considerations.) Scholarly retention criteria are beyond the scope of this book and of records management generally. Determination of scholarly value is the concern and responsibility of archival administration. Such determination, sometimes described as "archival appraisal," requires specialized knowledge about the scholarly disciplines and research activities for which particular electronic records may be relevant. Many archivists have advanced academic degrees in a subject discipline, such as history or public administration, as well as training in archival management or library science. In organizations that want to preserve records of scholarly value, archivists work closely with records managers to identify such records at the time retention schedules are prepared. In government agencies where preservation of records of scholarly value is required by law, archivists typically have review and approval authority over retention schedules.

Electronic Records as Official Copies

Whether legal, administrative, or research criteria apply, records managers must consider the relationship between electronic and nonelectronic records when preparing retention schedules. Much information maintained by corporations, government agencies, and other organizations exists in both electronic and nonelectronic formats. Some electronic records are the originating sources for paper documents, which fully replicate the content of electronic records in printed form. Electronic records as source records are the case, for example, with word processing documents, which are often printed for distribution, reference, filing, or other purposes. CAD files are another common example. They may be used to print copies of engineering drawings for reference, filing, or incorporation into bid packets. Electronic records that produce printed documents of identical content and functionality are termed *electronic source records*.

By definition, electronic source records precede paper documents of identical content and functionality, but in many situations, the opposite scenario applies. Information contained in paper documents, such as invoices or employee time sheets, is converted to computer-processable form by key-entry, scanning, or other means in order to create electronic records. In such cases, the paper documents are considered the source records. Often, however, the resulting electronic records are augmented through calculations or key-entry of additional information from other documents, so that a given electronic record and its associated nonelectronic source record cannot be considered identical copies. **Source documents** may likewise contain information that is excluded from data entry or added after creation of electronic records is completed. Printed copies of correspondence and contracts, for example, often have signatures that are absent from their word processing counterparts.

> *The program unit that has the official copy is the designated office of record for retention purposes. Copies maintained by other program units are considered duplicate records.*

Where a given record exists in multiple copies, the copy that will satisfy an organization's legal and administrative retention requirements is termed the **official copy**. The program unit that has the official copy is the designated office of record for retention purposes. Copies maintained by other program units are considered duplicate records. Where information is unique to an electronic records series, that series is necessarily an official copy, as is the case, for example, with many databases, which provide functionality that cannot be replicated in paper printouts, and with audio and video recordings, which cannot be printed. Where the same information exists in electronic and nonelectronic records, however, a corporation, government agency, or other organization may designate either the electronic record or the nonelectronic record as the official copy for retention purposes.

The official copy concept has a straightforward rationale: Not all copies of a given record need to be kept for the same amount of time. This principle, however, can be applied in several different ways:

1. Retention schedules may separately enumerate and specify retention periods for all copies of a given records series in all formats. Retention periods may differ among the copies, and, where legal or regulatory retention requirements exist, one copy is designated as the official copy. As its principal advantage, this approach is highly prescriptive, but it is impractical for records with unpredictable copying and distribution patterns. All copies of a record are rarely identifiable. A copy of a word processing document, for example, may have been widely distributed as attachments to an e-mail message. Recipients may forward the attachments to others or printed copies for filing.

2. One copy of a record is designated as the official copy for retention purposes. Other copies can be kept as long as the official copy or discarded sooner if no longer needed.

3. One copy of a record is designated as the official copy for retention purposes. A short retention period, perhaps 1 to 3 years, is mandated for all other copies.

4. Retention periods and offices of record are designated for specific types of information, such as accounts receivable records or product specification sheets, without prescribing the specific copy or format in which the information is to be retained. The office of record determines which copy will be the official copy.

Where the same record exists in electronic and nonelectronic formats, strong arguments can be made for making the electronic copy the official copy, especially where the record originates electronically. Electronic copies occupy much less physical space than an equivalent quantity of paper records and, given the cost factors discussed previously, they cost much less to store. Electronic copies can often be retrieved more quickly and conveniently than paper records. Where mission-critical information is involved, electronic copies are preferred for ease of backup.

Legally-Mandated Retention Periods

Various laws and government regulations contain recordkeeping requirements that specify minimum retention periods for certain types of records. Such laws and regulations apply to all private and public organizations that operate within a specific governmental jurisdiction. U.S. companies, for example, are subject to recordkeeping requirements contained in federal laws and in the laws of every state or locality where they do business. A multinational manufacturing company headquartered in the United States must comply with applicable recordkeeping requirements in all countries where its products are sold, and records managers must consider those requirements when preparing retention policies and procedures. An organization is considered to be doing business in a location if it maintains an office, employees, or property there.

Compliance with legally-mandated recordkeeping requirements is an important benefit of formalized retention schedules. Such recordkeeping requirements typically specify minimum retention periods for the records series to which they pertain. Retention periods determined by other criteria discussed in this chapter may be longer than those defined by legally-mandated recordkeeping requirements, but they can never be shorter.

Identification of applicable laws and regulations is the essential first step toward compliance with legally-mandated recordkeeping requirements. For organizations operating in the United States, recordkeeping requirements can be found in the **Code of Federal Regulations (CFR)**, which is updated by the Federal Register, as well as in various state codes and local government statutes and regulations. In many other countries, recordkeeping requirements are contained in similar compilations of legal statutes and government regulations. Organizations that operate in Canada, for example, must comply with recordkeeping requirements in Canadian Consolidated Statutes and Regulations and with provincial and local laws and regulations that specify retention periods for certain records. Similarly, organizations that operate in Australia must comply with recordkeeping provisions in Commonwealth Consolidated Legislation and Commonwealth Consolidated Regulations as well as records retention requirements in various state laws and regulations. In some countries, recordkeeping requirements can be difficult to identify. Advice from local legal counsel will usually be necessary.

The purpose of legally-mandated recordkeeping requirements and their associated retention specifications is to enable government agencies to monitor compliance with laws and regulations. As might be expected, various legally-mandated retention periods apply to financial records that are pertinent to tax assessments. Such retention requirements ensure that government agencies will have sufficient information to determine taxes owed and paid. Retention of specific personnel and payroll records are likewise mandated by laws and government regulations. They ensure the availability of information about hiring procedures, proper payment of wages, and other fair labor practices, as well as the health and safety of employees. A widely publicized group of recordkeeping requirements applies to specific industries or business activities regulated by one or more government agencies. Examples include banking, food processing, insurance, securities, public accounting, pharmaceuticals, communications, transportation, energy, healthcare, foreign trade, and waste management. In those industries, government regulations specify minimum retention requirements for many types of records.

Although they are most often associated with private businesses, some legally-mandated recordkeeping requirements apply to government agencies and not-for-profit organizations. In many countries, government agencies are subject to laws that specify the retention authority of archival agencies over public records. The National Archives and Records Administration has retention authority over records maintained by U.S. government agencies. State archival agencies have similar retention authority over state government records and, in many cases, records maintained by local governments, school districts, quasi-governmental authorities, public benefit corporations, and other entities. Many state archives have published general schedules that specify minimum retention requirements to which agencies within their jurisdiction must conform.

> *The general principle is easily stated but open to interpretation: U.S. law permits the retention of records in any form provided that a particular form is not specifically mandated or prohibited by legal statutes or government regulations.*

Electronic records offer significant functional advantages over paper documents in certain information management applications, but their acceptability as official copies to satisfy legally-mandated recordkeeping requirements has been the subject of much discussion and uncertainty. The general principle is easily stated but open to interpretation: U.S. law permits the retention of records in any form provided that a particular form is not specifically mandated or prohibited by legal statutes or government regulations. With many recordkeeping laws and regulations, requirements for storage formats and media are omitted or implied rather than clearly stated. Some records managers want a clear affirmation that electronic records are acceptable for retention purposes, but this requirement is not possible in every case. The text of individual laws and regulations must be studied and interpreted to determine the acceptability of electronic records for retention purposes in particular circumstances.

A complicating factor is that many recordkeeping requirements predate widespread computerization of business operations. Although they do not specifically prohibit electronic recordkeeping, they are written in a manner that implies or assumes that the required information will be contained in paper documents or, less commonly, in microfilm reproductions of such documents. As an example, the Uniform Preservation of Private Business Records Act (UPPBRA) uses the terms "records" and "business papers" synonymously. It cites books of account, vouchers, documents, and canceled checks as examples of business records. Electronic records are not mentioned. Laws and regulations of this type can impede the acceptance of electronic records as official copies. An organization's legal department, which often has approval authority over retention schedules, may interpret the mention of specific media to mean nonacceptance of others for retention purposes.

Increasingly, however, recordkeeping laws and regulations are being revised to accept electronic records for retention. The following examples are representative of the hundreds of examples from the Code of Federal Regulations that might be cited.

- **8 CFR 274a.2.** Employment Eligibility Verification Form I-9 can be signed and retained in an electronic format.

- **12 CFR 12.3.** Records pertaining to securities transactions executed by national banks for their customers must be retained for a minimum retention period of three years. The records may be retained in electronic form.

- **15 CFR 762.5.** The Bureau of Export Administration of the Department of Commerce will accept "electronic digital storage" as a substitute for paper records.

- **21 CFR 11.** Specifies the conditions under which the Food and Drug Administration (FDA) considers electronic records to be reliable equivalents of paper documents for regulatory submissions and other purposes. Public Docket No. 92S-0251 specifies the types of regulatory submissions the FDA will accept in electronic form under the federal Food, Drug, and Cosmetic Act and the Public Health Service Act. In other cases, paper records are considered official records and must accompany electronic submissions.

- **21 CFR 189.5.** Electronic records can satisfy retention requirements for records related to human food manufactured from or processed with material from cattle.

- **21 CFR 1304.04.** The Drug Enforcement Administration will accept computer media for retention of records and inventories pertaining to controlled substances.

- **29 CFR 516.1.** Does not prescribe specific formats for payroll records, employment contracts, collective bargaining agreements, and other records that employers must keep under the Fair Labor Standards Act, provided that retention requirements are met. It indicates that "automatic word or data processing memory" is acceptable for retention of required information.

- **29 CFR 1904.2.** The use of "data processing equipment" is permitted to maintain a log of occupational injuries and illnesses required by the Occupational Safety and Health Administration (OSHA).

- **29 CFR 2520.107-1.** Electronic media can satisfy retention requirements specified in Sections 107 and 209 of the Employee Retirement Income Security Act (ERISA). It further provides that paper records can be destroyed at any time after they are transferred to an electronic recordkeeping system.

- **29 CFR 4000.53.** Electronic records can satisfy retention requirements specified by the Pension Benefit Guaranty Corporation provided that "adequate records management practices are established and implemented" for labeling the records, establishing a secure storage environment, creating backup electronic copies, periodically evaluating the electronic recordkeeping system, and retaining paper copies of records that cannot be accurately and completely maintained in electronic form.

- **31 CFR 103.33.** Banks can retain payment orders in electronic formats.

- **48 CFR 4.703.** Federal Acquisitions Regulations allow government contractors to store records in computer-processable form to satisfy contract negotiation, administration, and audit requirements. In most cases, these records must be retained for three years after final payment under a given contract. Digital images can be substituted for paper documents, but original records must be retained for a minimum of one year following scanning "to permit periodic validation of the imaging systems."

- **49 CFR 40.333.** Electronic records can satisfy retention requirements for workplace drug and alcohol test results mandated by the U.S. Department of Transportation.

- **49 CFR 1220.3.** The Surface Transportation Board of the U.S. Department of Transportation permits preservation of records by "any technology that is immune to alteration, modification, or erasure," a requirement that limits electronic recordkeeping to certain media. The Department of Transportation accepts machine-readable media to satisfy recordkeeping requirements for railroads, freight carriers, and other companies subject to the Interstate Commerce Act. Such media must be accompanied by a statement indicating the type of information they contain.

Various state regulations increasingly recognize the suitability of electronic records to satisfy legally-mandated retention requirements. As an example, New York State Technology Law, Section 305(3) provides that electronic records have the "same force and effect" as nonelectronic records, subject to exceptions specified in Section 307. According to Section 1795.28 of the California Health and Safety Code, health service providers can retain patient records in electronic form and discard paper versions. The providers must implement safeguards for security and confidentiality of the electronic records. Hospitals that contract with the Texas Department of Health to provide managed care services to Medicaid recipients must keep records in the form in which they were originally created for at least two years; thereafter, electronic records can be substituted for nonelectronic records to satisfy retention requirements. According to the Uniform Electronic Transactions Act (UETA), which has been adopted by most states, electronic records can satisfy retention requirements for checks, communications, and other records associated with transactions conducted electronically. Recognizing that the concept of an "original record" may be problematic for electronic information, the Act states that retention issues must focus on the integrity of information rather than its "originality."

Some recordkeeping laws and regulations specifically disavow restrictions on records formats for retention, but exceptions may be noted. As cited in 29 CFR 1910.20, for example, the Occupational Safety and Health Act (OSHA) permits retention of employee exposure and medical records in any retrievable form, but it requires that X-rays be "preserved in their original state." As specified in 17 CFR 240.17a-4, the Securities and Exchange Commission (SEC) requires nonrewritable storage media for records retained in electronic form by exchange members, brokers, and dealers. Section 1500 of the California Corporations Code requires that minutes of board and shareholder meetings be maintained in "written form." Other corporate records can be kept in any form capable of being converted to written form. Section 224 of the Delaware Code allows corporate records to be maintained in various machine-readable formats, provided that such records can be converted to "clearly legible written form" within a reasonable time upon request of any person entitled to inspect the records. The State of Vermont's Insurance Division Regulation 99-1 states that computer records "shall be archival in nature only, so as to preclude the possibility of alteration."

Although the previous examples cited apply to the United States, the passage or revision of laws and government regulations to accept electronic records for retention of information is occurring internationally. A detailed listing is beyond the scope of this book, but many countries allow corporations to maintain accounting and tax-related records in electronic form. The Australian Securities and Investment Commission, for instance, permits electronic recordkeeping for accounting information as provided in the Corporations Act of 2001. Similarly, the Australian Tax Commissioner will accept electronic records for transaction-related information pertinent to tax law provided that the records are readily accessible and convertible to human-readable form. According to the Canadian Uniform Electronic Commerce Act, electronic records can satisfy requirements for retention of documents or other written information. In its Model Law on Electronic Commerce, the United Nations Commission on International Trade Law (UNCITRAL) specifies that retention requirements for documents, records, or information can be satisfied by "data messages." The Model Law, which was adopted by resolution of the United Nations General Assembly in December 1996, has influenced legislation in many countries.

> *Regardless of the countries in which they apply, most laws and regulations that accept electronic records for retention purposes stipulate that the records must be complete, readily available, and appropriately indexed for convenient retrieval; that required retrieval equipment and software must be available; and that paper copies must be produced in a reasonable amount of time on demand for audits or other purposes. Further, the laws and regulations typically require descriptive documentation for electronic records and the computer systems that create and maintain them.*

At the time this book was written, no laws or government regulations required the creation and retention of electronic records as the sole method of satisfying legally-mandated retention requirements. Paper records are always an option. Some laws and government regulations, however, specify retention periods for electronic records where such records exist. The SEC, for example, specifically lists electronic records among the audit records that must be retained by public accountants under the Sarbanes-Oxley Act of 2002. Over the past three decades, the U.S. Internal Revenue Service has required the retention of computer-processable accounting records for as long as their contents may be pertinent to the administration of federal tax law. Section 6001 of the Internal Revenue Code specifies that taxpayers must keep records to establish income, deductions, credits, or other matters relating to tax assessments. IRS Revenue Ruling 71-20 defines computer-processable accounting data as records within the meaning of Section 6001. As specified in IRS Revenue Procedure 98-25, computer-processable records must be maintained in a retrievable format that provides information necessary to determine tax liability. At a minimum, the records must be retained until the expiration of the limitation period for assessment, including extensions, for each tax year, although records that pertain to fixed assets, inventories, and certain losses may need to be retained longer. Computer-processible records must be accompanied by documentation that describes the electronic records and the computerized accounting system that produced them, including procedures and controls that prevent simple mistakes and preclude fraud. At the time of an IRS audit, taxpayers must furnish all computer resources required to access electronic records.

IRS Revenue Procedure 98-25 applies to all taxpayers with assets of ten million dollars or more, to insurance companies that use computer-processible records to determine losses, and to foreign corporations that do business within the United States. Because most medium-sized and larger corporations, partnerships, and other businesses have implemented computerized accounting systems, these electronic recordkeeping requirements have broad impact. IRS Revenue Procedure 98-25 also applies to taxpayers with fewer assets where records are kept exclusively in electronic form rather than hardcopy or where electronic records are used for calculations that require a computer for verification. Retention of computer-processible records does not supersede long-standing IRS retention requirements for human-readable accounting records. Taxpayers must also retain copies of such records, in paper or microfilm form, as long as their contents are pertinent to tax law.

Other countries have adopted similar regulations regarding computerized record-keeping systems for tax information. As an example, Revenue Canada's Information Circular IC78-10R3, issued in 1998, requires the retention of computerized tax records for time periods specified in income tax regulations, even if paper documents contain the same information. Taxpayers' retention practices must be appropriate to the medium on which electronic records are stored, and information must be reliably preserved when electronic records are converted to new formats. Procedure manuals, flow charts, and other documentation must describe controls that prevent unauthorized alteration or loss of electronic records. Electronic records must also show an audit trail from source documents to financial accounts. The Australian Taxation Office Ruling TR2005/9 specifies that electronic tax records should be retained for as long as they are material for tax purposes. The records must be in a form that the Taxation Office can access and understand. The computer system that produced the electronic records must be adequately documented, and the security provisions must safeguard the records against unauthorized access and alterations. Taxpayers are advised to test electronic storage media periodically to confirm that they are readable.

Legal Status of Digital Document Images

Digital document images, as a type of electronic records, are often singled out for special treatment in recordkeeping laws and regulations. Digital document imaging systems record electronic reproductions of documents on magnetic media or optical disks. In most cases, the digital images are produced by scanning paper records. Microfilm scanners are also available.

> *Digital document images are true copies of the documents from which they were made, a true copy being one that accurately reproduces an original document.*

Since the mid-1980s, all published discussions of the legal status of digital document images have been based on the following premise: **Digital document images** are true copies of the documents from which they were made, a true copy being one that accurately reproduces an original document. Consequently, digital document images have the same legal status as duplicate records produced by other reprographic processes such as photocopying and microfilming. In the United States, the Uniform Photographic Copies of Business and Public Records as Evidence Act—commonly abbreviated as the Uniform Photographic Copies Act or, simply, the UPA—permits the substitution of photographic copies for original documents in all judicial or administrative proceedings. As its title indicates, the UPA applies to copies of public records maintained by federal, state, and local government agencies. It also applies to business records maintained by corporations, partnerships, sole proprietorships, nonprofit institutions, and other nongovernmental organizations.

The UPA applies to records retention as an administrative activity. It does not override any legal statutes or governmental regulations that require the retention of original documents, however. Statutes and regulations must be examined individually and thoroughly to determine whether such requirements apply. Other UPA conditions are also pertinent: The copies must be accurate reproductions of the original documents, and they must have been produced in the regular course of business. This should be done in conformity with formally established retention schedules, which specify that original documents from specified records series will be copied at predetermined intervals. Similar provisions are contained in the Uniform Preservation of Private Business Records Act, which allows recordkeeping requirements to be satisfied by copies.

The UPA permits, but does not mandate, the destruction of original documents, thereby allowing organizations to rely solely on copies for whatever purpose the originals were intended. Destruction is prohibited, however, where preservation of the original documents is specifically required by law. Some states have added a clause to the UPA that prohibits destruction of original documents held in a custodial or fiduciary capacity. In such situations, their owners' permission is required prior to destruction. Examples include case files, account files, and other client records maintained by law firms, public accountants, and other professional service firms. In such situations, the owner's permission is required for destruction of original documents following conversion to digital images.

Written in 1949, the Uniform Photographic Copies Act predates the introduction of digital document imaging products. Although it specifically mentions photocopying and microfilming, it does not provide an exhaustive list of acceptable reprographic technologies, nor does it exclude technologies that are not mentioned. The UPA applies to any copying process that "accurately reproduces or forms a durable medium for so reproducing" original documents. Digital document images satisfy this requirement, but one might argue that the application of **data compression** and/or enhancement algorithms to digital images prior to recording affects the accuracy of reproduction. Application of the UPA to digital document images would be complicated if compressed or enhanced document images are determined to not constitute exact reproductions of original documents. Fortunately, the most common compression methods utilized by digital document imaging systems are lossless—that is, they achieve compression without omitting any information from document images. Lossless methods produce accurate reproductions. Few digital document imaging systems employ enhancement algorithms. Where they do, such algorithms affect only the quality of reproduction not the content of information. They merely minimize or remove minor blemishes that detract from the appearance and utility of digital images.

The Uniform Photographic Copies Act applies only in those legal jurisdictions where it has been adopted. At the time of this writing, it had been adopted by the U.S. federal government and approximately two-thirds of the states. Some states have developed and passed their own laws that address the substitution of copies for original documents. The scope and content of such laws is typically similar to that of the Uniform Photographic Copies Act. In a development that is likely to be repeated in other legal jurisdictions, several states have modified their existing laws concerning duplicate records to more specifically encompass digital document images. As examples:

- **Copy definition.** The definition of "copy" contained in section 8.01-391(F) of the Virginia Code Annotated has been changed to include "copies from optical disks" along with photographs, photostats, and microfilm. Copies of digital document images stored on magnetic media are not mentioned specifically, but the definition does not exclude them. It broadly embraces "any other reproduction of an original from a process which forms a durable medium for its recording, storing, and reproducing."

- **Reproduction processes.** Section 109.120 of the Missouri Revised Statutes addresses reproduction of documents by "photographic, video, or electronic processes." The resulting copies must be "of durable material" and "accurately reproduce and perpetuate the original records in all details."

- **Duplicate records.** Section 44.139(B) of the Louisiana Revised Statutes gives an "electronically digitized copy" equivalent evidentiary status with microfilm as a duplicate record. When properly authenticated, such copies are admissible in evidence in all courts and administrative proceedings in the jurisdictions governed by such law.

Government regulations that apply to specific business activities or industries often permit the substitution of copies for original documents to satisfy records retention requirements. Because some regulations predate the commercial availability of digital document imaging technology, they do not mention it specifically. Several regulating agencies have recently revised their retention requirements to incorporate guidelines or opinions concerning the acceptability of digital document images for certain types of records. In the United States, the Nuclear Regulatory Commission was the first regulating agency to accept digital document images for records storage by organizations within its scope of authority. The Securities and Exchange Commission authorizes the use of digital document images for records retention by brokerage firms, subject to certain conditions. Brokerages must provide prior notice to the examining authority of their intent to use electronic document imaging technology, and their systems must include appropriate indexing, display, and printing capabilities. Brokerages must have an audit system for accountability regarding input of records to the digital document imaging system. Federal Acquisition Regulations let contractors substitute digital document images for paper records, provided that the images are accurate reproductions of the original records and that they are conveniently indexed. Contractors must retain the original records for one year following scanning for periodic validation.

As previously noted, the retention practices of government agencies are subject to policies promulgated by archival authorities. The National Archives and Records Administration (NARA), which has retention authority over U.S. government agencies, accepts digital document images, which NARA describes as "scanned images of textual records," for permanent records to be transferred to the National Archives. The transferred images must comply with NARA's specifications for image format, image quality, image compression, transfer media, and accompanying documentation. Provisions for transfer of digital images are part of NARA's electronic records management (ERM) initiative, which also addresses the transfer of e-mail with attachments, PDF files, digital photographs, Web content records, and digital geospatial data records. In the past, paper and microfilm were the only acceptable media for transfer of permanent records to the National Archives, although federal government agencies could implement digital imaging systems for business process improvement or other reasons.

The acceptability of digital document images for retention of state and local government records varies. In most U.S. jurisdictions, state archives determine whether and to what extent digital images are acceptable as official copies of such records. An increasing number of state archives accept digital images as official copies of government records, including permanent records. Continuing an approach that was popular in the late twentieth century, some state archives limit digital imaging technology to records that will be retained for 10 years or less. If digital imaging is used for records with longer retention periods, the paper documents must be retained or microfilmed.

Admissibility of Electronic Records

The preceding section addressed the ability of electronic records, including digital document images, to satisfy recordkeeping requirements specified in legal statutes and government regulations. A different, much discussed group of legal considerations involves the admissibility of electronic records as evidence in courts cases or administrative proceedings, and the retention of specific electronic records series for that purpose. Compared to legally-mandated retention periods, admissibility issues will typically affect a greater number and variety of electronic records. Although they are critical for retention scheduling, statutes and government regulations that specify retention periods affect a subset of an organization's electronic records. By contrast, any electronic record might prove useful as evidence.

> *Evidence that a judge or jury can properly consider is termed "admissible."*

Broadly defined, **evidence** consists of testimony, documentation, or physical items submitted pertinent to alleged facts in judicial or quasi-judicial proceedings such as court trials or administrative hearings. The purpose of evidence is to prove or clarify a point at issue in a legal proceeding. Evidence that a judge or jury can properly consider is termed "admissible." Records managers, corporate and institutional attorneys, and others responsible for planning and implementing recordkeeping systems that will effectively support legal actions are understandably concerned about the admissibility of electronic records.

In court trials, the admissibility of records is determined by rules of evidence, which are embodied in legal statutes and court decisions (common law). Such rules apply equally to electronic and nonelectronic records. To be admissible as evidence, any record, regardless of form, must satisfy two foundation requirements that apply to all evidence: (1) The content of the records must be relevant to the matter at issue; and (2) The records' authenticity must be firmly established—that is, the court must be convinced that the records are what their proponents claim them to be. Relevance determinations are case-specific and typically fall outside the scope of records management responsibilities. The authentication of electronic records, however, is a direct concern of records managers.

Electronic Records Authentication

The purpose of authentication is to demonstrate the reliability of records to a court's satisfaction. General authentication considerations apply equally to electronic and nonelectronic records. To be considered reliable, a record, regardless of form, must meet the following criteria:

1. The record must have been created at or near the time of the event that is the subject of litigation.
2. The record must have been created by a person with knowledge of the event.
3. The record must have been maintained in the regular course of an organization's business.

The admissibility of electronic records is confirmed by widely publicized lawsuits and government investigations where e-mail messages have been admitted into evidence, often to the detriment of the organizations that created and maintained them. Questions may arise, however, about the nature and extent of authentication required to establish the reliability of electronic records in specific situations. Such questions may relate to the operation of hardware and software that generates electronic records, and to the potential for erasure, editing, or other alteration of contents.

Various judicial opinions have raised questions about inaccurate information attributable to hardware malfunctions or software errors. Hardware-related concerns are most commonly associated with emerging technologies of questionable or unproven reliability. During the 1960s, for example, a high incidence of equipment downtime raised doubts about the ability of computer systems to maintain accurate records. Continuing improvements in hardware reliability since that time have dispelled such doubts, but software defects remain notoriously widespread.

Concerns about the improper alteration of electronic records have been widely publicized in discussions of computer crime. In nonelectronic recordkeeping systems, such modifications are often difficult to make and easy to detect. The alteration of an organization's paper-based financial records, for example, may require tampering with various ledgers, balance sheets, invoices, and other source documents, some of which may be inaccessible to the perpetrator. As a further impediment, alterations to paper records involve physical changes, which may be detectable by specialists or even casual observers. Forensic scientists have decades of experience with the examination of suspect documents. Where records are stored on microfilm, undetectable alterations can prove particularly difficult to make.

By contrast, records stored on rewritable electronic media—such as magnetic disks, magnetic tapes, or certain optical disks—may be changed, erased, or otherwise manipulated with little or no trace. Character-coded text and quantitative values can be easily overwritten with new information. Advances in computer technology permit the undetected manipulation of digital images, computer-aided design files, video recordings, and audio recordings. In the case of electronic records maintained by networked computer systems, such alterations may be performed by a remote perpetrator, thereby circumventing physical accessibility requirements associated with the modification of paper records.

> *According to the Federal Rules of Evidence (FRE) and Uniform Rules of Evidence (URE), authentication requirements for computer-generated business records can be satisfied by describing the system or process used to produce a given electronic record and by showing that the system or process produces an accurate result.*

To successfully address these formidable concerns, records managers must develop and implement electronic recordkeeping systems and procedures that will facilitate authentication and dispel any doubts about the reliability of electronic records. According to the **Federal Rules of Evidence (FRE)** and **Uniform Rules of Evidence (URE)**, authentication requirements for computer-generated business records can be satisfied by describing the system or process used to produce a given electronic record and by showing that the system or process produces an accurate result. Similar authentication provisions are contained in the Canadian Uniform Electronic Evidence Act, the United Kingdom Civil Evidence Act, the Australian Evidence Act, and in comparable laws of other countries.

To demonstrate the accuracy and trustworthiness of electronic records created and maintained by a given computer, video, or audio system, an organization may be expected to provide testimony and/or documentation pertaining to system administration, input procedures, equipment, software, security, and the competency of employees who operate the system. The following records management procedures can facilitate compliance with such authentication requirements:

- **Designated administrator.** An administrator should be designated for each system that creates or maintains electronic records. The system administrator should be identified by job title rather than by personal name. The system administrator will typically be a management-level employee who is involved with one or more aspects of the system's operation such as the supervision of data entry or records retrieval. To be able to give the knowledgeable testimony required for authentication purposes, the administrator should become familiar with the entire system, including its technical and operating characteristics. The system administrator may also be given other responsibilities with legal implications such as control over the release or expungement of electronic records.

- **Hardware documentation.** The system's hardware and software characteristics must be documented in a manner that fully describes the role of each component in the creation and maintenance of electronic records being submitted as evidence. Hardware documentation should indicate the types, brand names, and model numbers of all hardware components and recording media used in the system, together with the dates that specific components were put into or taken out of service. Technical specification sheets provided by vendors will typically provide sufficiently detailed information to satisfy documentation requirements for hardware and recording media. To confirm that hardware is being maintained in proper working condition, records should be kept of equipment inspections and repairs.

- **Software documentation.** Software documentation should also include descriptions of all systems and application programs involved in the creation and maintenance of electronic records. For custom-developed application software, flowcharts, source code, program debugging procedures, and other developmental documentation should be included. Descriptions of prewritten (purchased) software packages should include version numbers and implementation dates for all software upgrades.

- **Procedures documentation.** The accuracy and trustworthiness of electronic records can be affirmed by thorough documentation of records creation procedures, as well as by descriptions of training given to data entry clerks, video camera operators, or other personnel responsible for creation of electronic records. Business processes that create electronic records must be documented through written procedures and work flow diagrams. Detailed written instructions should be prepared for operators of data entry terminals, document scanners, video cameras, audio recorders, and other input devices. They should delineate the records creation work steps to be followed in specific situations. Descriptions of input verification procedures—such as double-keying of data entries, computer-based validation of specified field values, or visual inspection of digitized images—should also be included. The written instructions should be used when training personnel who create electronic records. The nature and amount of such training should likewise be documented, and the training should emphasize compliance with established records creation procedures. Logbooks, employee time sheets, or other records should indicate the names of persons who operated input equipment on specific dates.

- **Records protection.** Electronic records must be protected from physical damage or tampering that could impair their accuracy or raise questions about their trustworthiness. Specific protection measures employed by a given electronic recordkeeping system should be fully documented. Detailed descriptions of media handling procedures and storage conditions, discussed in detail elsewhere in this book, will affirm the physical integrity of electronic records. Access control procedures for electronic records and security provisions, such as password protection and privilege controls in computer-based systems, should be documented. A list of all authorized users and their access privileges should be maintained. The list should differentiate those users who are authorized to create or edit electronic records from those who are restricted to retrieval of previously created records from specific files.

- **Compliance audits.** All aspects of system operation should be audited regularly for compliance with established procedures. Audit findings and the implementation of corrective actions should be fully documented.

These procedures and documentation requirements will increase the likelihood that electronic records will be admissible in evidence over objections that might be raised by an opposing party in a legal action. Historically, such objections have been based on the rule against hearsay and/or the best evidence rule. Typically, authentication questions are raised in the context of a hearsay objection. **Hearsay** is a statement made out of court that pertains to some matter raised in court. Because hearsay is not subject to cross-examination by the opposing party in a legal action, it is generally inadmissible under the rules of evidence that apply in federal and state courts. Because electronic records, like their nonelectronic counterparts, are usually created out of court, they are considered hearsay and will not be admitted in evidence unless they fall within one of the several exceptions to the rule against hearsay. Such exceptions exist for business and public records.

> *The business records exception to the hearsay rule covers records "in any form." It interprets business records broadly to include those created and maintained by institutions, associations, and nonprofit organizations.*

In U.S. federal courts, electronic records are admissible in evidence under Rule 803(6) of the Federal Rules of Evidence (FRE), the so-called business records exception to the hearsay rule. The exception is based on the premise that records created in the normal course of business activities possess a circumstantial probability of trustworthiness. Because organizations that create such records must rely on them, their accuracy is presumed. The business records exception to the hearsay rule covers records "in any form." It interprets business records broadly to include those created and maintained by institutions, associations, and nonprofit organizations. At the state level, an identical business records exception is included in the Uniform Rules of Evidence (URE), which have been adopted by approximately 60 percent of the states. A business records exception to the hearsay rule is similarly included in the **Uniform Business Records as Evidence Act (UBREA)** and in various state-specific evidence rules, as well as in common law.

Explicitly or through judicial interpretations, the business records exceptions to the hearsay rule have delineated certain requirements for authentication of electronic records. A qualified witness must provide foundation testimony concerning the records' reliability. The witness is sometimes termed a *custodian*, although that description is not elaborated. The witness's qualifications have been variously defined. In general, the witness must be familiar with the organization and understand the procedures and circumstances under which the electronic records are created, maintained, and retrieved. Courts have held that the witness need not be personally familiar with the subject of electronic records, but he or she must know how the records are processed and used. The witness need not have been employed by the organization at the time the electronic records in question were created, nor personally involved with the actual recording of information on magnetic or optical media.

Technical knowledge requirements vary. Some state courts, for example, have required that a qualified witness be a supervisor of computing activities. Where detailed technical knowledge is required, a consultant or industry analyst can provide expert testimony. Regardless of technical expertise, the witness must establish that electronic records were made in the regular course of business and testify to the method and circumstances of records creation and maintenance. In the absence of a qualified witness, these foundation requirements may be satisfied by other means such as examination of the electronic records themselves plus surrounding circumstances.

> *Courts and legal authorities have generally treated computer-generated printouts as electronic records, even though they are paper documents that contain human-readable information.*

Business records exceptions to the hearsay rule require that electronic records be made within a reasonable time after the transaction, business activity, or other event to which they pertain. Data entry should occur soon after the event, and records should not be retained in main memory or on interim media for long periods of time. Courts and legal authorities have generally treated computer-generated printouts as electronic records, even though they are paper documents that contain human-readable information. Several authorities contend that the requirement for timely creation of electronic records applies primarily to the entry and recording of information rather than to the interval between input and printing. Although a long delay prior to creating computer printouts may increase the potential for tampering or errors, such delay alone should not impede admissibility. In several cases, computer printouts have been judged admissible even though they were produced long after entry of the data they contain.

Several early court cases required proof of a computer's mechanical accuracy, but such issues are seldom raised today. Courts have likewise rejected the contention that admissibility depends on a demonstration that a given computer system was operating properly at the specific time when an electronic record was created.

If authentication requirements are satisfied, the business records exceptions described previously will overcome most hearsay objections to the admissibility of electronic records in evidence. Because they define business records broadly, such exceptions have also been applied to records created by government agencies, academic institutions, not-for-profit entities, and other organizations. Rule 803 (8) of the Federal Rules of Evidence and Uniform Rules of Evidence provide an additional exception, however, for public records. The relationship between the two exceptions has not been fully delineated. For records created by government agencies, the public records exception provides an additional method of overcoming hearsay objections. The Federal Rules of Evidence, Uniform Rules of Evidence, and various state-specific statutes also include residual exceptions to the hearsay rule. They can conceivably be used to admit electronic records that cannot satisfy the requirements of other exceptions.

Objections to the admissibility of electronic records in evidence may also be raised under the best evidence rule, which requires the introduction of an "original writing" into evidence unless its absence can be satisfactorily explained. If the original record is unavailable, a trustworthy copy may be received in evidence. An original record may be unavailable for various acceptable reasons. It may, for example, have been destroyed in conformity with an organization's established business practices, as embodied in formally approved retention schedules. In some cases, an original record is in the possession of a third party who is beyond the court's subpoena power. Alternatively, an adversary in a legal proceeding may fail to produce an original record, despite notice. The best evidence rule precludes admission of a copy in evidence if the original record is available.

Application of the best evidence rule to electronic records poses certain conceptual problems. The rule appears most obviously and directly relevant to digital document images recorded on optical disks or magnetic media. As previously discussed, such images are considered copies of the documents from which they were made. The best evidence rule has also been applied to computer printouts, which may be considered copies of original information stored on other media. However, Rule 1001(3) of the Federal Rules of Evidence and Uniform Rules of Evidence treats printouts as original records, thereby precluding an objection to their admissibility under the best evidence rule. Other provisions of the FRE and URE, however, suggest that computer printouts are duplicate records.

Where that view is sustained, best evidence objections to the admissibility of electronic records can be overcome in various ways. As previously discussed, the

Uniform Photographic Copies of Business and Public Records as Evidence Act, and various state-specific statutes of similar scope, permits the substitution of copies for original records to satisfy judicial and administrative requirements. They give copies and originals equivalent legal status, provided that the copies are accurate reproductions of the originals, that they are produced in the regular course of business, and that retention of the original records is not required by law. Rule 1003 of the Federal Rules of Evidence and Uniform Rules of Evidence permits the admission of duplicate records in evidence as substitutes for originals unless serious questions are raised about the authenticity of the original records or, in specific circumstances, it is judged unfair to admit a copy in lieu of the original. By recognizing the admissibility of copies, Rule 1003 places the burden of argument on the party seeking to exclude a copy rather than the party seeking to admit it. Under Rule 1003, the availability of an original record does preclude the admissibility of a copy. If computer printouts are considered copies, they may be admissible in evidence under FRE and URE Rule 1006, the voluminous writings rule. That provision allows admission of summaries, such as computer-generated tabulations or graphic depictions, for voluminous records judged too unwieldy to produce in court.

The foregoing discussion examined the rules of evidence that determine the admissibility of electronic records in federal and state courts. Many legal proceedings, however, are held before federal and state administrative agencies where court-oriented rules of evidence do not apply. Making generalizations about the admissibility of electronic records in such situations is impossible. Federal administrative agencies are bound by the Administrative Procedures Act, which gives such agencies considerable discretion in determining the admissibility of records. Some federal administrative agencies have informal rules of evidence that must be evaluated on a case-by-case basis to determine their application to electronic records. At the state government level, the admissibility of evidence in administrative proceedings is typically governed by state administrative procedures acts and agency procedural rules. Significant variations in admissibility rules may be encountered from one state to another and, within a given state, from one agency to another.

Retention periods appropriate to the use of records in evidence are influenced by statutes of limitations that prescribe the time periods within which lawsuits or other legal actions must be initiated. Statutes of limitations define the time period for when a person or organization can sue or be sued for personal injury or breach of contract, for example. Limitations of assessment periods are the fiscal counterparts of statutes of limitations. They prescribe the period of time that a tax agency can determine taxes owed. Once the period defined by a given statute of limitations or limitation of assessment has elapsed, no legal action can be brought for a specific matter. If the statute of limitations on personal injury lawsuits is three years in a given state, the injured party loses the legal right to sue after that time. As a complicating factor for retention decisions, statutes of limitations begin when an event, such as personal injury or breach of contract, occurs, not when records relating to that event are created. Electronic records pertaining to products manufactured today may be relevant for legal actions several decades in the future.

If electronic records are being retained specifically and exclusively to support legal actions, retention periods longer than pertinent statutes of limitations serve no purpose.

Although they can have a significant impact on a given agency's records retention practices, statutes of limitations do not mandate retention periods. They simply define the maximum period of time during which records being retained in support of an actual or possible legal action can be used for that purpose. If electronic records are being retained specifically and exclusively to support legal actions, retention periods longer than pertinent statutes of limitations serve no purpose. Electronic records can be destroyed in conformity with retention schedules while statutes of limitations are in effect, provided that no laws or government regulations mandate the retention of such records. If litigation is pending or imminent, however, no records can be destroyed, even if their retention periods elapse.

E-Discovery and the Amended Federal Rules

Discovery is a part of the pre-trial litigation process that gives opposing parties the opportunity to request relevant information, including records, from one another with the intent of discovering information to build their claims or defenses. Discovery is based on the premise that both parties to litigation should have access to as much information as possible and that no relevant information will be concealed. The **Federal Rules of Civil Procedure**, which are promulgated by the U.S. Supreme Court and approved by Congress, govern the discovery process in U.S. district courts. Most states have adopted similar rules.

Requests for production of records are an important component of discovery. **Electronic discovery (e-discovery)** is the process of seeking electronic records during the discovery phase of a legal action. In 2006, the Federal Rules of Civil Procedure were amended to specifically address e-discovery issues. Collectively, the 2006 amendments recognize and formalize the importance of electronic records in litigation. They draw upon ideas and guidelines developed by the Sedona Conference, a legal research and educational institute that deals with laws and policies related to complex litigation and other matters. The amendments are designed to bring order and consistency to discovery of electronic records. In this sense, they fulfill the purpose of Rule 1, which is designed to simplify and reduce the cost of litigation.

The following discussion summarizes the 2006 amendments, emphasizing those that have implications for an organization's records management practices or that create opportunities for records management involvement in the discovery process as it relates to electronic records. The e-discovery provisions of the amended Federal Rules apply to civil litigation in U.S. district courts. They do not apply to criminal trials or to civil litigation in state courts, but some states have adopted their own provisions for electronic discovery that are similar to the amended Federal Rules. E-discovery initiatives are not limited to the United States. In all Canadian jurisdictions, for example, court rules provide for discoverability of electronic records. Several provinces, notably Ontario, are also involved in e-discovery initiatives. Similarly, the Federal Court of Australia has taken an active role in the development of practice rules relating to e-discovery.

From a records management perspective, the amended Federal Rules deal with litigation not retention. The amended rules do not specify how long electronic records must be kept; but, in the context of discovery, all organizations have an obligation to preserve evidence—that is, they must retain records (including electronic records) that are relevant for reasonably foreseeable or ongoing litigation. This obligation, which is well established in common law, predates the 2006 amendments. The amended rules merely reemphasize the obligation as it pertains to electronic records. They do not impose new retention requirements for such records. An organization will continue to determine retention periods for electronic records based on factors discussed elsewhere in this chapter.

Rule 34(a)

Rule 34(a) as amended is the foundation for the other amendments discussed next. The amended version broadens the discovery process to include electronic records of all types. It affirms that discovery of electronic records is on an equal footing with discovery of paper documents. Given the pervasiveness of computerization, all litigation is likely to have an e-discovery component.

As originally adopted, Rule 34(a) pertained to the discovery of "documents" and "things." Reflecting the increasing importance of computerized recordkeeping, Rule 34(a) was amended in 1970 to add "data compilations" to the list of discoverable items, but that addition does not definitely encompass the growing variety of electronic records produced by computer, audio, and video technologies. The 2006 amendment replaces "data compilation" with "electronically stored information," which broadens the scope of discovery to include electronic records of any type. Henceforth, a request for production of "documents" should be understood to apply to electronic as well as paper records, unless the discovery order is limited to records of a particular type.

The newly amended Rule 34(a) also gives the requesting party the right to inspect, test, or sample electronically stored information. This right, sometimes described as the "quick peek" provision, was not clearly stated in previous versions of the rule. It applies to paper documents as well as electronic records.

Amended Rule 34(a) has several implications for an organization's records management policies, procedures, and operations:

- **Broader electronic records definition.** Rule 34(a) affirms a broad definition of an organization's electronic records. Electronic records in all formats and media—including word processing documents, spreadsheet files, database records, Web pages, e-mail, voice mail, instant messages, text messages and surveillance tapes—are considered records from a legal perspective and are subject to discovery.

- **Evidence preservation.** The obligation to preserve evidence in all formats must be considered when defining retention policies for electronic records.

- **Legal holds.** Electronic records in all formats must be included when suspending destruction of records potentially relevant for litigation.

Rule 34(b)

Amended Rule 34(b) addresses the manner in which electronic records are to be produced in response to a discovery order:

- **Format requests.** The amended rule permits a requesting party to specify the format for production of electronic records in response to a discovery order. If the responding party objects to the format specified by the requesting party or if no format is specified, the responding party must state the format it intends to use. That format must be the format in which the electronic records are ordinarily maintained or a format that is "reasonably usable."

- **Ease of use.** The responding party must produce electronic records in a manner that does not pose unnecessary obstacles for the requesting party. The electronic records must be organized and labeled to correspond to categories in a discovery request.

An organization's IT unit will presumably play an instrumental role in providing electronic records in a format acceptable to the requesting party. In some cases, companies that offer file conversion services may be hired to assist with this process. An organization's records management program may be asked to assist attorneys in categorizing and labeling electronic records during the discovery process.

Rule 16(b) and Rule 26(f)

As amended, Rule 16(b) and Rule 26(f) are designed to address issues related to the discovery of electronic records at an early stage in litigation. Rule 16(b) deals with electronic records issues in the context of pretrial conferences and schedule management. Rule 26(f) specifies that opposing parties must confer to consider, among other things, the following issues related to discovery of electronic records:

- The subjects about which discovery of electronic records are likely to be needed
- The preservation of discoverable evidence
- The time frame for discovery
- The accessibility of specific types of electronic records
- The format in which electronic records will be produced to satisfy discovery orders
- Any issues related to privileged information in electronic records

This mandated meeting of opposing parties must occur at the earliest opportunity but not later than 21 days before a scheduling conference is held or a scheduling order is due.

These so-called early meet and confer amendments are of the greatest concern to attorneys because they impose new requirements that the attorneys must satisfy. Compared to the other amendments discussed in this book, they have the most important implications for records management involvement in the litigation process. The amendments to Rule 16(b) and Rule 26(f) place a premium on advance planning and early preparation. In order to adequately prepare for a prescheduling conference, attorneys must be knowledgeable about a client's IT infrastructure and electronic record-keeping practices. At a minimum, attorneys should understand the following:

1. Types of computers and other information technologies employed by the client organization.

2. Types of software applications in use.

3. Categories of data repositories and electronic records associated with those applications.

4. Policies, procedures, and practices for preserving (retaining) electronic records needed for specific business purposes.

5. Policies, procedures, and practices for destroying electronic records no longer needed.

6. Locations where electronic records are stored by personal computers in the client's offices or elsewhere, by network servers in centralized or departmental installations, by mainframe computers, in storage area networks, by hosted systems, by mobile computing devices, by personal digital assistants, in offsite repositories, or elsewhere.

7. Procedures for identifying and retrieving electronic records when needed.

The principal concern is that this information may not be readily available to attorneys. External counsel, in particular, may be unfamiliar with an organization's computing environment. Even where the information is available, many attorneys lack the technical background required to understand detailed descriptions of information technology installations and electronic recordkeeping practices. They are trained to understand the legal aspects of a case rather than the technical infrastructure that supports the creation, use, and preservation of electronic information. However, federal courts will likely expect attorneys to be well informed about their clients' electronic recordkeeping practices.

Standing orders and local rules issued by some state and local U.S. district courts have made availability a requirement. For example, in New Jersey, where U.S. District courts adopted electronic discovery amendments prior to the federal amendments. According to District of New Jersey Local Rule 26.1(d), attorneys have a duty to investigate their clients' information management and electronic recordkeeping systems and practices in order to understand how information is stored and retrieved. This investigation must be done prior to the pretrial conference, and it must encompass current, historical, and backup information. Attorneys must also identify knowledgeable persons within the client organization or elsewhere who can facilitate the discovery process.

Since the 2006 amendments were announced, many organizations and their attorneys have been evaluating their litigation readiness. To guide its attorneys, an organization should consider preparing a "map" of its information technology infrastructure and electronic recordkeeping environment. The map, which is similar to the map created during the inventory process discussed in Chapter 4, will enable attorneys to identify potential sources of discoverable information. The map must be prepared in sufficient detail and with appropriate clarity to be understandable by attorneys and others who may lack extensive technical backgrounds. It will describe hardware and software components that create and store specific types of electronic records and identify the organizational units responsible for specific computing resources and electronic records. An organization's records management program, working in cooperation with knowledgeable persons in the information technology unit, is a logical choice to create such a map, although consulting services may be required to assist with the mapping process and help attorneys interpret it. The mapping process should be performed in the broader context of an organization's need to revise, expand, and clarify its policies, procedures, and practices for retention and destruction of electronic records.

Rule 26(a)(1)

Amendments to Rule 26(a)(1) contain general provisions governing discovery and the duty of disclosure by organizations that are parties to litigation. These amendments require that an organization disclose information about certain records, including paper documents and electronic records, at an early stage in the litigation process, and identify the employees or other persons who have such records in their custody. This disclosure must be done prior to receiving a discovery request from the opposing party. Specifically:

- Rule 26(a)(1)(A) as amended specifies that an organization involved in litigation must, without awaiting a discovery request, disclose to the other parties the names, addresses, and telephone numbers of individuals who are likely to have discoverable information of any type that the disclosing party may use to support its claims or defenses.

- Rule 26(a)(1)(B) as amended specifies that the organization must provide a copy or description of all documents or electronically stored information in its possession, custody, or control and that it may use to support its claims or defenses.

The records management implications of these amendments are limited, and their scope and impact have been misunderstood and/or exaggerated by some commentators. The amendments do not require an organization to disclose the locations and characteristics of all its records. The disclosure requirements apply only to documents or electronic records that the organization intends to use to support its case. Further, this requirement does not apply to electronic records that the opposing party may request through a discovery order.

Most organizations should be able to comply with these amended rules. Presumably, attorneys responsible for a case will have located the records they intend to use in the course of developing their claims or defenses. The amended rule merely requires that the existence, characteristics, and locations of these records be disclosed to opposing parties at an early stage in the litigation process. An organization's records management program may assist attorneys in locating this information, but the amendment does not impose any additional records management responsibilities or burdens.

Rule 26(b)(2)

Amendments to Rule 26(b)(2) limit an organization's obligation to disclose electronic records in certain circumstances. Specifically:

- Rule 26(b)(2)(B) as amended specifies that an organization need not provide discovery of electronic records from sources that are "not reasonably accessible because of undue burden or cost." The organization must demonstrate to the court's satisfaction that the records are not reasonably accessible. Even then, the court may order discovery of such records if the requesting party can show good cause. In some cases, the requesting party may be willing to share or bear the cost of discovery in order to obtain information from sources identified as not reasonably accessible.

- Rule 26(b)(2)(C) specifies conditions that might be considered too burdensome or costly. For example, the discovery request may be unreasonably cumulative or duplicative, the requested records may be more conveniently available from another source, or the cost of the proposed discovery may outweigh the likely benefits.

These amendments will have no impact on disclosure requirements for electronic records produced by active applications that operate on an organization's mainframe, network servers, PCs, or other computing devices. Typically such records are stored on hard drives, which renders them readily accessible. The amendments may limit the discovery of backup tapes or archive tapes stored in offsite locations, although such tapes may be judged to be readily accessible if they are stored by a commercial provider with reliable inventorying, retrieval, and delivery services. The amendments may also apply to legacy databases, older word processing files, or other electronic records created by application programs that have been taken out of service and where retrieving the records is not easily possible.

> *An organization is obligated by legal statute and common law to preserve all records relevant for litigation, regardless of whether they are readily accessible.*

The scope of these amendments is limited to discovery of electronic records. They do not affect retention requirements for inaccessible records. An organization is obligated by legal statute and common law to preserve all records relevant for litigation, regardless of whether they are readily accessible. Further, an organization must be prepared to identify, by category or type, any sources that contain potentially responsive information that it is neither searching nor producing. This work must be done in sufficient detail to enable the requesting party to evaluate the burdens and costs of discovery for such information, as well as the likelihood that the identified sources may contain useful information.

Other Amended Rules

The following amended rules deal with legal issues that are not significant for an organization's records management practices:

- Rule 26(f)(5)(B) addresses the inadvertent disclosure of privileged information in response to discovery orders. Given the large quantity of electronic records maintained by an organization, co-mingling privileged information with other information when organizations respond to discovery orders is a realistic risk. The amended rule provides that, upon notification from the producing party, the party receiving allegedly privileged information must take steps to prevent its use or disclosure until the claim is resolved.

- Rule 33(d) provides that an answer to an interrogatory involving review of business records should include a search of electronically stored information.

- Rule 37(f) creates a "safe harbor" to protect a party from sanctions for loss of electronic records destroyed by routine, good-faith operation of an electronic information system—for example, by accidental overwriting of data files.

- Rule 45 summarizes the other amendments in the context of subpoena practice.

Legal Status of Electronic Signatures

Signatures are used to authenticate documents, to signify intent or approval, and to prevent repudiation. To be considered valid and enforceable, certain business documents must be signed. Contracts, leases, purchase orders, and payment authorizations are obvious, commonplace examples. In many applications, such documents are printed from databases, word processing files, or other computer-processible sources for the sole purpose of creating a signed file copy to satisfy retention and evidentiary requirements. The substitution of electronic records for such purposes depends on the acceptability of electronic signatures.

Broadly defined, an **electronic signature** denotes any electronic method of signing a computer-processible record. An electronic signature need not resemble a handwritten signature. The possibilities range from straightforward typing of the author's name at the end of an electronic message or document created by word processing software to sophisticated biometric identifiers based on a signer's physical characteristics such as hand geometry or fingerprint recognition. Other approaches include a personal identification number (PIN), a digitized image of a handwritten signature, or user selection of an icon in a dialog box possibly supplemented by a password or other verification. The phrase "digital signature" denotes a specific type of electronic signature that employs signer verification and encryption technology.

In the United States, the Electronic Signatures in Global and National Commerce Act (15 U.S. Code §7001-7031), also known as the *E-Sign Act*, became law on October 1, 2000. It clarifies the legal status of electronic signatures and records in the context of signing requirements imposed by law. It provides that agreements, contracts, or other transactions cannot be rendered invalid solely because they are signed electronically. The law defines an electronic signature broadly as "an electronic sound, symbol, or process attached to or logically associated with a contract or record and executed or adopted by a person with the intent to sign the record."

Exclusions are limited to wills and other testamentary instruments, matters relating to family law, certain sections of the Uniform Commercial Code, court orders and other judicial documents, insurance cancellation notices, certain records relating to product recalls, and records relating to the transportation of hazardous substances.

> *According to the UETA, the legal significance of a record or signature is not affected by its format.*

State laws may modify, limit, or supersede the E-Sign Act under certain conditions. The Uniform Electronic Transactions Act (UETA), approved in 1999, by the National Conference of Commissioners on Uniform State Laws, facilitates and promotes e-commerce and other electronic transactions by eliminating uncertainties about the legal status of electronic signatures and records associated with such transactions. According to the UETA, the legal significance of a record or signature is not affected by its format. The UETA broadly defines an electronic signature as "an electronic sound, symbol, or process attached to or logically associated with a record and executed or adopted by a person with the intent to sign the record." Like the E-Sign Act, the UETA affirms the equivalency of manual and electronic signatures for authenticating records in business transactions where the parties have agreed to conduct the transactions by electronic means. The UETA addresses some issues, such as the attribution of electronic signatures, and records that are not covered in the E-Sign Act. It also states that electronic signatures and records satisfy evidentiary and audit requirements, although it allows individual states to limit the acceptability of electronic records and signatures for audit purposes. Like the E-Sign Act, the UETA excludes testamentary documents, which are unlikely to be subject to electronic transactions, but it permits electronic signatures and records for certain family law matters such as property settlements and post-nuptial agreements.

Some states have enacted their own laws regarding electronic signatures. Such laws resemble the UETA and E-Sign Act in concept, but they may differ in scope and detail. As an example, the New York Electronic Signatures and Records Act (I NYCRR Part 540), also known as the *NYESRA*, establishes standards and procedures for the use and authentication of electronic signatures by government entities in New York State. Generally, the NYESRA provides that an electronic signature has the same validity as a conventional hand signature. It defines an electronic signature broadly as an electronic identifier "that is unique to the person using it, capable of verification, under the sole control of the person using it, attached to or associated with data in such a manner that authenticates the attachment of the signature to particular data and the integrity of the data transmitted, and intended by the party using it to have the same force and effect as the use of a signature affixed by hand." Exclusions include wills, trusts, powers of attorney, deeds, mortgages, and negotiable instruments.

In the United States and elsewhere, electronic commerce initiatives and projects for electronic delivery of government services are important motivators for electronic signature legislation. Internationally, the UNCITRAL Model Law on Electronic

Commerce allows for a variety of electronic signature technologies, provided that they identify the signer and are appropriately reliable for their intended purposes. The UNCITRAL Model Law has influenced electronic signature and electronic transaction legislation in a number of countries. The Canadian Uniform Electronic Commerce Act, for example, extends the UNCITRAL Model Law to any business transaction or legal relationship that involves documentation. Like the U.S. laws described previously, it equates electronic and handwritten signatures for many purposes, as does the United Kingdom Electronic Communications Act of 2000, the Australian Electronic Transaction Act of 2000, the South African Electronic Communications and Transactions Act of 2002, the Singapore Electronic Transaction Act of 1998, the Turkey Electronic Signature Law of 2004.

Operational Retention Requirements

Although laws and government regulations can have a significant impact on records retention practices, legally-mandated recordkeeping requirements affect a small percentage of most electronic records. In some organizations, large numbers of records may be retained for possible use in evidence, but retention decisions for many electronic records are based on operational (business) needs rather than legal considerations.

> *For each electronic records series, operational and legal requirements should be defined separately. The applicable retention period is determined by the longer of the two requirements.*

Even where a regulatory requirement to retain records for a specific number of years or until the resolution of litigation or other legal matters exists, an organization's business needs may dictate a longer retention period. For each electronic records series, operational and legal requirements should be defined separately. The applicable retention period is determined by the longer of the two requirements. In some organizations, as previously noted, research-oriented retention criteria are also considered. Scholarly considerations may lead to retention periods that exceed legal or operational requirements. Electronic records that have no continuing business value may be significant to historians or other scholars.

Retention Principles

Operational retention parameters are variously described as *administrative retention parameters or user retention parameters.* As their name suggests, they are determined by the operational requirements of users who reference records to support an organization's daily business operations or long-term goals. As with paper documents, operational retention decisions for electronic records are based on their content and business purpose rather than their format, but some electronic records have special attributes that complicate retention decisions. Significant differences exist, for example, between Web pages and other types of records, including other electronic records. The dynamic content of Web pages makes version control critical and raises questions about retention of superseded information. Given the interrelationships among pages at a given Web site, retention actions can have a ripple effect throughout a Web site. In particular, modification or deletion of one or more Web pages can adversely impact site navigation on an intranet or the Internet. Similarly, some Web pages contain links to external sites, which may be modified or deleted by their originators.

Like their legal counterparts, operational retention periods are usually measured in years following the occurrence of a specified event such as the end of a fiscal year or calendar year, the completion of an audit, the fulfillment of a contract, the completion of a project, or the termination of employment. Operational retention periods for electronic records are typically negotiated through meetings or other consultation with persons who must use the records to fulfill their assigned work responsibilities. A fundamental records management assumption is that users of records are uniquely qualified to determine their reference value, based on their experience with a given records series and their knowledge of the business operations and objectives that the records support. Through questions and discussion, records managers can help users clarify the relationship between reference value and retention requirements.

Meetings about operational retention requirements are attended by one or more representatives of the departments or other program units that create and use electronic records. Often, the department's records management coordinator takes the lead in explaining the program unit's operational requirements at such meetings. Other interested parties, including managerial and administrative employees who create and use specific records series, may also be involved. Electronic records created by one program unit are often used by others. In the case of computer-processible records, for example, such information-sharing is encouraged by the implementation of enterprise-wide databases, data warehouses, intranets, and other centralized information resources that serve the needs of multiple departments. It is facilitated by the widespread implementation of computer networks that provide convenient remote access to electronically-stored information.

As previously discussed, a thorough inventory of electronic records includes questions about frequency of consultation and retention practices associated with specific records series. Responses to such questions provide a useful starting point for the determination of operational retention periods, which should be based on the reasonable probability that a given electronic records series will be needed in the future to support specific business objectives or activities. Operational retention designations are based on the concept of an **information life cycle**. Decades of records management theory and practice indicate that the operational utility of many, if not most, records varies inversely with the age of the records. Typically, records maintained by consultants, government agencies, and other organizations are most valuable and are referenced frequently for a relatively brief period of time following their creation or receipt. As the records age and the matters to which they pertain are resolved, their business value and reference activity diminish, either gradually or abruptly. When, and if, their business value falls to or approaches zero, the records can be discarded. This life cycle concept applies equally to records in electronic and nonelectronic formats.

Operational retention periods are essentially estimates of life cycle duration for specific records series. For example:

- Certain electronic records, such as e-mail distributed by listservices, have very short life cycles—they are often discarded after an initial reading.

- Other records, such as drafts of word processing documents and reminder files stored by PDAs, are updated by replacement at similarly brief intervals.

- Some electronic records, such as routine office documents created by word processing programs and financial planning documents stored as spreadsheet files, may be retained for a brief period then discarded, usually within several years of creation.

- Many transaction-oriented records, such as database records pertaining to purchase orders and insurance claims, are referenced frequently for several weeks or months following their creation or receipt, but only occasionally after the matters to which they pertain are resolved. Total retention periods for such electronic records may range from 6 to 10 years.

Certain electronic records are retained for much longer periods. Their retention requirements may be determined by the life cycles of objects or persons to which the records pertain. For example:

- CAD files and digitized engineering drawings pertaining to facilities or equipment are retained as long as the facilities or equipment remain in service.

- Test results, statistical data, and other electronic records related to pharmaceutical products are retained as long as the products are marketed and often longer as continuing proof of safety or efficacy.

- Academic records maintained by a high school or college are retained for as long as former students may reasonably be expected to request a transcript of grades or certification of graduation.

- Medical records maintained by a hospital are retained for as long as a former patient might require follow-up care.

- Payroll records maintained by government agencies are retained for as long as they may be needed to verify past employment for calculation of pension credits or eligibility for Social Security benefits.

- Some electronic records have continuing operational value that warrants indefinite retention.

In some cases, the time-dependent operational utility of electronic records can be established with confidence. Retention periods for student records, medical records, and employee benefits records may be based on human life expectancy or a reasonable percentage thereof. Past experience with a particular records series is often a reliable basis for retention determinations. Experience may confirm, for example, that mechanical and electrical drawings stored as CAD files contain information essential to future building repairs and must be retained as long as the building remains in service. Similarly, word processing files pertaining to closed contracts may have been used in the past to prepare subsequent contracts or contract amendments. They will likely prove useful in the future for that purpose.

As a helpful feature, some computer programs keep track of the frequency or last date of reference activity for specific types of records. Certain office applications, for example, indicate the dates when a word processing file, spreadsheet, or presentation was created and last opened. Similarly, accounting and database management programs may create an audit trail by recording the dates of file entries and revisions. Whenever possible, similar features should be incorporated into the design plan for new or updated computer applications. As a complicating factor, many electronic records series are relatively new entities, and organizations may consequently have little long-term reference experience to guide their retention decisions. In some cases, however, electronic records are replacements or adjuncts for paper files for which reference patterns are well understood.

> *When an organization is involved in litigation or government investigations, retention of obsolete electronic records may ultimately prove harmful.*

Because the future utility of specific electronic records series cannot be predicted with certainty, some risk is inevitably associated with operational retention decisions. Because destruction is irreversible, some program units may be reluctant to discard electronic records, and long retention periods are often established by default to allow for improbable contingencies. The decreasing cost of computer storage appears to favor this approach, but such conservative retention practices entail their own risks. When an organization is involved in litigation or government investigations, retention of obsolete electronic records may ultimately prove harmful. The opposing party in a legal action builds its case on information obtained through discovery, as previously explained. Drafts of word processing documents and poorly-worded or ill-informed e-mail messages are subject to misinterpretation that can pose significant problems. Even where electronic records contain no damaging information, the organization that maintains large quantities of them must bear the often substantial cost of locating the required information and providing copies in response to a subpoena.

Retention of E-mail

According to Ferris Research, over 6 trillion nonspam e-mail messages were sent by business users in 2006. At an average length of 5 kilobytes each, these messages require 30 petabytes (30 quadrillion bytes, the equivalent of one million gigabytes) of computer storage. If spam is included, the total may be even greater. According to SoftScan, a European e-mail security provider, the average size of spam e-mails, which account for over 85 percent of an organization's e-mail traffic, increased from

6.62 kilobytes in 2006 to 11.76 kilobytes in 2007. Admittedly, any given organization has only a fraction of these amounts, but those numbers are nonetheless daunting. As an example, the Office of Information Technology at the University of Tennessee-Knoxville processes over one million e-mail messages per day, of which 90 percent are blocked as spam. According to a survey reported at the Yale University Web site, the university's Information Technology Services unit processed 63 million nonspam messages from September through December 2007. That total included e-mail coming into the university via the Internet plus e-mail originating within Yale. During the same period, the university's e-mail system filtered or deleted an average of 3.5 million spam messages per day.

Given this enormous volume, corporations, government agencies, academic institutions, and other organizations are understandably concerned about the retention and timely disposition of e-mail. E-mail management in all of its aspects—including retention of e-mail, legal and e-discovery issues, storage and archiving of messages, e-mail backup, e-mail classification, spam blocking, e-mail indexing and tracking, and e-mail security—is arguably the most widely acknowledged records management problem. At the time this chapter was written, a Google search for the phrase "e-mail management" retrieved 912,000 matching items, while a search for the more specific phrase "e-mail retention" retrieved 66,800 matching items. Although a comprehensive examination of e-mail management is beyond the scope of this book, the following discussion examines issues and approaches related to retention of e-mail. To obtain a manageable focus, related policy topics, such as proper use of e-mail for business communications or reduction in number of copies of e-mail messages, are omitted.

ANSI/ARMA TR-02, *Procedures and Issues for Managing Electronic Messages as Records* contends that policies for retention of e-mail messages and their associated metadata are essential for compliance with legal / regulatory requirements and to support the continuing conduct of an organization's business. An organization must identify e-mail messages that are considered official copies and preserve them in a reliable, secure manner that will ensure accessibility throughout the retention periods. An organization must also establish methods and timetables for disposition of e-mail messages that are not considered official copies.[1] Yet a 2007 survey by Osterman Research, a market analysis firm that serves the electronic messaging industry, found that 53 percent of responding companies lack an e-mail retention policy, and 67 percent allow individual end users to determine how long messages are kept. Further, retention practices vary considerably, with over one-third of responding companies retaining messages for less than one year and an equal number retaining some messages for longer than 10 years.

> *To be operationally acceptable, an e-mail retention policy must provide reasonable assurance that messages will be available when needed for decision-making, project management, transaction processing, and other business purposes.*

To be legally acceptable, an e-mail retention policy must comply fully with all applicable laws and regulations to which an organization is subject, and it must ensure the preservation of messages relevant for litigation, government investigations, or other legal matters. To be operationally acceptable, an e-mail retention policy must provide reasonable assurance that messages will be available when needed for decision-making, project management, transaction processing, and other business purposes. It must be applicable to an organization's existing accumulation of e-mail messages, including messages stored apart from e-mail servers, as well as messages that employees will create and receive in the future. It must also be applicable to messages that were sent and received by terminated employees. In some organizations, mailboxes of terminated employees outnumber those of current employees. In the absence of their original owners, their contents can be difficult to evaluate for retention. Further, an e-mail retention policy must be fully compatible with an organization's information technology infrastructure.

In theory, retention of e-mail should be based on the previously discussed principle that retention decisions are based on the content and business purpose of a given record rather than its format. Electronic mail technology is a means of transmitting written communications. Depending on the circumstances of creation or receipt, e-mail messages are the electronic counterparts of interoffice memoranda or of conventional mail. Some corporations, government agencies, and other organizations have developed retention guidelines for correspondence based on its content and business value. As a typical example:

- Correspondence that documents significant policies, decisions, actions, events, or business relationships is retained permanently.

- Correspondence that relates to a project or contract is retained for the same period of time as other records that deal with the same matters.

- Correspondence that deals with fiscal or administrative transactions is retained for six or seven years or for some comparable period of time after the matters to which the correspondence pertains are resolved.

- Correspondence that deals with routine business operations, such as confirming a meeting, may be discarded within a few years if it is saved at all.

Such guidelines, where they exist, apply to all forms of correspondence. The mere fact that a written communication is transmitted by e-mail rather than by conventional delivery methods is irrelevant for retention decisions.

In practice, however, this retention guidance can be difficult to apply. Categorization of correspondence is a subjective process that must be performed on an item-by-item basis. Given the huge quantity of e-mail in employee inboxes, time-consuming examination and evaluation of individual messages in order to determine their retention periods is impractical. At two minutes per message, it will take over 16 hours to review an inbox containing 500 messages, a relatively small accumulation for many e-mail users. At that rate, an organization with 1,000 e-mail users will expend the equivalent of eight person-years of effort to categorize existing messages for retention. Conservatively assuming an average hourly wage of $25 including benefits, this retention initiative will cost $400,000 or $400 per mailbox. This amount is many times the cost to retain these messages for many years, if not indefinitely. However, although long or indefinite retention of e-mail is technically possible and may be economically feasible given the declining cost of computer storage, such a policy will complicate an organization's discovery burden and will likely pose significant operational problems for its computing operations. In particular, the efficient operation of e-mail servers is compromised as the quantity of stored messages increases, backup operations become more difficult to complete in a timely manner, and upgrade or replacement of e-mail software or servers will be complicated by the burdensome migration of large quantities of saved messages.

To be successful, an e-mail retention policy must be readily understood and easily implemented with a minimum of employee training. As a simplified yet systematic alternative to item-by-item categorization of messages, an organization should consider a uniform retention period for all e-mail messages sent or received by its employees. Such a policy is based on the following retention rules:

1. **Two categories of messages—official copies and duplicate copies—will be differentiated for retention purposes.** For intraorganizational e-mail, the official copy will be the senders' copy—that is, the copy held by the mailbox owner identified in the "from" portion of a message. This approach will reduce the quantity of e-mail to be retained. Typically, a message has one sender, but it may have multiple recipients. For e-mail that employees receive from external sources, the recipient's copy will be the official copy for retention purposes. The recipient is the employee identified in the "to" portion of a message. Where multiple employees are listed as recipients, the first one named can be designated as the recipient of the official copy. All other copies (cc and bcc) are considered duplicate records for retention purposes.

2. **The uniform retention period for official copies should range from 3 to 10 years.** A uniform maximum retention period shorter than three years is not advisable from an operational or legal perspective. To be considered legally acceptable, an organization's retention practices must be reasonable for the types of records involved and for the circumstances in which they are used. In records management work, three years is widely regarded as a reasonable minimum retention period where a longer period is not required by law and a shorter period cannot be confirmed as permissible. Some basis for this practice exists in statutory law: According to the Uniform Preservation of Private Business Records Act (UPPBRA), business records can be discarded after three years unless a longer time period is required by law.

3. **Ten years is the longest practical retention period for e-mail messages.** Within a 10-year period, most statutes of limitations for initiation of litigation will have elapsed, as will statutes of limitations on federal, state, and local tax audits, but 10-year retention of e-mail is too long for most purposes. Within a 10-year period, an organization will likely change its e-mail application, which may render older messages unreadable. No one can provide reasonable assurance that messages created by e-mail applications in use today will be readable by future e-mail products. If a uniform maximum retention period of three years is considered

too short to satisfy legal and operational requirements, six years is a reasonable alternative. A six-year period is long enough to encompass statutes of limitations for many breaches of contract, personal injuries, and employment-related legal matters for which an e-mail message may be relevant. It also exceeds the time period during which tax returns are subject to audit.

4. **Official copies of e-mail messages will be retained for the uniform retention period.** This standard will be enforced unless the organization's retention schedule or related policies specifies a shorter retention period for specific types of messages or the message is being retained in another way—as a printed copy, for example—in which case the e-mail message is considered a duplicate copy for retention purposes. To support the retention policy, an organization should develop a list of types of messages, such as confirmation of meetings or other calendar items, that need not be retained for the uniform retention period.

5. **A uniform retention period of one to three years can be implemented for duplicate copies of e-mail messages, where a duplicate copy is any copy other than the official copy.** Employees should be encouraged to delete duplicate copies of e-mail messages at the earliest opportunity when they are no longer needed. Duplicate copies of e-mail messages should be automatically deleted 30 days after termination of employment of a mailbox owner.

6. **Messages will be deleted automatically unless they are relevant for litigation, investigations, or other legal purposes.** Whether they are considered official copies or duplicate records, messages will be deleted automatically, without notification to the mailbox owner, when the uniform retention period elapses unless the message has been identified as relevant for pending or ongoing litigation, government investigations, audits, arbitrations, or other legal or quasi-legal purposes.

7. **Messages must be printed or transferred into an approved electronic record-keeping system for retention if they contain information eligible for longer-term storage.** An organization's e-mail is not a suitable repository for messages and attachments that must be retained longer than the uniform maximum period. Messages that contain such information must be printed or transferred into an approved electronic recordkeeping system for retention. This transfer must be done before the uniform retention period elapses.

8. **Attachments can be separated from messages at any time and stored apart from the e-mail system.** If this transfer is not done, attachments will be deleted with their associated messages when the uniform maximum retention period elapses. If an e-mail message merely conveys an attachment that must be retained longer than the uniform maximum period, and the attachment is considered an official copy, the attachment must be separated from the e-mail message and stored outside the e-mail system.

9. **Delete nonbusiness messages 10 days after receipt or creation.** Personal e-mail, unsolicited e-mail, spam, and other messages unrelated to an organization's business must be deleted at the earliest opportunity but not longer than 10 days after creation or receipt.

This e-mail retention policy complies fully with all laws and regulations to which an organization is subject. As a matter of policy, an organization will never knowingly alter or destroy e-mail messages that must be kept for pending or ongoing litigation, government investigations, tax audits, arbitrations, or other legal matters until those matters are fully resolved.

The concept of a uniform retention period for e-mail is easy to understand, requires little decision-making, and can be implemented quickly with a minimum of employee training. It can be applied to an organization's existing accumulation of e-mail messages, including messages that have been transferred to external files, as well as to messages that will be created or received by an organization's employees in the future. Employee retention action will be required only for e-mail messages that must be kept longer than the uniform retention period. If a uniform retention period of six years is selected, employee retention action will seldom be required. As its principal concern, a uniform retention period will result in the retention of some messages that do not need to be kept. This situation will increase storage costs, which, as previously discussed, have declined significantly and are likely to continue to do so. More significantly, however, a greater number of e-mail messages will be subject to e-discovery and freedom-of-information law inquiries, which will increase the cost of those activities. This problem must be balanced against the protection that a uniform retention period provides against inappropriate destruction of specific e-mail messages, which may lead to an inference of obstruction of justice.

The retention concept outlined previously is compatible with e-mail archiving software and services. Typically marketed as e-mail archiving solutions, such products and services create a centralized repository for retention of messages and attachments external to an organization's e-mail system, thereby improving the performance of e-mail servers without sacrificing convenient access to messages. Designed to complement and supplement an organization's e-mail infrastructure, an e-mail archiving solution may be implemented on an organization's own server or as a hosted service. Although specific characteristics and capabilities vary, most e-mail archiving solutions support some combination of the following features and functions:

- Automatic or user-initiated transfer of messages and their associated metadata from mailboxes or external files to the archiving repository
- Journaling to ensure the automatic, tamper-proof capture of all inbound, outbound, and internal e-mail when required for regulatory compliance, or other reasons
- Integration with e-mail client software for transparent access to archived messages by mailbox owners and other authorized persons
- Full-text indexing of messages for e-discovery or other purposes
- Cross-mailbox searching by authorized persons
- Ability to delete messages and attachments by age or file type based on an organization's predefined retention rules
- Litigation or audit holds for specific mailboxes or messages

- Single-instance storage (de-duplication) of messages and attachments received by multiple employees

- Compression of messages and attachments to conserve storage space and to prevent unauthorized access by persons external to the organization

- Replication of folder and subfolder structures from user mailboxes

- Ability to separate message and attachments for storage external to the centralized repository

- Ability to generate reports and graphs about e-mail patterns and traffic in aggregate or for individual users

Media Stability and System Dependence

Long operational retention periods for electronic records are complicated by the limited storage stability of certain electronic recordkeeping media and their dependence on specific configurations of computer, video, or audio hardware and/or software. Limited media stability and hardware/software dependence also have obvious and significant implications for research-oriented retention criteria, many of which require the permanent preservation of records. Used in this context, stability denotes the extent to which an information storage medium retains physical characteristics and chemical properties appropriate to its intended purpose. The stable life of a given medium is the period of time during which it can be used for reliable recording (writing) and playback (reading) of information. With electronic media, reliability is determined by the preservation of signal strength and the absence of permanent read/write errors. In the computer industry, for example, the long-standing de facto standard of error-free operation specifies that electronic media must contain less than one permanent read/write error per trillion recorded bits (approximately 120 gigabytes). Given the increasingly high capacities of computer storage media, a more meaningful measure of media stability specifies that the error rate for a given medium must not exceed the error correction capabilities of the device in which the medium will be recorded or read.

> *Retention periods for specific electronic records series are obviously limited by the playback life of the media on which the records series are stored.*

In their product specifications, media manufacturers may differentiate recording stability from playback stability. **Recording stability** denotes the period of time that a given magnetic or optical storage medium permits reliable recording of new information. **Playback stability**—the ability to retrieve previously recorded information—is more significant for this discussion of records retention. Retention periods for specific electronic records series are obviously limited by the playback life of the media on which the records series are stored.

Discussions of stability are most relevant for electronic records stored on removable media such as magnetic tapes or optical disks. Hard drives are the storage devices of choice in high-performance computing applications, but information recorded onto hard drives is continuously vulnerable to damage from equipment malfunctions. As discussed elsewhere in this book, electronic records stored on hard drives are usually copied onto removable media for backup protection. In many computer applications, database records, word processing documents, and other information stored on hard drives will be replaced or overwritten with new information or updated versions at regular intervals. In such situations, media stability is of limited concern, since the information—being changeable—has a relatively short useful life.

The stability of a given information storage medium depends on various factors, including the medium's chemical composition and the conditions under which it is stored and used. Although magnetic tapes and optical disks are sometimes described in product advertisements and other promotional literature as archival media, they do not offer the permanence implied in that description. As applied to magnetic and optical media, the term *archival* conforms to historical data processing usage, where to *archive* means to transfer inactive information from relatively expensive online storage devices, such as hard drives, to presumably less expensive removable media for offline storage. This data archiving activity is defined in Chapter 2.

National and international standards provide lifetime estimates for specific paper and photographic records media, no comparable published standards address the stability of electronic records stored on magnetic or optical media. In the case of magnetic tapes, anecdotal evidence based on operational experience with older media suggests the possibility of long life. For example, some audio and video recordings created several decades ago remain playable today. Computing facilities have likewise successfully retrieved information from magnetic tapes that have been in storage for more than a decade. Various journal articles, technical reports, and other scientific publications suggest that magnetic media will retain their utility for one to three decades, depending on media composition.

On the other hand, audible and visible distortions attest to the deterioration of many older audio and video recordings on magnetic tape reels and cassettes, although such media may remain playable despite impaired quality. In the case of computer-processable information, however, physical or chemical changes in magnetic media can render data unreadable. Many personal computer users, for example, have had the disturbing experience of being unable to retrieve information recorded onto diskettes, even though the recording was performed just a few weeks or months before the attempted retrieval. Serious concerns have been voiced about the integrity of information stored on magnetic tapes in large data archives. In a widely reported development, a 1990 study by the General Accounting Office questioned the integrity of magnetic tapes maintained by the National Aeronautics and Space Administration. The tapes, containing data generated by unmanned space missions undertaken since the late 1950s, were judged to have undergone significant deterioration in storage, making their continued utility suspect.

Factors that influence the stability of electronic media have been documented in many scientific and technical publications. Computer, video, and audio information recorded onto magnetic media are vulnerable to accidental erasure by magnetic fields of sufficient strength. Information recorded onto magnetic tapes can be damaged by print-through effects—that is, the migration of recorded signals from one layer of tape to another. Magnetic recordings are also imperiled by changes in the physical and chemical characteristics of a given medium. The most significant physical changes result from media wear and improper media handling. The physical and chemical characteristics of magnetic tapes and diskettes are adversely affected by improper storage environments. These effects can be minimized, and media stability extended, by implementing storage and handling procedures and precautions discussed later in this book.

Among optical media, compact disc-recordable (CD-R) and nonrewritable DVDs (DVD-R and DVD+R) are the most stable. Manufacturers claim playback stabilities of 75 to several hundred years for these media. These claims are based on accelerated aging tests. Stability periods for other optical disks range from 10 to 50 years, with 30 years being a typical claim for rewritable CDs and DVDs.

Magnetic tapes and optical disks may remain stable for several decades, but few magnetic recording and playback devices are engineered for a useful life longer than 10 years, and most will be removed from service within a shorter time.

Even if the stability of magnetic and optical media were to improve to levels comparable to those of high rag content papers or silver gelatin microfilm, retention periods for electronic records would still be limited by complications resulting from the interdependence of media, recorded information hardware, and software. Media stability is rarely the limiting factor for long-term storage of computer-processible information, audio recordings, or video images. The service lives of magnetic and optical storage devices is typically shorter than that of media intended for use in such devices. Magnetic tapes and optical disks may remain stable for several decades, but few magnetic recording and playback devices are engineered for a useful life longer than 10 years, and most will be removed from service within a shorter time. Computer storage peripherals are usually replaced with newer equipment within five years. Audio and video recorders may have longer service lives, but the enhanced capabilities and attractive cost-performance characteristics of new models provide a powerful motive for replacement at relatively short intervals.

New magnetic and optical storage devices typically support higher-density recording formats than their predecessors; for example, with successive generations of magnetic tape and optical disk drives intended for computer applications. To preserve the utility of previously recorded information, successor products may offer backward compatibility—that is, they can read media recorded by older models. Such backward compatibility is not guaranteed to be continued in all future products. In fact, the history of magnetic and optical storage technology suggests that backward compatibility provides a bridge between two or, at most, three generations of equipment. Eventually support for older formats is phased out. As an example, magnetic tape units available at the time of this writing do not support low-density recording formats such as 200 and 550 bits per inch. Even nine-track magnetic tapes recorded at 800 bits per inch, which were widely encountered in the 1970s, are no longer supported by some newer tape drives, most of which operate at 1,600 or 6,250 bits per inch.

Backward compatibility does little, if anything, to address problems of discontinued media. Eight-inch and 5.25-inch diskettes, for example, have been supplanted by the 3.5-inch size, but drives that support that format are no longer standard equipment with newer personal computers. The eight-track magnetic tape cassette is an obvious example of an obsolete audio recording medium for which playback equipment is difficult to obtain. U-matic videocassettes were driven from the market by half-inch video tape formats, which will someday be supplanted by digital recording technologies. Since the early 1980s, manufacturers of optical disk drives and media have discontinued certain models or entire product lines without providing replacements. As an example, none of the 5.25-inch write-once optical disks manufactured before 1988 could be read by optical disk drives available for sale 10 years later.

In computer applications, problems of hardware dependence are compounded by software considerations. Electronic records are intended for retrieval or other processing by specific application programs that, in turn, operate in a specific systems software environment. Even more than equipment, software is subject to changes that can render previously recorded information unusable. Successor versions of a given program may not be able to read data, text, or images recorded by earlier versions. Customized software is particularly susceptible to changes in recording media or hardware characteristics.

Data Migration

As discussed elsewhere in this book, many computer, audio, and video records exist only in electronic formats. They cannot be converted to human-readable representations without prohibitively high cost or significant loss of functionality. In such cases, the media stability and hardware/software considerations described previously pose formidable, but not necessarily insurmountable, obstacles to long-term retention. **Data migration**, the process of periodically converting electronic records to new file formats and/or new storage media, can satisfy long retention requirements. Conversion of electronic records to new file formats will maintain the usability of recorded information when computer systems and/or software are upgraded or replaced. Conversion of electronic records to new storage media will maintain the usability of recorded information where the stable life span of a given storage medium is shorter than the retention period for recorded information or where product modifications or discontinuations render a given storage medium unusable.

> *The longer the retention period for recorded information, the greater the need for data migration to ensure the future usability of electronic records.*

Data migration requirements should be determined when retention periods are defined for electronic records. The longer the retention period for recorded information, the greater the need for data migration to ensure the future usability of electronic records. Data migration will typically be required where *any* of the following conditions apply:

- **The scheduled destruction date for electronic records is greater than five years from the initial installation date or last major upgrade of the computer storage device or software that reads, processes, or maintains the records.** Thus, if electronic records must be read by a magnetic tape drive installed in 2006, data migration will likely be required if the records will be retained until 2011 or later. Similarly, if electronic records must be processed by database management software upgraded in 2007, data migration will likely be required if the records will be retained until 2012 or later.

- **The total retention period for the electronic records is greater than 10 years from the date that the records were created.** Thus, electronic records created in 2005 will likely require data migration if they will be retained until 2015 or later.

- **Upgrades and changes will affect the usability of electronic records.** Usability will be affected by upgrades or other changes in computer hardware or software components before the specified retention periods for the records elapses.

Data Migration Plan

As part of its retention initiatives for electronic records, an organization must review data migration requirements and, where indicated, develop a data migration plan for all existing applications. Data migration requirements must also be considered when new applications are planned and implemented. At a minimum, the data migration plan for a given application must:

1. Identify the data to be migrated;
2. Identify data, if any, to be excluded from migration;
3. Identify the organizational unit that will be responsible for performing data migration;
4. Specify anticipated migration intervals, where required, for conversion of electronic records to new file formats;
5. Specify anticipated migration intervals, where required, for copying electronic records onto new media;
6. Specify functional requirements for data migration tools to be developed or acquired;

7. Specify functional requirements for electronic storage media to be used in the migration process;

8. Provide a method for testing and verifying that data migration was performed accurately and reliably without loss of information from the original electronic records;

9. Mandate retention of the original electronic records until accurate, reliable data migration is confirmed.

Data migration plans must be reviewed periodically and revised, if necessary, based on experience or other considerations. At a minimum, data migration plans must be reevaluated whenever computer hardware and/or software components are upgraded or replaced or whenever recorded information is transferred to new storage media. When upgrading or replacement of system components is planned, the cost of data migration should be included in the project budget.

> *A data migration plan is not required for electronic records that are considered duplicate copies.*

Data migration requirements apply only to electronic records designated as official copies to satisfy retention requirements. A data migration plan is not required for electronic records that are considered duplicate copies.

Alternatives to Data Migration

Where the usability of electronic records is affected by upgrading or replacing computer hardware or software components, data migration can be avoided by keeping the superseded hardware or software components in service for the limited purpose of retrieving older electronic records when needed. This practice should be limited to electronic records that are subject to very occasional retrieval and that will be eligible for destruction within three years, assuming that the superseded hardware or software components can be kept in service for that entire time.

Where electronic records are subject to long retention periods, data migration plans will involve a significant future commitment of personnel, technological, and financial resources through multiple iterations of file format conversion and/or storage media conversion. Where electronic records are designated for permanent retention, the commitment is perpetual. The practicality of such data migration commitments must be carefully considered when designating electronic records as official copies for retention purposes.

Where the same information exists in electronic and nonelectronic formats, or where information can be converted easily and reliably to nonelectronic formats through printing or transcription, records managers may prefer paper or microfilm for information designated for long-term retention. Although conceptually unattractive, this method is easily implemented and minimizes the risk that required information will be unreadable in the future. Compared to most magnetic and optical media, paper and microfilm are more stable. Because paper and microfilm records contain human-readable information, problems of hardware and software dependence are minimized or eliminated. The conversion of electronic records to human-readable formats is unacceptable, however, where future reprocessing of the records into machine-readable form is anticipated.

Summary

Retention schedules establish the infrastructure on which many other records management activities are based. They enumerate electronic records series and indicate the period of time that each is to be retained. They may also indicate the physical storage media to be used, the locations where electronic records are to be stored, and the disposition of electronic records when their retention periods have elapsed. Retention schedules vary in scope and content. They may be prepared for electronic records maintained by individual program units within a given organization or for electronic records maintained by the organization as a whole. The same retention schedules may cover electronic and nonelectronic records. Properly formulated, retention schedules will ensure the availability and utility of electronic records for appropriate periods of time, while preventing the unwarranted accumulation of obsolete records. Retention schedules also promote the efficient use of electronic storage media and devices.

Retention periods for electronic records are determined by legal, administrative, and research criteria. Recordkeeping requirements presented in various laws and government regulations specify minimum retention periods for certain information. Some laws and regulations permit the retention of electronic records to satisfy such requirements. No laws or regulations require the creation and retention of electronic records as the sole method of satisfying legally-mandated recordkeeping requirements, but certain laws do specify retention periods for electronic records where they exist.

A broader group of legal considerations involves the admissibility of electronic records as evidence in court trials, administrative hearings, or other legal proceedings. To be admissible, electronic records must satisfy authentication requirements. The purpose of such authentication is to demonstrate the reliability of electronic records to the court's satisfaction. Records managers must develop and implement electronic recordkeeping systems and procedures that will facilitate authentication and enable organizations to overcome objections to the admissibility of electronic records. An administrator capable of providing knowledgeable testimony for authentication purposes should be designated for each system that creates or maintains electronic records. All system characteristics and operating procedures should be fully documented. Security provisions must be implemented to protect electronic records from tampering or other modifications that may impair their trustworthiness.

Operational retention parameters for electronic records are determined by administrative reference requirements. They are typically negotiated through meetings or other consultation with persons who must use the records to fulfill their assigned work responsibilities. The limited storage stability and hardware/software dependence of electronic media generally argue against long operational retention periods. Lifetime estimates for most magnetic and optical storage media are typically shorter than those for paper records and photographic films.

The future utility of electronic records is further limited by the interdependence of media, information, hardware, and software. Electronic media are designed to be recorded and read by specific devices. In most cases, the service lives of such devices are much shorter than that of electronic recording media. The continued utility of electronic records is consequently imperiled by equipment obsolescence and product discontinuations. In computer applications, problems of hardware dependence are compounded by software dependence. Even more than equipment, computer software is subject to changes that can render electronic records unusable. Data migration plans can address these complications, but records managers may prefer paper or microfilm for long-term retention of information in some situations.

Notes

1 These guidelines apply to e-mail in all forms, including attachments and instant messages. By extension, they also apply to recorded voice messages.

Chapter 6

Managing Vital Electronic Records

Vital records, as briefly defined in preceding chapters, contain information essential to an organization's mission. Put another way, vital records contain information needed for mission-critical business operations—operations that an organization must perform. All mission-critical business operations depend to some extent on recorded information. If a vital record is lost, damaged, destroyed, or otherwise rendered unavailable or unusable, such operations will be curtailed or discontinued, with a resulting adverse impact on the organization. For example, without vital records:

- An equipment manufacturer would be unable to build, ship, or repair its products.
- A pharmaceutical company would be unable to develop, test, or prove the safety and efficacy of chemical compounds.
- A government agency would be unable to provide essential services to citizens.
- A financial institution would be unable to answer questions about customer accounts.
- An insurance company would be unable to process claims.
- A hospital would be unable to render effective medical care.
- A school or college would be unable to document the academic achievements of students.
- A law, accounting, or architectural firm would be unable to serve its clients.

Vital records are considered vital specifically and exclusively for the information they contain. Vital record status is not necessarily related to other record attributes. Format is immaterial. Vital records may be paper documents, photographic films, or electronic media. They may be active or inactive records, originals, or copies. Vital record status is independent of retention designations. Vital records need not be permanent records; they may, in fact, be retained for brief periods of time and replaced at frequent intervals. Furthermore, some records may be considered vital for only a portion of their designated retention periods. Records in an accounts receivable database, for example, are vital until paid, but they are often retained for several years following receipt of payment for legal reasons, internal audits, or other purposes.

Specific record attributes aside, a **vital records program** is a set of policies and procedures for the systematic, comprehensive, and economical control of losses associated with vital records. Traditionally, records management has emphasized the protection of vital records against accidental or willful damage, destruction, or misplacement. The last of these protections encompasses a spectrum of events ranging from misfiling to theft of records. An organization may also be harmed by misuse of, alteration of, or unauthorized access to vital records, especially those records that contain confidential or personally-identifiable information. In the case of computer-stored electronic records, such considerations have been widely discussed by public policy analysts, legal scholars, and others.

The relationship between disaster preparedness and records management is well established. ISO 15489-1, *Information and Documentation—Records Management—Part 1: General,* the international records management standard, includes risk assessment and protection of records among the requirements for records management operations. The development, implementation, and operation of policies, programs, and procedures to protect vital records have traditionally been considered a records management responsibility. In most organizations, however, vital records protection is closely related to other loss control and risk management activities. Many businesses, government agencies, and other organizations, for example, have developed contingency plans for the protection of personnel, buildings, machinery, inventory, and other assets in the event of an unplanned calamitous event such as a fire or flood. Properly implemented, such contingency plans can reduce exposure to loss and increase the likelihood of an organization's survival. They provide formalized procedures to help an organization withstand and limit the impact of adverse events, enabling it to continue essential business operations—though possibly at a reduced level—following a disaster. Vital records protection is an indispensable aspect of such contingency planning. For U.S. government agencies, for example, 36 CFR 1236 states that the management of vital records must be part of every federal agency's plan for continuity of business operations in the event of emergencies. For many organizations, the information contained in vital records is their most important asset. In some cases, the loss of information can have more devastating consequences for continuity of business operations than the loss of physical plant or inventory.

In computer installations, vital records protection is often viewed as a facet of the broader, much publicized field of computer security and disaster recovery, which is concerned with preventing or limiting potentially disastrous events and implementing effective measures for resumption of computer operations following a disaster. In the typical organization, planning for computer security and disaster recovery is the responsibility of a centralized information technology department. Often, committees or task forces, composed of information technology staff and representatives of key user departments, are formed to address issues of loss control, including the replacement of computing equipment and restoration of computer operations following a disaster, the protection of computer resources against electronic intrusion, and the detection and prevention of computer fraud. Computer security and disaster recovery committees may also include internal auditors, security personnel, legal counsel, and risk management specialists.

> *In a given organization, the records manager is the employee most likely to have a broad understanding of the nature and importance of vital electronic records and the ways in which they relate to other information resources that support an organization's mission.*

Records management participation in such contingency planning activities is essential to facilitate the coordination of vital records protection with other aspects of computer security. Vital records protection is a critical element in any disaster recovery plan. The rapid restoration of computing operations following a disaster serves little purpose if the information needed to support specific applications is unavailable. In a given organization, the records manager is the employee most likely to have a broad understanding of the nature and importance of vital electronic records and the ways in which they relate to other information resources that support an organization's mission.

A vital records protection program for electronic records includes the following components:

1. Formal establishment of the program by senior management with responsibility and authority for protection of vital electronic records assigned to the records management activity—to be coordinated, where appropriate, with related contingency planning activities;

2. The identification and enumeration of vital electronic records;

3. Risk analysis to determine the extent to which specific vital records are threatened by hazards and to calculate exposures;

4. The selection and implementation of appropriate loss prevention and records protection methods; and

5. Employee training and compliance auditing.

The following sections explain and discuss these program components. Although the discussion emphasizes vital electronic records, many of the concepts and methods presented here also apply to vital nonelectronic records in paper or photographic formats. A comprehensive disaster recovery plan must encompass such nonelectronic information resources.

Establishing the Vital Records Protection Program

Citizens have a reasonable expectation that government agencies will safeguard records that support essential public services. Similar expectations apply to corporate shareholders, to a financial institution's customers, to an insurance company's policyholders, to a professional services firm's clients, to medical patients, to students, and to any other persons or organizations affected by the recordkeeping practices of others. These expectations are based on the legal concept of "standard of care," which is the degree of care that a reasonable person would exercise to prevent injury to another. Failure to do so constitutes negligence. In U.S. law, the calculus of negligence is based on a straightforward principle: if precautionary measures cost less than the losses they are intended to prevent, then the precautionary measures should be taken.

Although standard of care is most often discussed in the context of medical malpractice, it is relevant for other professional disciplines, including records management. An organization's electronic records, as previously discussed, are assets that contain potentially valuable, sometimes vital information. In any organization, senior management has ultimate responsibility for the protection of assets, including the formulation and implementation of risk management and business continuity plans. Information contained in vital electronic records is an asset. It follows, then, that senior management is ultimately responsible for the protection of vital electronic records. If the destruction or misuse of vital electronic records results in the interruption of critical business operations, senior management must accept responsibility for the ensuing financial losses or other consequences.[1]

Protection of vital records is not merely a good idea; it is a statutory obligation in some circumstances. In the United States, senior management's responsibility and obligation to protect vital electronic records is implied or explicitly stated in several laws and government regulations:

1. Within the U.S. government, 36 CFR 1236.12 makes agency heads responsible for protecting vital records, which are defined as records needed to meet operational responsibilities under emergency conditions or to protect the legal and financial rights of the government and those affected by government activities.

2. For corporations, partnerships, and other private businesses, the most frequently cited legal statute is the Foreign Corrupt Practices Act (FCPA) of 1977 (as amended in 1988 and 1998). Originally intended to prevent the destruction of records in order to conceal bribery or other crimes, the FCPA imposes significant penalties for failure to keep accounting records and other information pertaining to certain assets. The FCPA's recordkeeping provisions apply to all domestic and foreign companies that list their securities on U.S. exchanges. Violations of recordkeeping provisions can be enforced or prosecuted without regard to any violation of the FCPA's anti-bribery provisions.

3. Among laws and regulations that specifically address the protection of computer-stored records, the Federal Information Management Security Act (FISMA) of 2002 mandates that U.S. government agencies develop information security protections "commensurate with the risk and magnitude of the harm resulting from unauthorized access, use, disclosure, disruption, modification, or destruction of (i) information collected or maintained by or on behalf of the agency and (ii) information systems used or operated by an agency or by a contractor of an agency or other organization on behalf of an agency." As defined by FISMA, information security must provide safeguards against improper destruction of

information and ensure timely and reliable access to information. FISMA has replaced the Computer Security Act of 1987, which required the development and implementation of security plans for "sensitive" information maintained by computers operated by U.S. federal government agencies and federal government contractors.

4. OMB Circular A-130, issued by the Office of Management and Budget, defines policies to secure information, including electronic records, maintained by federal government agencies. Although many of its provisions are concerned with privacy protection and prevention of unauthorized access to computer systems, Circular A-130 requires U.S. government agencies to ensure that "information is protected commensurate with the risk and magnitude of the harm that would result from the loss, misuse, or unauthorized access to or modification of such information." Agencies must provide effective mechanisms for maintaining continuity of computer operations. Manual backup procedures are not a viable option.

5. Organizations in specific industries are subject to records protection and computer security requirements promulgated by regulating agencies. As an example, financial institutions insured by the Federal Deposit Insurance Corporation (FDIC) are required to have organization-wide disaster recovery and business continuity plans for their computer installations. Review of financial institutions' business continuity plans is a well-established component of examinations performed by the Federal Financial Institutions Examination Council (FFIEC), which prescribes principles and standards for federal examination of financial institutions. Its examination procedures include detailed questions about the development, implementation, testing, and oversight of disaster recovery policies and procedures, including provisions for data backup and offsite storage. Other regulatory bodies that require contingency plans for depository institutions include the Comptroller of the Currency, the Federal Home Loan Bank Board, the Office of Thrift Supervision, and the National Credit Union Administration.

6. As part of the administrative simplification provisions of the Health Insurance Portability and Accountability Act (HIPAA) of 1996, the Department of Health and Human Services makes data backup and disaster recovery planning mandatory components for security standards for electronic information maintained by healthcare providers and plans. As specified in 45 CFR 164.306, healthcare organizations must "protect against any reasonably anticipated threats or hazards to the security and integrity of such information." According to 45 CFR 164.308, data backup and disaster recovery plans are required "to create and maintain retrievable exact copies of electronic protected health information."

7. IRS Revenue Procedure 86-19 required offsite protection of computer-processible tax records. It has been supplanted by IRS Revenue Procedure 98-25, which recommends but does not require offsite storage.

8. Protection against unauthorized or unintentional disclosure of computer-stored records is maintained by various privacy statutes. Among U.S. laws, the Privacy

Act of 1974 (5 U.S. Code 552A) is the best-known example. Other federal statutes with privacy provisions for recorded information include the Fair Credit Billing Act (15 US. Code 1637); the Fair Credit Reporting Act (15 U.S. Code 1681); the Family Educational Rights and Privacy Act (20 U.S. Code 1232); the Right to Financial Privacy Act (12 U.S. Code 3401); the Financial Services Modernization Act (15 U.S. Code 6801), also known as the Gramm-Leach-Bliley Act; the Electronic Communications Privacy Act of 1986 (18 U.S. Code 1367), the Drivers Privacy Protection Act of 1994 (18 U.S. Code 2721), the National Information Infrastructure Protection Act of 1996 (18 U.S. Code 1030, and the Children's Online Privacy Protection Act (COPPA) of 1998 (16 CFR 312).

Similar privacy laws have been passed by various states. Medical records and adoption records, in particular, are subject to state-specific privacy legislation. Privacy legislation with restrictions on access to recorded information has also been passed in certain other countries. Examples include the Canadian Privacy Act of 1983 and Canadian Personal Information Protection and Electronic Document Act of 2000, the United Kingdom Data Protection Act of 1998, the Swiss Federal Law on Data Protection of 1992, the Australian Privacy Act of 1998, the New Zealand Privacy Act of 1993, and the New Zealand Health Information Privacy Code of 1994. In Directive 1995/46/EC, the European Commission provides a regulatory framework for basic privacy principles related to collection, storage, and processing of personal data.

Organizations have been held liable for damages associated with inadequate provisions for the security of electronic records. Reported cases have dealt with the failure to prevent unauthorized disclosure of computer information such as consumer credit records or medical records. Comparable civil liability could conceivably result from an organization's failure to protect specific operating records from accidental or willful loss or destruction. Accidental deletion of computer-stored medical records, for example, could complicate treatment and damage a patient's health. Similarly, a university's failure to implement a disaster recovery plan could render it unable to provide academic transcripts should such computer-stored records be destroyed, thereby placing its graduates at a disadvantage when competing for employment or seeking further education. A corporation's failure to protect its personnel records could make it impossible to determine retirement eligibility or other benefits. Destruction of birth, death, marital, or land records maintained by state or local government agencies can have widespread adverse consequences for individuals and organizations.

Some legal actions related to incidents of this type may have occurred but were not reported, having been settled out of court in favor of the injured party to avoid publicizing an organization's computer security problems. The legal outcome in such situations is far from certain, however. Arguments in favor of liability are based on the previously discussed concept of standard of care, with its presumed duty to secure electronic records against destruction or misuse, including unauthorized access. However, the nature and scope of such a duty have not been firmly established in statutory provisions or case law. Until recently, the lack of industry-wide standards for computer security has complicated agreement about reasonable measures to protect electronic records. Addressing this problem, the ISO/IEC 27002 standard, *Information Technology—Security Techniques—Code of Practice for Information Security Management*, provides a starting point for the development of computer security policies by corporations, government agencies, and other organizations. Similarly, guidelines developed for federal government computers by the National Institute of Standards and Technology are applicable to nongovernmental organizations.

> *Vital records protection is costly, but it makes no direct contribution to revenues, product development, or the delivery of services. It provides no benefits unless and until a disaster occurs.*

Legal requirements and liabilities aside, a vital records protection program is, in effect, an insurance policy for essential information. Like any insurance policy, vital records protection can be difficult to sell to decision makers. Vital records protection is costly, but it makes no direct contribution to revenues, product development, or the delivery of services. It provides no benefits unless and until a disaster occurs. As discussed next, many threats to vital records have a low probability of occurrence. Senior management may consequently ignore them in favor of more pressing business concerns, but vital records protection is justified by the intolerable consequences that follow an adverse but improbable event. Senior management must be made to appreciate the potential for tangible and intangible damages associated with the loss, destruction, or misuse of vital electronic records, however unlikely that loss, destruction, or misuse may seem. The damages may include, but are by no means limited to:

- Loss of customers resulting from the inability to fulfill orders and contracts, complete transactions, support products, or provide services

- Loss of revenue or interruption of cash flow due to lack of records and resulting inability to determine amounts to be billed to specific customers or to process payments

- Loss of opportunity because information needed for contracts, partnerships, joint ventures, or other business agreements is unavailable

- Negligence lawsuits associated with dereliction of duties and the failure to protect essential records from accidental or willful loss or destruction

- Fines or other penalties for failure to provide records needed for government investigations

- Increased assessments, plus penalties and interest, following tax audits because of inadequate documentation of business expenses, depreciation, and other deductions, allowances, and tax credits

- Delayed compliance with governmental reporting requirements for public companies

- Lack of records needed for litigation support

- Inability to document insurance claims with resulting delay or reduction in settlements
- Reduced employee productivity with longer completion times for information-dependent business operations
- High cost to reconstruct lost information
- Tarnished reputation and loss of customer goodwill

By initiating and supporting a program to protect vital electronic records, senior management acknowledges that these consequences are intolerable. Although an organization's senior management bears ultimate responsibility for safeguarding vital electronic records, its involvement is typically and properly limited to delegating authority for the creation, implementation, and operation of a systematic vital records program. To formalize a protection program for vital electronic records maintained by a business, government agency, or other organization, senior management should issue a written directive that:

- Acknowledges the importance of protecting vital electronic records as a component in the organization's contingency planning efforts;
- Formally establishes a program for the systematic, comprehensive, and economical protection of vital electronic records;
- Solicits the cooperation of personnel in all program units where vital electronic records are maintained.

If the organization does not have a program to protect its nonelectronic vital records, or if an existing program for such records is in need of revision, the scope of the management directive should be broadened to include information resources in paper and photographic formats.

As with other records management activities, the development and implementation of a successful vital records program depends on the knowledge and active participation of program unit personnel who are familiar with the nature and use of vital electronic records in specific work environments. An advisory committee of program unit representatives provides a formal structure for such participation. The committee will support the records management department in planning, implementing, and operating a program to protect vital electronic records.

Identifying Vital Records

To be considered vital, a record must be essential to a mission-critical activity, its unavailability must have a significant adverse impact on that activity, and its contents must not be fully duplicated in other records from which essential information can be recovered or reconstructed. Protection of these essential information assets is an indispensable component of emergency preparedness, business continuity, and disaster recovery initiatives.

Vital electronic records are typically identified by surveying individual program units to determine which, if any, vital records they create and maintain. The end product of such a survey is a list of the vital electronic records created and maintained by each program unit. For those electronic records series identified as vital, the list should include the following data elements:

1. The series title;

2. A brief description of the series' purpose, scope, and operational and physical characteristics;

3. The reason that the series is considered vital, including a clear, convincing statement of the mission-critical activity that will be disrupted if the records series is lost, destroyed, or otherwise rendered unavailable;

4. The name of the program unit responsible for protecting the vital records series;

5. The method of protection to be implemented.

> *At a minimum, vital record designations for electronic and non-electronic records series should be coordinated. If exactly the same information exists in electronic and nonelectronic records, one of the formats should be selected for vital records protection.*

Lists prepared for individual program units may be combined to form a master list of vital electronic records maintained by an entire organization or by a specific administrative entity such as a division, subsidiary, or field office. As with retention schedules, electronic and nonelectronic vital records may be integrated into a single listing, and that approach is often advisable. At a minimum, vital record designations for electronic and nonelectronic records series should be coordinated. If exactly the same information exists in electronic and nonelectronic records, one of the formats should be selected for vital records protection. If purposeful duplication and offsite storage will be used, protecting electronic records will typically prove faster and more economical than paper or photographic records that contain the same information. Compared to their nonelectronic counterparts, electronic records are more compact and easier to duplicate.

As noted in Chapter 4, a vital records survey can be combined with an inventory of electronic records performed for purposes of preparing retention schedules. That approach is recommended where practical. A combined records inventory/vital records survey will minimize duplication of effort. Vital record status can be evaluated for each records series identified during a records inventory. Vital records protection measures can also be coordinated with retention-oriented management actions such as offsite storage of specific machine-readable media.

Where a separate vital records survey must be conducted, the procedures are similar to those employed in a conventional records inventory. Based on interviews with program unit personnel, a records manager prepares a tentative list of vital electronic records for consideration and comment by interested parties, both within and outside the program unit that maintains the records. A series of meetings or other consultations will resolve concerns and disagreements, leading eventually to a final approved list of vital electronic records for each program unit or, if desired, a master list. Several drafts may be required before a final version is obtained, however. As with retention scheduling, the records manager coordinates the meetings, directs the discussion, redrafts the vital records lists, and provides a broad perspective on information management issues that transcend the responsibilities and requirements of specific program units.

In corporations, government agencies, or other organizations, most program units maintain one or more electronic records series that contain useful information. Program unit personnel rely on such records to perform specific tasks. When asked to identify vital electronic records, they will include most, if not all, records they routinely utilize. This response is understandable—program unit personnel value records information that they reference frequently and would not want to lose any of it. A given series of electronic records may be important but not truly essential, however. Records managers must help program unit employees distinguish vital records from important ones.

Important records support a program unit's business operations and help it fulfill its assigned responsibilities. Unavailability of such records may cause delays or confusion, but it will not render a program unit inoperative. The loss of important records may impede a program unit's work, but it will not prevent it. Some important records are replaceable—their contents may be reconstructed from other records, although such reconstruction may involve considerable time, inconvenience, and expense. In some computer applications, operations supported by important electronic records may be performed—though, admittedly, less quickly or efficiently—by reversion to manual procedures. Truly vital electronic records, by contrast, are essential and irreplaceable. Their contents cannot be reconstructed, and the operations they support cannot be performed without them. Reversion to manual procedures is impossible.

Vital records are always associated with mission-critical operations—those operations that pertain to an organization's fundamental responsibilities and most essential activities. For records to be considered vital, the business operations they support must be essential. In most organizations, a small percentage of nonelectronic records are properly considered vital. By contrast, a somewhat higher—but not necessarily large—percentage of an organization's electronic records may be vital records. In businesses, government agencies, and other organizations, mission-critical operations have historically been priority candidates for computerization or other forms of automation. Certain mission-critical operations, such as accounts payable, accounts receivable, and payroll processing, are encountered in a broad range of work environments. Those activities have been computerized for decades. Other mission-critical operations are associated with specific types of organizations or industries. Examples include claims processing and policy management in an insurance company, maintenance of customer accounts in a bank or other financial institution, inventory control in a retail organization, development and testing of drugs in a pharmaceutical company, creation and maintenance of patient records in a hospital, and creation and maintenance of student records in a school, college, or university.

Electronic records essential to mission-critical operations are, by definition, vital records, because the operations cannot be performed without them. The identification of vital electronic records consequently begins with the identification of an organization's mission-critical operations. Once mission-critical operations are identified by program unit personnel or others, records managers must determine which electronic records are required by those operations. All vital records are associated with mission-critical operations, but nonvital records may be employed in those operations as well. When determining that a given electronic records series is vital, the records manager must be able to clearly and convincingly state which mission-critical operations would be prevented by loss, destruction, or other unavailability of the indicated records series—the ultimate test of a vital record.

As a complicating factor, the records manager must differentiate the electronic records that are vital to a corporation, government agency, or other organization as a whole from those records that are vital to a specific program unit within that organization. Records series in the former group support truly mission-critical operations, while those in the latter group support valuable but not mission-critical activities. In many organizations, certain program units perform useful functions that are not critical to the organization's mission. Loss or destruction of electronic records may cause a temporary or permanent disruption of business operations in such program units, but the organization's mission will not be imperiled. Such records cannot be considered vital, because the activities they support are not vital to the organization as a whole. As an example, a hospital's community relations department may maintain a database of information about community groups with which it is involved. If the database is damaged, the department's work will be impeded or rendered impossible, but patient care—the hospital's mission—will not be affected.

Risk Analysis

As an important part of vital records planning, records managers must consider the risks to which specific electronic records are subject. The purpose of **risk analysis,** sometimes termed *risk assessment,* is to determine and evaluate exposure to particular risks. Its outcome provides the basis for protection planning and other records management decisions.

The following discussion is based on the common business definition of *operational risk* as a danger of damage or loss to an organization resulting from inadequate internal processes, including inadequate information management practices, or from external events. This definition, which was originally developed for the banking industry, has since been widely applied to other types of organizations.[2] Operational risk is a function of three variables:

1. Threats or hazards that may harm an organization

2. Vulnerabilities that render an organization susceptible to threats

3. Consequences or negative impacts associated with specific threats

The next section surveys threats and vulnerabilities that an organization must consider when developing a program to protect vital electronic records. Adverse consequences associated with the loss of vital electronic records were discussed earlier in this chapter.

Threats and Vulnerabilities

Vital electronic records may be threatened by destruction, loss, or corruption from a variety of causes. For example:

- **Malicious destruction.** This type of destruction of recorded information may result from warfare or warfare-related activities such as terrorist attacks and civil insurrections. Vital electronic records are also subject to purposeful or seemingly aimless vandalism by disgruntled employees, former employees, intruders, or others. An organization's vulnerability to these threats depends on various factors, including the nature of the organization's business, the local socio-political environment, and security provisions in place.

- **Accidental destruction.** Potentially catastrophic agents of accidental destruction include natural disasters such as violent weather, floods, and earthquakes. An organization's vulnerability to these disastrous events depends on unpredictable and unpreventable geographical, geological, and meteorological factors. Vulnerability is obviously increased by close proximity to airports, military bases, power plants, and major highways and railway lines used for transport of hazardous materials. Vital electronic records can also be damaged or destroyed by human-induced accidents such as fire or explosions that may result from carelessness, negligence, or lack of knowledge about the consequences of specific actions. Often, these adverse effects will destroy computer hardware and software components as well as vital records. Vulnerability is increased in rural locations that are remote from firefighting services.

- **Careless handling.** More likely causes of accidental records destruction are less dramatic and more localized but no less catastrophic in their consequences for mission-critical operations. Magnetic tapes and other electronic media can be damaged by careless handling. With very active media, the potential for such damage is intensified by use. As discussed elsewhere in this book, magnetic and optical media can be damaged by improper environmental conditions and careless handling. Information recorded on magnetic media and certain optical disks can be erased by exposure to strong magnetic fields. Careless work procedures, such as mounting tapes or diskettes without write protection, can expose vital electronic records to accidental erasure by overwriting. Mislabeled media may be inadvertently marked for reuse, their contents being inappropriately replaced by new information. The implementation of systematic procedures for media storage, care, and handling can reduce an organization's vulnerability to these threats.

- **Hardware/software failures.** Computer hardware and software failures can damage valuable information. Head crashes or other hardware malfunctions, while much less common than in the past, can destroy valuable information recorded on hard drives. Improperly adjusted equipment, such as misaligned tape guides, can cause scratches or other media damage. An organization can minimize its vulnerability to these problems by keeping its computer hardware in good working order and replacing aging equipment, but hardware malfunctions cannot be eliminated completely. Software failures are more difficult to control. When a computer program locks up or terminates abnormally, information may not be properly recorded. Similarly, computer records may be accidentally deleted during database reorganizations or by utility programs that consolidate space on hard drives.

- **Lost or misfiled media.** Electronic media can be misfiled or misplaced. Like any valued asset, recorded information can be stolen for financial gain or other motives. An organization's vulnerability to misplacement or theft of media is increased by the widespread storage of electronic records in users' work areas where systematic handling procedures are seldom implemented and security provisions may be weak or absent. The use of compact, easily concealed electronic media, such as high-density magnetic tapes and solid-state memory devices, facilitates theft, and the high capacity of such media increases the amount of information affected by a single incident of theft. In fact, the inherent and continuously improving compactness and high storage density of all electronic media, when compared to paper documents, exposes more information to loss-related incidents.

- **Unauthorized access.** The potential for unauthorized tampering with electronic records has been widely discussed in publications and at professional meetings. Records stored on rewritable media—such as magnetic disks, magnetic tapes, and certain optical disks—are subject to modification by unauthorized persons in a manner that can prove very difficult to detect. Such unauthorized modification may involve the deletion, editing, or replacement of information. Password protection, encryption, and other countermeasures can reduce but not entirely eliminate an organization's vulnerability to such data tampering.

- **Records corruption.** Viruses and other malicious software are much publicized causes of corruption of computer-stored records. Broadly defined, a **virus** is a computer program that can insert a copy of itself into another program. The virus then performs operations specified by its developer. The operations often involve the modification or destruction of information stored by the computer that the virus infiltrates. Viruses can also prevent the recording of information, consume system resources required by other programs, cause software failures, and damage hardware components. Depending on the virus, such effects may be immediate or delayed. Because they replicate themselves, computer viruses can spread in a geometric progression through a computer system or network. Among related types of malicious software, a *worm* travels through a computer installation or network without replicating itself, while a *Trojan horse* is a program that performs a desirable task and some unexpected, usually destructive functions. *Logic bombs* infiltrate a computer installation but remain dormant until triggered by a specified event, at which point it may erase a hard drive, delete files, or otherwise destroy recorded information. Software that detects malicious software is constantly improving, but it is not completely effective.

- **Improper disclosure.** Improper disclosure of electronic records, whether accidental or intentional, has been the subject of considerable discussion by a variety of interested parties, including records managers, computer specialists, lawyers, public policy analysts, and civil rights advocates. Although such discussions have typically warned against the unauthorized disclosure of sensitive personal information protected by privacy legislation, electronic records may also store business plans, pricing information, trade secrets, or other proprietary technical, strategic, or financial information of interest to an organization's competitors. Certain government computers similarly store electronic records with national security implications. Improper disclosure of vital electronic records may result from espionage-related activities such as unauthorized access to computer systems, electronic eavesdropping, or bribery of employees who have access to desired information. Computer networks are vulnerable to intrusion by hackers. Accidental disclosure is also possible when computer output is routed to the wrong device in a local or wide area network, when electronic messages are incorrectly addressed or distributed, or when incompletely erased rewritable media are distributed for reuse.

Qualitative Risk Assessment

Regardless of the specific threats involved, risk assessment may be based on intuitive, relatively informal qualitative approaches, or more structured, formalized quantitative methods. Qualitative approaches rely principally on group discussions. They are particularly useful for identifying and categorizing physical security problems and other vulnerabilities. A risk assessment team or committee, possibly lead by a records manager, evaluates the dangers to specific vital electronic records series from catastrophic events, theft, and other threats. The team typically produces a prioritized list of vital electronic records judged to be at risk and for which protective measures are recommended.

A qualitative risk assessment is usually based on a physical survey of locations where electronic records are stored, combined with an examination of reference activity and patterns that may increase vulnerability and a review of security procedures already in place. Geophysical and political factors, such as the likelihood of destructive weather or the possibility of warfare or civil unrest, are also considered. In the case of electronic records stored on hard drives in centralized or decentralized computing installations, the team may examine the following factors:

- Physical security and supervision in the computer area
- The number and types of employees who have access to the computer area

- The number and locations of online workstations
- Password protection or other precautions against unauthorized access
- Network security arrangements
- The use of surge protectors or uninterruptible power supplies to prevent electrical damage
- The availability of fire control apparatus
- The implementation of backup procedures and offsite storage arrangements for recorded information
- The frequency of hardware or software malfunctions that can damage electronic records

Similarly, a risk analysis of magnetic tapes or other removable media stored offline will be concerned with the appropriateness of environmental conditions, security provisions to prevent unauthorized access to storage areas, and the proximity of the storage areas to flammable materials or other hazardous substances.

> ***Threats may be categorized as unlikely, likely, or very likely to occur, while vulnerabilities may be categorized as limited, acceptable, or high.***

By definition, a **qualitative risk assessment** does not estimate the statistical probabilities associated with destructive events or the financial impact of the resulting losses. The intent is to develop an understanding of the interplay of threats, vulnerabilities, and consequences as they relate to an organization's vital electronic records and the mission-critical activities they support. Typically, the likelihood of a given threat and the extent of an organization's vulnerability are evaluated in general terms, although the nature and frequency of adverse historical events, such as destructive weather, power outages, network security breaches, infiltration of computer systems by malicious software, or reported theft of computer storage media, are considered. Threats may be categorized as unlikely, likely, or very likely to occur, while vulnerabilities may be categorized as limited, acceptable, or high. The adverse impact associated with a particular combination of threat and consequences may be similarly described as *low* (little or no disruption of mission-critical activities), *medium* (some disruption but mission-critical activities will continue, although possibly at a lower level of effectiveness), or *high* (mission-critical activities will terminate or be severely disrupted).

In the project team's report, these evaluative designations should be accompanied by definitions or clarifying narrative. The greatest concern is for the vital electronic records with high vulnerabilities to threats that have a high likelihood of occurrence with sudden, unpredictable onset—magnetic tapes containing vital information stored in laboratory areas where flammable materials are used in scientific experiments, for example, or confidential product specifications and pricing information stored on desktop computers in unsecured areas.

Quantitative Risk Assessment

Quantitative risk assessment is based on concepts and methods originally developed for product safety analysis and subsequently adapted for computer security applications. Like its qualitative counterpart, quantitative risk assessment relies on site visits, discussions, and other systems analysis methods to identify vulnerabilities, but it uses numeric calculations to measure the likelihood and impact of losses associated with specific vital records series. The calculations are expressed as dollar amounts, which can be related to the cost of proposed protection methods. If the calculated cost of a given loss exceeds the cost of protective measures, those measures should be implemented. As an additional advantage, quantitative risk assessments provide a useful framework for comparing exposures for different vital records series and prioritizing them for protection.

Various quantitative assessment techniques have been proposed by risk analysts and others, but all are based on the following general formula:

$$R = P \times C$$

where:

R = the risk, sometimes called the *Annualized Loss Expectancy (ALE)*, associated with the loss of a specific vital records series due to a catastrophic event or other threat;

P = the probability that such a threat will occur in any given year; and

C = the cost of the loss should the threat occur.

This formula measures risk as the *probable annual dollar loss* associated with a specific vital electronic records series. The *total annual expected loss* to an organization is the sum of the annualized losses calculated for each vital electronic records series.

Quantitative risk assessment begins with the determination of probabilities associated with adverse events and the calculation of annualized loss multipliers based on those probabilities. Information systems specialists, program unit personnel, or others familiar with a given electronic records series are asked to estimate the likelihood of occurrence for specific threats. Whenever possible, their estimates should be based on the historical incidence of adverse events. Reliable probability estimates are easiest and most conveniently obtained for events such as power outages, equipment malfunctions, software failures, network security breaches, and virus attacks for which maintenance statistics or other documentation exists. Statistical data about potentially destructive weather events, such as hurricanes or floods, is available in books, scholarly journals, newspapers, and other reference sources, including a rapidly increasing number of Web sites. At its Web site, for example, the Federal Emergency Management Agency (FEMA) (www.fema.gov) will display flood hazard maps for any U.S. location. Various Web sites provide information about the frequency of hurricanes, tornadoes, earthquakes, landslides, volcanic eruptions, and tsunamis worldwide. Similarly, accident data is available for specific airports.

In the absence of written evidence or experience, probability estimates must be based on informed speculation by persons familiar with the broad information management environment within which a given vital records series is maintained and used. In this respect, quantitative risk analysis resembles the qualitative approach. Often, the records manager must ask a series of probing questions, followed by lengthy discussion, to obtain usable probability estimates. As an example, the records manager may ask an information technology manager or user whether file damage resulting from hardware malfunctions is likely to occur once per year. If the answer is yes, the records manager should ask whether such an event is likely to occur once every half year, once per quarter, once per month, and so on. This procedure can be repeated until a satisfactorily specific response is obtained.

Once probabilities are estimated, annual loss multipliers can be calculated in any of several ways. Using one method, a calamitous threat to vital electronic records with a given probability of occurrence is assigned a probability value of 1. Other threats are assigned higher or lower values, based on their relative probability of occurrence. As an example, a threat estimated to occur once per year is assigned a probability value of 1, which serves as a base line for other probability estimates. An event estimated to occur once every three months (four times per year) is assigned a probability value of 4, while an event with an estimated frequency of once every four years is assigned the probability value of 0.25.

Applying the previous formula, the probability value is multiplied by the estimated cost of the loss should the event occur. Factors that might be considered when determining costs associated with the loss of vital electronic records include, but are by no means limited to, the following:

1. The cost of file reconstruction, assuming that source documents or other input materials remain available;

2. The value of canceled customer orders, unbillable accounts, or other losses resulting from the inability to perform specific business operations because needed electronic records are unavailable;

3. Labor costs associated with reversion to manual operations, assuming that such reversion is possible;

4. The cost of defending against or otherwise settling legal actions associated with the loss of vital electronic records.

Quantitative risk assessment is an aid to judgment not a substitute for it. The risk assessment formula is an analytical tool that can help records managers clarify their thinking and define protection priorities for vital electronic records. Assume, for example, that a hospital estimates the probability of one chance per year that a database of patient records essential to mission-critical medical care will be corrupted, though not extensively damaged, by unauthorized modification, defective software, minor hardware malfunction, or infiltration by computer viruses. A probability (P) of 1 is assigned to that risk. The adverse event will affect a subset of patient records. The cost (C) to reconstruct the corrupted records by rekeying information from paper documents is estimated at $2,000 when the adverse event occurs. Applying the formula, the risk (annualized loss expectancy) is 1 times $2,000, or $2,000.

Assume further the probability of one chance in 10 years that the same database of patient records will be extensively damaged by a catastrophic hardware or software failure. A probability (P) of 0.1 is assigned to that risk because it is one-tenth as likely to occur as the base case cited previously. If the cost (C) to reconstruct the database following hardware failure is estimated at $40,000, the risk is 0.1 times $40,000, or $4,000. These calculations indicate that catastrophic hardware failure, while having a much lower probability of occurrence, poses a more significant risk than corruption of patient records by unauthorized modification, minor hardware malfunctions, software defects, or computer viruses. Consequently, hardware protections should be made a higher priority for vital records protection.

Risk Control

Whether qualitative or quantitative analysis is employed, an organization may decide to accept a given risk associated with the loss of specific vital records. Alternatively, an organization may transfer risk by purchasing specialized insurance coverage for reconstruction of valuable papers and records, but that approach is rarely practical or affordable for large quantities of electronic records. The organization is better advised to control risk by taking steps to safeguard its vital electronic records. Where vital records protection is part of a broader computer security, business continuity, and disaster recovery plan, risk control measures may also safeguard equipment, software, and networking components necessary to retrieve or process vital electronic records. Regardless of scope, *risk control* encompasses preventive and protective measures.

> **Prevention is the first line of defense against risk.**

Although some recorded information may be reconstructable in the event of a disaster, the high cost of such reconstruction makes it a last-resort component of risk control. Prevention is the first line of defense against risk. Preventive measures are designed to minimize the likelihood of damage to vital electronic records from one or more of the threats enumerated in the preceding discussion. Preventive measures apply to both working copies and security copies of vital electronic records. For purposes of this discussion, protective measures are designed to facilitate the reconstruction of files and the restoration of business operations should one or more vital records series be damaged. Protective measures typically apply to **security copies**, sometimes described as *backup copies*, of vital electronic records.

Whether prevention or protection is involved, risk control begins with heightened security awareness formalized in organizational policy and procedures, which must be communicated to every employee who works with vital electronic records. Security of automated systems and the information they store is the responsibility of every employee. A directive from senior management, in the form of a memorandum sent to managers of program units, should acknowledge the critical nature of vital electronic records and emphasize the need to safeguard them. Risk control guidelines should be conspicuously posted in areas where vital electronic records are stored or used. One person in each program unit should be assigned specific responsibility for the implementation of risk control guidelines; ideally, that person will also serve as the program unit's records management liaison. Program unit managers should review risk control policies and procedures at staff meetings. The records manager should be available as a resource person to address such meetings and clarify risk control policies and procedures. To publicize the vital records initiative, the records manager can prepare articles on vital electronic records and the importance of risk control for employee newsletters, intranet Web pages, or other in-house publications.

Preventive Measures

Preventive risk control measures address the physical environment where electronic records are stored and used. To the greatest extent possible, storage facilities for vital electronic records should be located in areas where floods and destructive weather are unlikely. Locations near chemical manufacturing facilities, power plants, airport landing routes, and other potential hazards should also be avoided. Often, records managers have little control over the geographic locations where working copies of vital records are maintained, but they can specify the locations of storage copies. Because electrical system failures can lead to equipment failures that may damage vital electronic records, electrical outlets should be protected by circuit breakers and surge suppressers. Such controls are routinely encountered in centralized computer installations, but they may not be implemented at decentralized departmental sites. Storage areas for vital electronic records should contain zone-controlled smoke detection and fire extinguishing equipment that conforms to requirements outlined in local fire codes. Environmental controls and media handling precautions discussed elsewhere in this book also apply to vital electronic records.

Certain preventive risk control measures promote the physical security of vital records against malicious destruction, corruption, theft, or access by unauthorized persons.

- **Centralized filing repositories.** Securing one storage location is easier than securing many storage locations. Whenever possible, centralized filing repositories should be designated for offline storage of working copies of vital electronic records contained on removable magnetic or optical media. Commonly encountered examples of such filing repositories include the magnetic tape libraries associated with centralized computer installations and the videotape libraries associated with corporate or institutional television studio facilities.

- **Media repositories.** Media repositories should be situated away from high traffic locations, preferably in areas without windows.

- **Authorized access.** Access to media repositories should be restricted to authorized individuals who have a specific business reason for entering such areas. Badges should identify authorized individuals. Employees in the vicinity of a media filing area should be instructed to challenge and report suspect persons who enter the area. Media filing areas should not be included in building tours designed to impress visitors.

- **Access entrance.** Access to media repositories should be limited to a single supervised entrance. Other doors should be configured as emergency exits with strike bars and audible alarms.

- **Vital records media.** All media that contain vital records should be stored in the designated repository when not in use. Media should not be removed from the repository until they are ready for processing, and they should be returned to the repository immediately following processing. All media and containers should be examined on entry into or removal from the repository.

- **Circulation control records.** Circulation control records should be kept for every medium removed from the repository. For each transaction, such circulation control records should contain:

  - A medium identifier;
  - A borrower identifier;
  - The time and date the medium was removed;
  - The purpose for which the medium was removed;
  - The location to which the medium was taken; and
  - The time and date when the medium is to be returned.

Several vendors offer media tracking software that employs bar codes to facilitate entry of media and borrower identifiers. Such products resemble library circulation control systems, which have been computerized for several decades. They will track the locations of specific media, block unauthorized removals, and generate lists of media scheduled to be returned or are past due.

- **Unattended repositories.** Media repositories should never be accessible when unsupervised. They should be locked when unattended.

> *Where vital electronic records are maintained in user areas, security is difficult to enforce and easily compromised.*

The foregoing security procedures are most easily implemented in centralized installations where media repositories are located within a computer room that is itself secure. Similar conditions may apply to centralized storage facilities for video or audio recordings. Where vital electronic records are maintained in user areas, security is difficult to enforce and easily compromised. Desktop computers and departmental servers may be unavoidably located in high-traffic office areas, and their media may be stored at individual workstations rather than in supervised, centralized repositories where access can be controlled. Mobile computing devices and associated media that contain vital electronic records are obviously vulnerable to theft, misplacement, or other loss when used out of the office.

Despite these complications, certain security precautions can effectively reduce the vulnerability of vital electronic records created and maintained by desktop computers and departmental servers as shown in Figure 6.1.

Security
Precautions for
Vital Electronic
Records

Figure 6.1

Precautions for Securing Vital Electronic Records on Desktop and Departmental Servers

- **Authorized employees.** Access to computer workstations must be restricted to authorized employees. To the greatest extent practical, the installation of computer workstations should be limited to supervised areas. Employees should be instructed to challenge and report unauthorized persons who attempt to use them.

- **Usernames and passwords.** Access procedures for remote computers or network file servers should not be posted near computer workstations or discussed with unauthorized persons. An effective method of user authentication is critical to prevent electronic intrusion. Access to vital electronic records and their associated software should be controlled by passwords or personal identification numbers. Such identifiers typically consist of strings of alphanumeric characters that may be system-assigned or specified by individual users. Where users are allowed to construct their own passwords, they should be instructed to avoid personal names or other easily guessed character strings. Group passwords should be avoided.

- **Password protection.** Access software should blot out or otherwise suppress the display of passwords when they are entered. Passwords should not be posted near terminals or LAN workstations. They should not be printed on reports, listings, word processing documents, or other computer-generated output. If a master list of passwords is maintained in a computer file, it should be encrypted. Passwords should be changed at regular intervals and immediately invalidated on transfer, retirement, resignation, or termination of employees to whom they were assigned. Passwords should automatically expire if not used for a specified period of time.

- **Password levels, limitations, and supplements.** Passwords should be associated with specific privileges such as the ability to retrieve records (read privileges) or to add records to a file (write privileges). The ability to edit or delete vital records should be limited to those employees with a demonstrable need to perform such operations in the execution of assigned work responsibilities. Continuing need for specific access privileges should be verified at regular intervals. In applications requiring high security, two or more levels of password protection can be utilized. Alternatively, password protection may be supplemented or replaced by other user authentication and access control procedures such as hardware-based access methods that require possession of special keys or bionic verification methods. Examples of the latter include systems that recognize signatures, voiceprints, fingerprints, palm geometry, or eye retinal patterns.

- **Computer workstations.** Computer workstations should be turned off—and locked, if possible—when not in use. They should never be left unattended while operational. System software should automatically terminate a computer session after a predetermined period of inactivity. For organizations connected to the Internet, mission-critical applications and vital electronic records should be isolated from publicly-accessible computer resources.

- **Desktop computers.** Desktop computers should be attached to work surfaces to avoid loss of information stored on internal hard drives. Where physical attachment of computers is impractical, the computer's system unit should be secured against the removal of hard drives. All computer equipment should bear ownership tags or similar identification. Employees should be instructed to challenge and report persons who attempt to remove computer equipment from work areas.

- **Network drives.** Vital electronic records should be stored on network drives rather than in desktop computers. Thin clients, which lack local storage capabilities, force such procedures. Alternatively, local hard drives can be disabled to prevent their use for data storage.

- **Removable media.** Magnetic tapes, optical disks, and other removable media should never be left unattended on work surfaces. Such media should be kept in locked drawers or cabinets until ready for processing and returned to their storage locations immediately after use.

- **Mobile devices.** Confidential personal data, trade secrets, or other sensitive information should not be stored in mobile computing devices. If this practice is unavoidable, the devices should never be left unattended.

Special security procedures and precautions are necessary to prevent contamination of computer programs and vital electronic records by viruses and other malicious software. Because most viruses are believed to enter computer systems through software, a centralized authority should be established to approve software procurement and installations for all computers in the organization. Software should not be purchased or installed on any computer without authorization. Software should be purchased new in sealed packages from known suppliers. Computer programs downloaded from publicly-accessible information services or bulletin boards are widely suspected as sources of viral contamination and should be avoided. Newly acquired software should be processed by anti-viral programs that can detect and remove viruses. While such programs can identify and/or disable many viruses, they are not completely effective and must be combined with other preventive and protective measures outlined here.

Clues to the presence of viruses include changes in directory entries, file modification dates, volume labels, and program file sizes. Computer users should be instructed to monitor such indicators and report any suspect conditions immediately. Infected computers and all copies of potentially infected programs should be removed from service. Infected workstations should be disconnected from computer networks.

Protective Measures

Protective measures for vital electronic records are designed to support the restoration of mission-critical operations in the event of a disaster. Whether electronic or nonelectronic vital records are involved, such protective measures have historically relied on specially-designed storage enclosures and purposeful duplication of records for offsite storage. These measures are most effective when combined.

Specially-designed filing cabinets, vaults, and other storage enclosures provide onsite protection of vital electronic records against certain threats enumerated previously. Vital electronic records can be protected against theft, for example, by storing them in locked file cabinets, safes, or vaults. Underwriters' Laboratories rates file cabinets for their resistance to tampering. Insulated storage containers offer some protection against fire by limiting the records' exposure to potentially destructive heat. Underwriters' Laboratories rates the fire-resistant properties of insulated storage containers in terms of the hours of protection they provide against specified temperatures and humidity conditions. For effective protection of magnetic and optical media, fire-resistant containers should bear the UL Class 125 designation. During a fire, such containers will maintain an internal temperature below 125 degrees Fahrenheit at an ambient temperature of 1,700 Fahrenheit, which is thought to be a safe level for magnetic and optical media. A cabinet, safe, or vault with a UL Class 125-1 rating will provide effective protection against damaging heat for one hour, but a UL Class 125-2 rating, which provides two hours of protection, is preferable. Insulated enclosures should also protect vital electronic records against vapor penetration and fire hose streams for the indicated periods. Because insulated filing cabinets, safes, vaults, and other fire-resistant enclosures can be damaged by severe impact, the buildings in which they are installed must be able to resist structural collapse for the UL-rated exposure period. To further reduce vulnerability to damage, fire-resistant storage enclosures should be locked in areas where they will not be exposed to heavy falling objects.

> *The production of backup copies of essential files at predetermined intervals is routine operating procedures in centralized computer installations.*

Tamperproof and fire-resistant storage containers can prove useful in certain situations, but the most effective approach to vital records protection involves the purposeful preparation of backup copies for storage at secure offsite locations at a sufficient distance from the originals as not to be affected by the same disasters. The production of backup copies of essential files at predetermined intervals is routine operating procedures in centralized computer installations. In desktop computer and departmental server installations, where procedures are less routinized, backup operations may be performed sporadically, if at all. For effective vital records protection, backup responsibilities must be clearly delineated. Backup schedules must be established and rigidly enforced.

Backup procedures have historically been considered essential for information stored on hard drives, because such devices are vulnerable to head crashes and other hardware malfunctions that imperil recorded information. Backup is also important for magnetic tapes, optical disks, and other removable media which, while not subject to head crashes, can be damaged in various ways discussed elsewhere in this book. Backup media selected for vital electronic records must satisfy the security and recoverability requirements of applications with which they are associated. In some computer installations, files stored on one hard drive are copied onto another. RAID arrays, as described in Chapter 2, provide redundant recording for fault-tolerant operation. For reliable vital records protection, however, backup copies are typically made on removable media, which can be stored offsite. Historically, magnetic tapes have been the dominant media for hard drive backup in centralized computer installations. Optical disks, which may be used to backup data stored by personal computers, typically lack sufficient capacity to backup network hard drives.

Some computers may be backed up completely on a daily basis, but most computer installations employ a combination of full and incremental backup operations. A full backup tape contains copies of all data files recorded on a given hard drive. Incremental backup tapes contain copies of files that have changed since the last backup of any type. Full backup operations are typically performed weekly, with incremental backups being performed daily, usually at the close of business or at another predetermined time, in the interval between weekly full backups. The contents of a hard drive can be restored from the latest full backup copy followed by the incremental backup copies in the order in which they were produced. In a variation on this approach, differential backup tapes cumulate the contents of previous incremental backups. A hard drive can be restored from the full backup copy and the latest differential backup tape.

Backup tapes are intended specifically and exclusively for data recovery. They should not be confused with *archival tapes*, which contain inactive data transferred from hard drives. To minimize media and storage costs, backup tapes should be retained for the shortest time necessary and recycled—that is, made available for reuse—promptly when their purpose is fulfilled. Retention of backup copies is defined by an organization's backup rotation plan. The following is a typical rotation and retention plan for backup copies:

- For each computer to be backed up, 10 magnetic tapes are labeled with the following designations:

Incremental Daily Backup	Full End-of-Week Backup	Full Monthly Backup
Monday	Friday 1	Month 1
Tuesday	Friday 2	Month 2
Wednesday	Friday 3	
Thursday	Friday 4	

- Each label should also indicate the date the tape was first used, the computer being backed up, and the backup software employed.

- Incremental backups are performed Monday through Thursday at a predetermined time, using the tapes labeled for those days. The resulting backup media are sent to offsite storage at the close of each business day or as soon as possible thereafter.

- A full end-of-week backup is performed on the first, second, and third Friday of each month, using the appropriate labeled media. For months that have five Fridays, a backup tape is prepared on the fourth Friday of the month. These end-of-week backup tapes are sent to offsite storage.

- On the last Friday of each month, a full backup is performed on one of the monthly tapes, beginning with the medium labeled "Month 1." This tape is sent to offsite storage.

- Backup tapes for Monday through Thursday are removed from offsite storage and recycled at the end of the following week. End-of-week and end-of-month tapes are each recycled after 30 days.

Offsite storage repositories for vital electronic records may be established and operated by a business, government agency, or other organization on its own behalf. Alternatively, a commercial storage facility designed specifically for vital electronic records may be utilized. In either case, the offsite storage facility should be located in a secure site. Some vital records repositories are located underground. They feature stringent perimeter security with bonded guards and electronic surveillance apparatus.

Backup copies of vital electronic records should be stored at a sufficient distance from the working copies to be unaffected by the same natural disasters or destructive events. The storage facility must be close enough, however, for convenient delivery of vital electronic records as well as timely retrieval of backup copies to support disaster recovery. For pickup and delivery of records, some in-house and commercial storage facilities offer courier services equipped with environmentally-controlled trucks or vans. Some facilities also support electronic vaulting in which backup copies of vital records are transmitted to offsite storage over high-speed telecommunications facilities. Most storage facilities for vital electronic records are designed for computer-generated media, but they are suitable for video and audio recordings as well. Environmental specifications outlined elsewhere in this book must be observed. Backup electrical generators should be available to maintain environmental controls in the event of power outages. Some facilities will also accept paper documents or microfilm, although the former—being combustible—may be excluded to minimize the danger of fire.

Most storage facilities provide one or more large vaults in which the vital electronic records of different program units or, in the case of commercial repositories, different customers are stored. In some cases, safe-deposit containers or separate rooms may be provided for records requiring special security precautions. To make the best use of available storage space, backup copies of vital electronic records should be made on the densest, most compact media compatible with application requirements. Media compactness is particularly important for customers of commercial vital records storage facilities that base their charges on the type and amount of space consumed.

Real-Time Backup

Real-time backup—variously known as *real-time replication, continuous backup,* or *mirrored backup*—is a disaster recovery method that employs simultaneous or nearly simultaneous recording of information by multiple computers. Changes to a database that resides on one computer, for example, are automatically made in a copy of the database that resides on another computer. Typically, the two computers are located at different sites. Data is recorded on hard drives at both sites. If data processed by a specific application is damaged or otherwise rendered unavailable at the primary site, it can be accessed through the secondary site.

Compared to scheduled tape backup, real-time backup permits faster, more convenient data recovery with only a momentary interruption of mission-critical operations. As an inherent limitation, tape-based backups can recover only data back to the last scheduled backup operation, which was typically performed at the close of business on the previous day. Changes that have occurred since the last backup interval are not recoverable. By contrast, real-time backup permits complete recoverability of changes. It is the only backup method that is well-suited to round-the-clock computer operations that have no "off hours" and tape backup intervals cannot be readily defined by the close of business. Among its other advantages over tape backups, real-time backup requires no media handling and very limited manual intervention.

Backup Computing Arrangements

As previously noted, offsite storage of vital computer records is one component in a risk control plan that includes disaster recovery provisions for computer hardware and software. Those aspects of risk control are typically the responsibility of computer specialists. However, records managers should be aware of available protection options. Hardware recovery provisions are based on the availability of a backup computer site that can be utilized to maintain computing operations if an organization's primary site is destroyed. The backup site must provide hardware identical to or compatible with the organization's own equipment. In businesses, government agencies, or other organizations with distributed data processing operations, compatible backup computing capabilities may exist in branch locations or field offices. In the event of a disaster, processing can be shifted to such alternate sites. Although this approach may apply to minicomputer- and microcomputer-class systems, rarely is a large, costly mainframe computer facility replicated at two or more locations within the same organization.

Some organizations have established reciprocal backup arrangements with a subsidiary, an affiliated company, or an independent organization that employs compatible computer hardware. The reciprocating parties agree to make their computing facilities available to one another in the event of an emergency. Such mutual aid agreements provide a relatively inexpensive means of obtaining backup computing capabilities, but they are often criticized as ineffective. Reciprocal obligations must be clearly established in contracts or other formal agreements signed by responsible officials of both organizations. Terms of the agreement should be reviewed periodically and an implementation plan developed jointly by both parties. Each organization's exposure to risk is, in effect, increased since both organizations must operate with diminished computing capacity if a disaster strikes either of them. Critical processing operations must consequently be identified and prioritized in advance of an emergency. Despite the best intentions, heavy workloads at the reciprocating site may impede effective implementation. Even where reciprocal obligations are specified in writing, they may be difficult to enforce. Legal remedies are possible, but they are unlikely to provide relief in the short time frame essential to restore an organization's computing capabilities.

In most emergency scenarios, disaster recovery plans based on hot sites or cold sites will typically prove more effective than reciprocal backup agreements. A **hot site** is a fully equipped standby computing facility designed for emergency use on short notice, typically within 24 hours of a disaster. Hot sites may be operated by computer manufacturers, commercial service bureaus, or other vendors who specialize in disaster recovery capabilities. They are intended for organizations that cannot tolerate an interruption of computing services. Access to hot sites is typically sold by annual membership fees or subscriptions that allow an organization to use the facility for a specified period of time following notification of an emergency. In addition to subscription fees, daily occupancy and resource usage charges may be imposed during the period of utilization. To minimize the potential for conflicts associated with simultaneous need, the number of subscriptions to a given site is limited. In most cases, use of the hot site is contractually restricted to several weeks or months. Computing equipment at the hot site must be compatible with the customer's own hardware. In some cases, the hot site also provides offsite storage facilities to which backup copies of vital electronic records can be sent in anticipation of an emergency.

A **cold site**, sometimes described as an empty shell, is an unfurnished space suitable for the installation of computing and telecommunications equipment in the event of an emergency. A cold site is a computer-ready facility. It includes raised flooring, utilities, air conditioning, and telecommunication lines. The occupying organization must provide the required hardware, perform installation, and make the facility operational. In an emergency, this task may be accomplished by purchasing new computing and telecommunications equipment for delivery to the cold site or by salvaging hardware from a damaged data processing facility. A cold site may be owned by a single organization and reserved for its own use or shared by several organizations for occupation upon notification of an emergency. In the latter case, access is sold by subscription with daily occupancy charges also imposed. Regardless of the occupancy arrangement, the implementation and activation of a cold site can require considerable advance planning to ensure timely delivery, installation, and testing following an emergency. As an interesting variant of the cold site, some vendors offer computer-ready mobile facilities and modular buildings that can be installed at a customer's own location, usually within several days.

The disaster recovery approaches described previously were developed principally for centralized computer installations. Damaged desktop computers, in stand-alone or networked implementations, are typically replaced by new ones. Although computer replacements can often be accomplished quickly, replacement is rarely immediate. An organization may have spare desktop computers, but network connections and servers take time to install and activate. A period of computer downtime, however brief, is consequently inevitable. During that time, reversion to manual operations based on nonelectronic paper or microfilm records may be necessary. Temporary reversion to manual operations may also be part of a disaster recovery plan for larger computers. In such situations, records managers can make a significant contribution to disaster preparedness by determining the types and locations of paper records likely to be needed in specific applications and developing plans to make them quickly available in an emergency.

The discussion to this point has emphasized protection of vital electronic records and restoration of computer processing capabilities in the event of a disaster. To be effective, however, a disaster recovery plan for computer-processable records must also include provisions for protection of custom-developed software and documentation. As with vital records, software is typically protected through a combination of backup and offsite storage. Magnetic tapes, diskettes, and optical disks are commonly utilized as backup media.

Documentation can be broadly defined as the written information recorded during the development of a computer system. It explains pertinent aspects of that system. Its purpose is to ensure that the details of a system are understood by those persons who have a need to know those details. Documentation may address both hardware and software characteristics of a given system. Vital records protection and disaster recovery plans are most concerned with software documentation, including both developmental and occupational documentation.

As its name suggests, *developmental documentation* provides narrative and graphic descriptions of computer programs. It includes, but is not necessarily limited to, a statement of purpose for a given program; a description of the hardware configuration for which the program is intended, including memory and peripheral equipment requirements; a list of required system software and support programs, including operating systems, assemblers, compilers, interpreters, and utility programs; a discussion of the algorithms employed, including flowcharts or other graphic representations of programming logic; and the program source code as written in assembler or higher-level languages. Operational documentation includes installation and operating instructions for a given program. User training and reference manuals are examples of operational documentation. Regardless of content, documentation may be recorded on paper, on microfilm, or in machine-readable, computer-processible form on magnetic or optical media.

Auditing for Compliance

Once vital electronic records have been identified and appropriate loss control methods specified, the implementation of preventive and protective measures for designated records series will usually be the responsibility of personnel in the program unit that maintains the records. Periodic audits should be performed to confirm compliance. Such audits may be conducted by records management staff or delegated to another organizational unit, such as an internal audit department, that has other compliance-oriented responsibilities. In such cases, auditing for vital records compliance can be coordinated with financial or other auditing activities, thereby simplifying the scheduling of audits as well as saving both time and labor. Internal auditors can report the results of vital records compliance audits to the records manager for follow-up and corrective action where indicated. To gain the attention of top management, the internal audit reports should also be distributed to those persons who receive reports of important financial audits.

Summary

A vital records program is a set of policies and procedures for the systematic, comprehensive, and economical control of losses associated with vital records. Vital records contain information essential to an organization's mission. If such records are damaged, lost, or otherwise rendered unavailable, critical business operations will be curtailed or discontinued, with a resulting adverse impact on the organization. A vital records program involves the identification of vital records, the assessment of risks to which such records are subject, and the implementation of appropriate protection methods. Although traditionally considered a records management responsibility, vital records protection is closely related to other loss-control and contingency-planning activities. The protection of computer-generated records, in particular, is often viewed as a facet of the broader field of computer security and disaster recovery.

In any organization, senior management has ultimate responsibility for the protection of assets, including the protection of vital records. Such responsibility is implied or explicitly stated in several laws and government regulations. In the United States, examples include the Foreign Corrupt Practices Act of 1977, the Federal

Information Management Security Act of 2002, and OMB Circular A-130. Provisions against unauthorized disclosure as a facet of records security are contained in various privacy statutes.

Vital electronic records are typically identified by surveying individual program units. The end product of such a survey is a descriptive list of vital electronic records series. The list should indicate the reason each series is considered vital, the name of the program unit responsible for protecting the series, and the method of protection to be implemented. Because substantial costs are often involved, vital records protection must be limited to those records that are truly essential to mission-critical operations. Vital records must consequently be distinguished from important records. The latter may be very useful to a given program unit, but their loss will not render the unit inoperative. For convenience, a vital records survey can be combined with an inventory of electronic records performed for purposes of preparing retention schedules.

Risk analysis begins with the identification of threats and vulnerabilities to which vital electronic records are subject. Typical risks include malicious or accidental destruction, loss of electronic storage media through theft or misplacement, corruption of electronic records through unauthorized tampering or contamination by computer viruses, and improper disclosure of electronic records through unauthorized access. Risk assessments may be based on qualitative or quantitative methodologies. In either case, assessment considers the probability of loss for specific vital records series and estimates the damage should a given loss occur.

A risk control program for vital electronic records includes preventive and protective measures. Preventive measures are the first line of defense against risk. Properly implemented, they minimize the probability of loss. Addressing the physical environment where vital electronic records are stored, preventive measures involve safeguards against malicious destruction, theft, corruption, or unauthorized access. Such safeguards apply to both security and working copies of vital electronic records. Protective measures, in contrast, facilitate the reconstruction of vital electronic records in the event of loss. Applying principally to security copies, protective measures rely on specially designed media enclosures and purposeful duplication of electronic media for offsite storage. Whether prevention or protection is involved, effective risk control depends on heightened awareness of security concerns, as formalized in organizational policies and procedures communicated to all employees who work with vital electronic records.

For computer-processible information, vital records protection is one component in a risk control plan that also includes disaster recovery provisions for computer hardware and software. Hardware recovery procedures are usually based on the availability of a backup computer site that can be utilized in the event that an organization's primary site is damaged. Software recovery plans rely on offsite storage of backup copies of programs and documentation.

To be effective, a vital records protection program must include compliance auditing. Rather than being performed by records management staff, audit responsibilities can be delegated to another organizational unit such as an internal audit department. In such cases, vital records compliance can be coordinated with financial or other auditing activities.

Notes

1   This idea is forcefully stated in Corpus Juris Secundum, a comprehensive legal encyclopedia that presents the principles of U.S. law as derived from legislation and reported cases. According to Volume 19, Section 491, corporate officers "owe a duty to the corporation to be vigilant and to exercise ordinary or reasonable care and diligence and the utmost good faith and fidelity to conserve the corporate property; and, if a loss or depletion of assets results from their willful or negligent failure to perform their duties, or to a willful or fraudulent abuse of their trust, they are liable, provided such losses were the natural and necessary consequences of omission on their part."

2   Operational risk encompasses legal risks resulting from failure to comply with laws, regulations, or contractual obligations.

Chapter 7

Managing Electronic Files and Media

The task of organizing electronic records resembles its paper counterpart in certain respects. As described in Chapter 3, computer-processible electronic records pertaining to a particular business operation or activity are grouped in files, which are created by a computer's operating system and application programs at the time the records are entered and saved. Depending on the application and the type of information being stored, a computer file may contain one or more records. A data file, for example, typically consists of multiple records, while a word processing file often contains the equivalent of a single document. An image file may similarly contain one or more graphic images. Depending on the application, files may be recorded on magnetic disks, magnetic tapes, optical disks, or other media. Although the term "file" is seldom applied to audio and video recordings, parallels can be drawn with individual audio selections or video programs recorded on magnetic tapes, optical disks, or other media. As computer-stored audio and video information becomes more commonplace, "audio file" and "video file" are likely to be more widely utilized as descriptive terms. The following discussion emphasizes computer files, but some points are also applicable to audio and video records.

Within a given computer storage medium, files are organized into directories created and managed by the computer's operating system under which the files were created. A **directory** is a table of contents for a specific medium. Directory information varies with the operating system employed in a given computer configuration. File name, file size, and the date the file was last modified are typical directory data elements. Certain media, such as magnetic tapes and diskettes, usually have a single directory. The higher the storage capacity of a given medium, however, the more likely it is to contain multiple directories, each storing files of a particular type. Such multiple directories are commonly termed *subdirectories*. They can be effectively utilized to group logically related files recorded on hard drives, hard disk cartridges, high-capacity floppy disks, and optical disks. Often, subdirectories are themselves subdivided, thereby creating a hierarchy of logically subordinate and superordinate directories. The permissible number and structure of such hierarchical subdivisions is determined by the operating system in use in a particular installation.

In some cases, a given magnetic or optical disk is partitioned into segments called **volumes**. Each volume is treated as the logical equivalent of a disk drive, even though it shares a physical drive with other volumes. Volumes are sometimes created to divide high-capacity storage devices into smaller, more manageable units. A multigigabyte hard disk drive or optical disk cartridge, for example, may be partitioned into two or more volumes, each of which will be used for a specific application. In some cases, a computer's operating system imposes limits on volume size. Where the capacity of a given storage device exceeds the permissible volume size, the device must be partitioned into multiple volumes; for example, with early versions of the MS-DOS operating system. Newer operating systems are designed to accommodate very high-capacity storage peripherals, and they rarely have such a problem. As discussed in Chapter 2, the capacities of storage devices and media are increasing rapidly, and new computers must support the latest models.

In computer configurations, files, directories, volumes, and physical storage media are sometimes equated with cabinets, drawers, folders, and other familiar components of paper-based filing systems. The comparison, while useful, is necessarily forced. In graphical computing environments, such as Microsoft Windows or the Macintosh operating system, the information displayed when a computer is first turned on is described as a *desktop*. Storage peripherals, such as local and network hard drives, floppy disk drives, and optical disk drives—or predefined logical volumes within those devices—are represented by labeled icons in the desktop display. If the computer's desktop is analogous to a file room, the storage peripherals, and their fixed or removable recording media, are the computer-based counterparts of file cabinets. Depending on the computer configuration, they may be locally installed or network resources.

When a given storage device is selected, usually through mouse operations, the computer's operating system displays a directory for the device's recording medium. A root directory, which is displayed first, provides an overview of the medium's contents. Although the root directory may contain files, it is typically divided into subdirectories, based on specific computing tasks or business operations. With most graphical operating systems, subdirectories are depicted as folders, but they are more properly compared to file drawers, or portions of drawers. Subdirectories may contain application programs or files. The latter are represented by icons that depict their formats or associated application programs. Alternatively, subdirectories may contain folders, which represent hierarchically subordinate directories. Those folders may contain files or additional folders. With some computer operating systems, directories and subdirectories can be displayed in a tree-like structure that reflects their hierarchical relationships. Subdirectories can be nested to many levels, but complex hierarchical structures can prove difficult to understand and navigate.

Labels and Names

The effective management of electronic records requires careful attention to directory organization, file grouping and naming practices, and media labeling. In centralized computing facilities, such tasks may be highly formalized. Directory structures and file names are determined by programmers, while media labels are prepared by tape librarians and others responsible for offline storage of removable media. File names may be abbreviated, but they usually reflect the file's purpose or content. Many personal computer users, however, have developed their own, often idiosyncratic, approaches to file and media management. Directory and file names may be cryptic, giving little indication of either purpose or content. Subdirectories may be created haphazardly, with little regard for hierarchical relationships. Unrelated files may be stored in the same subdirectory, while related information is scattered among multiple subdirectories at several hierarchical levels. Problems associated with these practices are similar to those encountered with poorly managed paper files. Information needed for a given purpose cannot be located, necessitating time-wasting searches through directories and tedious examination of individual files.

> *Clear, complete labeling is essential to the identification of removable storage media such as magnetic tapes, hard disk cartridges, floppy disks, and optical disks.*

To minimize or eliminate such problems, a systematic program for the management of electronic records must provide guidelines for labeling media, organizing directories, and naming files. Clear, complete labeling is essential to the identification of removable storage media such as magnetic tapes, hard disk cartridges, floppy disks, and optical disks. Descriptive information about computer, video, and audio media should include, but will not necessarily be limited to, the following:

- Name of the program unit that created the removable storage medium or on whose behalf it was created.

- Name or type of computer, video, or audio system on which the medium is to be used, unless it can easily be determined by physical examination of the medium itself (as is the case, for example, with certain video and audio tapes).

- Name and version number of the application software with which the recorded information is to be used—for computer media.

- A list of files, applications, video programs, audio recordings, or other information recorded on the medium. For computer media, file locations are automatically recorded in directory listings generated by the computer's operating system. The directory is recorded on the medium itself. In graphical operating environments, distinctive icons typically identify the computer programs that were used to create specific files. For video and audio tapes that contain more than one program, media labels should indicate the physical locations where particular programs begin. The location may be expressed as an odometer reading that represents the distance from the beginning of a tape. Alternatively, some video and audio tape recorders generate electronic codes that mark the starting locations of individual programs. In either case, a list of odometer settings or program numbers must be manually prepared.

- Media capacity and/or recording density, if not indicated on the medium itself.
- Serial number of other unique identifier.
- Date or span of dates during which information was recorded onto the medium.
- Special storage and handling instructions, including security classifications and access restrictions where applicable.
- The medium's status as a working copy, backup copy, storage copy, etc.
- Special recording procedures that can affect the way in which a given medium will be played back or otherwise utilized. Examples include the use of Dolby noise reduction with audio tapes, stereo mode recording of VHS video tapes, or compressed recording of files onto computer media.

As a practical consideration, the data elements listed above will not fit on the relatively small labels provided with most computer, video, and audio media. In such cases, label contents can be limited to a serial number or other brief identifiers, with more complete information being recorded in a separate database or logbook. Various vendors offer color-coded adhesive labels that can identify magnetic tapes, optical disk cartridges, and other media by serial number. Where the shelf-type filing cabinets described later in this chapter are utilized, such color-coded labels can facilitate detection of misfiled media in large collections. Internal volume labels should be assigned to removable computer media to permit identification if their physical labels become detached or defaced. Volume labels can consist of serial numbers or other unique identifiers. In addition to maintaining descriptive information about an electronic medium in human-readable form, it can be stored as a word processing document or other text file on the medium itself.

As noted previously, low-capacity computer media, such as conventional diskettes, usually contain a single directory. Unrelated files should not be intermixed within such media. Low-capacity diskettes should be dedicated to specific applications or business operations. A given diskette might be reserved for files created by a specific word processing program, for example. More restrictively, a diskette might be limited to files created with a specific word processing program and pertaining to a particular business activity such as a specific project. If voluminous information is involved, additional restrictions may be appropriate. Separate diskettes may be maintained for specific types of word processing documents such as project correspondence or project reports. Alternatively, files produced by different computer programs may be combined on a single medium, provided that they are logically related. A diskette may contain word processing files and spreadsheet files pertaining to a specific business activity, such as budget preparation, or a specific project. Storage of interrelated files on a given medium is made practical by the availability of office suites and other integrated software packages that can exchange files created by different application programs.

With higher-capacity media, such as hard drives and optical disks, similar restrictions should be applied to directories and subdirectories. Computer users should not mix unrelated files within directories. Separate directories should be created for specific programs or business operations. Such directories can be divided into subdirectories that reflect the logical interrelationships of file types associated with specific computer applications or business activities. As an example, a separate directory might be established for each computer program installed on a personal computer. In a graphical operating environment, each directory would be pictorially represented as a folder labeled with the name of the computer application, such as Microsoft Word, WordPerfect, or Excel. Each directory might be organized into subdirectories, which are pictorially represented as labeled folders within directory folders. One subdirectory might contain the application program such as Microsoft Word for Windows and its related files (help files, spelling dictionaries, thesauri, grammar checkers, and so on). Additional subdirectories might be established for specific types of word processing documents—such as correspondence, memoranda, and reports—that are created and processed by the program. These subdirectories might be further divided topically, chronologically, or in some other way.

Some computer users prefer to group application programs in a single directory, with separate subdirectories for each program and its supporting files. Data, text, or other files created and processed by those application programs can be logically organized in other directories by business activity. As another example, an engineer who works on four projects simultaneously might create a single directory for application programs and separate directories for each project. The application directory might be divided into subdirectories for individual programs—such as Microsoft Word for Windows, Excel, and AutoCAD—that support project-related tasks. In a graphical operating environment, the four project directories would be represented by folders, labeled with the project name or other identifier. Subdirectories might be created for specific project-related information such as word processing files, spreadsheet files, and CAD design files.

Regardless of organization, meaningful, informative directory and file names are critical for convenient, accurate identification of desired electronic records stored on a given medium. Most operating systems display the contents of directories and subdirectories in a tree-like structure that reflects their hierarchical interrelationships. Alternatively, directories, subdirectories, and files may be listed alphabetically, by name, or chronologically, by the date they were created or last modified. In any case, folder labels or other names assigned to media directories and subdirectories should clearly indicate their scope, enabling users to determine the likely directory and subdirectory locations of desired files. File names should likewise indicate the contents and/or purpose of programs, documents, databases, images, or other information that the files contain.

With commercially available software packages, directory and file names are assigned automatically when a given package is installed onto a hard drive or other storage medium. Default names, determined by the software's developer, can be modified by computer users, but this change is seldom done. Other directories and subdirectories must be named by computer users when they are created. Files created by specific programs are similarly named when they are initially saved. Rules for naming directories and files are defined by computer operating systems. Older operating systems, some of which remain in use, impose significant restrictions on file names. With MS-DOS, for example, file names are divided into two parts: the file name proper and an optional extension. File names can be one to eight characters in length. They may contain alphabetic characters, numeric digits, selected punctuation marks, and certain other symbols. The optional extension usually describes the type of information that an MS-DOS file contains. As described in Chapter 3, it consists of one to three characters and is separated from the file name by a period. Widely encountered MS-DOS extensions include "exe," "com," and "bat" for program files; "doc" for word processing files; "txt" for ASCII text files; "wks" for spreadsheet files; "dat" and "dbf" for databases; and "bak" for backup files. Image files are often identified by extensions, such as "tif" or "gif," that indicate the graphic format utilized for image recording. These MS-DOS extensions are so widely recognized that they are sometimes employed for files created by other computer operating systems, including those that do not specify rules for file extensions.

Given the eight-character limit on MS-DOS file names, it could prove difficult, though not impossible, to construct mnemonic names that adequately reflected file contents and were readily comprehensible. A name like "Q1PROG97.RPT" might be assigned to a word processing file that contained the first quarterly progress report of 1997 for a particular project. Word processing files that contained subsequent quarterly reports for that year could be named "Q2PROG97.RPT," "Q3PROG97.RPT," and "Q4PROG97.RPT." Similarly, spreadsheet files that contained quarterly budget estimates might be named "Q1BDGT97.WKS," "Q2BDGT97.WKS," and so on. Newer computer operating systems impose fewer restrictions on the length and character content of file names. As their principal advantage, long file names permit the construction of informative labels that meaningfully describe a file's purpose. Windows file names can contain up to 255 characters, including letters of the alphabet, numeric digits, spaces, and many other symbols, subject to some restrictions. Windows file names are displayed as typed, but upper- and lowercase characters are considered identical when selecting file names. Unix file names can contain up to 256 characters, including letters of the alphabet, numeric digits, and many other symbols. Certain symbols, reserved by the Unix operating system for other purposes, are excluded. Unix file names are case-sensitive. With the Macintosh operating system, file names can contain up to 255 characters, including any character except the colon.

Formalized guidelines for media and volume labeling, directory structures, and file names can simplify and routinize the organization of information recorded on computer media; however, it often happens that a given file, known to be recorded on a given medium, cannot be found. The file name may have been forgotten or misunderstood, for example, or the file may have been renamed or moved to another subdirectory. Similar problems, typically attributable to misfiling, can arise in well-organized paper filing installations. When they do, users must manually search through all or part of a file drawer or group of drawers to locate a desired document. With computer storage media, such manual searches—which necessitate the sequential inspection of individual files—can prove prohibitively time-consuming and logistically impractical. The number of files stored on a given diskette is limited by media capacity, but hard drives, hard disk cartridges, and optical disks may contain thousands or tens of thousands of files.

This problem is addressed by utility programs that can locate specified files recorded on a given magnetic or optical medium. Such utility programs are often bundled with computer operating systems. The user specifies a filename to be matched and the storage medium to be searched. Depending on the program, the user may specify an exact match of the filename or a substring match, the latter including left or right truncation as well as embedded character strings. Some utility programs can also perform or limit searches by file type, date created or last modified, size, or other attributes. Certain utility programs will search the complete contents of files, rather than file labels, for specified words, phrases, or other character strings. Such programs display segments of files that contain the specified character string and its surrounding context for operator examination.

Document Management and ECM

As an alternative to directory and subdirectory schemes based on a computer operating system's file management capabilities, document / content management software can organize, store, retrieve, track, provide controlled access to, and otherwise manage electronic records. Document management products date from the late 1980s and early 1990s when software developers began introducing programs to create and maintain organized, searchable repositories of digital documents in text and image formats. Going beyond document storage and retrieval, however, document management products offered additional functionality to support the document preparation and approval process. As their most notable innovation, they integrated document storage and retrieval with word processing programs, spreadsheet software, presentation aids, desktop publishing tools, and other document authoring components.

Successive generations of document management products have enhanced this capability. Electronic documents can be saved in a designated repository from within their originating applications at the time they are created. When a document is retrieved, it can be reviewed and edited by authorized persons within its originating application. Among their other features, document management products allow electronic documents to be annotated, and they will track changes and conclusively identify the latest versions of documents that are subject to multiple revisions. These capabilities are particularly useful for legal briefs, contracts and agreements, engineering specifications, regulatory submissions, standard operating procedures, and other documents that are subject to multiple revisions and a prescribed approval process.

Since the late 1990s, document management software developers have reconceptualized and enhanced their products to accommodate a wider variety of digital content, including Web pages, blogs, wikis, video clips, and audio clips. These broader configurations are collectively described as *electronic content management (ECM)* products or *content management systems (CMS)*. Document management, including digital imaging and text retrieval functionality, is one of their components. At the time of this writing, available ECM software supported various combinations of the following features and capabilities as standard or optional components:

- **Multiple repositories.** Customers can create multiple repositories for collections of digital documents or other types of electronic records. Individual repositories can be established for specific business operations or document collections.

- **Content aggregation.** ECM software can populate a repository by aggregating electronic records from multiple sources. The electronic records can be stored on local or network drives in any accessible locations. One purpose of content aggregation is to establish an ECM platform as the single source for storage and retrieval of electronic records that come within the scope of an organization's content management initiatives.

- **Multiple file formats.** Content management software can accommodate digital content in multiple file formats, including text and graphic formats. A content management repository can accommodate, but is not limited to, word processing documents, spreadsheets, presentations, digitized document images, digital photographs, CAD files, Web pages, computer-generated reports, digitized video recordings, and digitized audio recordings. Electronic records in different formats can be comingled within folders and subfolders.

- **Content translation.** Content management software can convert digital content from one file format to another. All documents entering a repository can be automatically converted from their native formats to the PDF format, for example.

- **Version control.** Content management software can track successive revisions of electronic records. Revision histories are tracked, and the latest versions of word processing documents, spreadsheets, presentations, CAD files, and other digital content will be clearly identified. If desired, content management software can restrict or prohibit access to obsolete versions. Content management software can also store multiple renditions of an electronic record. The renditions may differ in file format, language, or other characteristics.

- **Customer-defined taxonomies.** Content management software can organize digital content according to customer-defined file plans (file taxonomies) consisting of folders with multiple levels of subfolders. Depending on the implementation, digital content can be assigned to specific folders and subfolders by batch transfers, dragging and dropping individual files, or from their originating applications at the time a file is saved. Some content management vendors offer pre-built file taxonomies for specific applications such as biomedical research, human resources, sales and marketing, finance, and engineering project management.

- **Customer-defined indexing.** Content management software can index digital content according to customer-defined categories. Digital content can be indexed at the folder, subfolder, and/or individual file levels.

- **Full-text indexing.** Content management software can index the character-coded content of word processing documents, presentations, email messages, and other text files.

- **Automatic categorization.** Content management products can analyze the characteristics of specific electronic records and assign them to folders and subfolders within a user-defined file plan without human intervention. Categorization products, sometimes described as *categorization engines*, employ synonym lists, pattern-matching algorithms, word clustering, word frequencies, word proximities, and other lexical and statistical concepts and tools to analyze an electronic record's content and identify words or phrases for categorization purposes. Some categorization engines employ rule-based approaches in which certain words or phrases are associated with specific categories in a customer-defined file taxonomy. Other categorization engines use an example-based approach in which electronic records are compared to a training set of documents previously categorized by a knowledgeable person.

- **Controlled access.** Content management software can assign and monitor access privileges for specific digital content. It can limit input, retrieval, and/or modification of digital content to authorized persons or groups of persons at the folder, subfolder, and file level. The software will also create an audit trail of all successful retrieval operations and failed access attempts.

- **Repository browsing.** Authorized users can search for digital content by browsing through folders and subfolders. To facilitate such browsing, the file plan for a given repository will be displayed as a tree-like hierarchy.

- **Metadata search.** Authorized users can search for digital content by assigned values in specific metadata fields at the folder, subfolder, and individual file level. Such metadata may contain descriptive or index information. For a word processing document, for example, metadata may include the file name, the name of the author, the dates the document was initially created or last edited, the size of the file, the language in which the document was written, a subject heading, and keywords. Boolean operations can be used to combine multiple metadata values in a single search.

- **Full-text search.** When full-text indexing is applied, authorized users can search for word processing documents, e-mail messages, and other character-coded files that contain specific words or phrases.

- **Federated search.** Much discussed in library applications, **federated searching** involves simultaneous searching of multiple information resources. Results obtained from the various sources are merged and presented to the searcher in consistent format. In some cases, duplication is eliminated. When supported by content management software, authorized users can search multiple repositories in a single retrieval operation, thereby creating a virtual unified repository as a composite of individual information silos. With some ECM products, federated searches can encompass external information sources, such as databases, Web sites on the public Internet or an organizational intranet, blogs, listservices, shared files stored on network drives, SharePoint sites, and online information services.

- **Automated summaries.** Content management software will extract relevant passages to create abstracts of retrieved records. The summaries display high-lighted search terms and their surrounding context.

- **Webtop client:** Authorized persons can use a Web browser to add documents to specific repositories, initiate searches, and perform other software functions. Special client software is not required. Some content management software also allows authorized persons to use popular e-mail clients, such as Microsoft Outlook, to perform repository searches.

- **Collaboration space.** Content management software permits document-based, private collaboration among designated persons—for example, in-house attor-neys and external counsel working on a legal matter, engineers and external con-sultants working on a technical project, or investment bankers and clients work-ing on a merger or acquisition deal. In effect, this function establishes a separate virtual repository for collaboration purposes. Contents of the collaboration repository may be drawn from other ECM repositories. The collaboration space also supports instant messaging, real-time computer conferencing, or other functionality.

- **Web content management.** Content management software allows authorized persons to incorporate digital content into Web pages on the public Internet and organizational intranets. Some products also support version control function-ality for Web site content.

- **Digital asset management.** Content management software manages rights and permissions for photograph collections, digitized art works, video recordings, conference call recordings, recorded depositions, and other audio-visual media. Some products also facilitate the incorporation of such media into documents, presentations, or other electronic records.

- **Enterprise reports management.** Content management software creates a repository of computer-generated reports for online retrieval by authorized per-sons. In this respect, ECM software is a more functional successor to **computer-output laser disk (COLD)** technology, which formerly used optical disks to store electronic versions of computer-generated reports.

When an electronic record is retrieved from a content management repository, it is opened by the application that created it. Where that application is not available to the retrieval workstation, the record may be opened by a viewer program that can accommodate multiple file formats, including old or obsolete formats associ-ated with supplanted versions of specific software products or with discontinued software.

Records Management Application Software

Like the ECM products a **records management application (RMA)** is a category of computer software that organizes, stores, retrieves, and otherwise manages records. As its distinctive characteristic, however, RMA software provides retention functionality that is absent from ECM products, which are principally intended for active electronic records that are subject to frequent retrieval and, in many cases, changes. By contrast, RMA software manages records in the inactive phase of the information life cycle. Specifically, RMA software provides a reliable repository for retention of inactive records. RMA software can identify records eligible for destruction in conformity with an organization's retention policies. Although RMA products can track the retention status of paper and photographic records stored in file rooms or offsite locations, they are more closely associated with electronic records.

Baseline functionality and desirable characteristics of RMA software are delineated in DoD 5015.2-STD, *Design Criteria Standard for Electronic Records Management Software Applications*, which was first issued by the U.S. Department of Defense in 1997. The Defense Information Systems Agency's Joint Interoperability Test Command tests RMA products to verify compliance with requirements specified in DoD 5015.2-STD. The U.S. National Archives and Records Administration has endorsed DoD 5015.2-STD for use by U.S. government agencies when selecting RMA software to store electronic records as official copies and to facilitate the transfer of permanent electronic records to the National Archives. Other organizations, including businesses, not-for-profit institutions, and state and local government agencies, have also found DoD 5015.2-STD useful in establishing criteria for evaluation and selection of RMA products. The Model Requirements for the Management of Electronic Records (MoReq), developed for the European Commission by Cornwell Affiliates, provides specifications that can be used to evaluate RMA products.

> *An RMA repository is organized into folders that correspond to categories in a user-defined file plan, which is based on a hierarchical folder / subfolder model.*

RMA software is compatible with many types of digital content, including database records, digital documents, Web pages, audio files, and video files. It creates an organized repository for electronic records, which may be transferred to the repository from office productivity software, e-mail systems, CAD programs, imaging software, workgroup collaboration software, or other originating applications. An RMA repository is organized into folders that correspond to categories in a user-defined file plan, which is based on a hierarchical folder / subfolder model. As an example, a file plan for contract records might provide a master folder for each contract with subfolders for proposals, signed contracts, amendments, invoices, payment authorizations, and other types of contract-related documents. Similarly, a file plan for archived e-mail might provide a master folder for each mail user with subfolders for each year or other time period when e-mail is transferred into the repository.

A carefully designed file plan for electronic records is a precondition for successful implementation of RMA software. File plan development is a significant effort that involves investigative, prototype, and test phases:

1. **Investigative phase.** The developer must identify record types to be stored in an RMA repository, as well as issues and concerns to be addressed by the file plan. For contract documents, for example, the investigative phase will require a detailed examination of records and filing methods for selected active and/or terminated contracts. The developer must also interview persons who are knowledgeable about contract documentation requirements and filing practices. Whenever possible, the developer will obtain and study file plans developed by government agencies and other organizations for comparable document collections.

2. **Prototype phase.** The developer will prepare a draft file plan, accompanied by instructions and appropriate supporting procedures. The draft file plan will specify how the RMA repository will be organized and indexed as well as retention periods keyed to file categories at the folder, subfolder, or document level. The draft plan should also include procedures that define responsibilities for transferring electronic records to the RMA repository and instructions for filing specific types of electronic records. The draft file plan will be circulated among knowledgeable persons for review and suggestions. One or more group meetings may be needed to clarify the reviewers' comments and criticisms, which will be incorporated into a revised draft to be recirculated for further review and comment. Several additional drafts may be required to produce an acceptable prototype file plan.

3. **Test phase.** The prototype file plan will be implemented using the selected RMA product and tested on several collections of electronic records. The developer will monitor this pilot implementation, discuss the prototype plan with users and other interested parties, and make further revisions to the file plan in order to ultimately produce an operational version, which will be reviewed periodically and modified as necessary to address changing requirements.

RMA repositories can import electronic records in a variety of file formats. The records may be transferred into a repository in batches, or files may be individually dragged and dropped into appropriate subfolders from their originating applications. The latter approach is suitable for small quantities of electronic records or where an entire folder from an originating application can be dragged and dropped into one of the repository's subfolders. Depending on the method employed, an RMA repository may contain the actual records, or it may store links to word processing files, PDF files, e-mail messages, spreadsheets, or other records located elsewhere—on a network file server, for example.

Regardless of format and storage location, electronic records transferred to an RMA repository are considered the official copies for reference and retention purposes. As determined by an application planner, authorized persons have read-only access to specific records, and they cannot modify, replace, or delete them. Access privileges can be defined for individuals or groups at the folder, subfolder, or document level. Electronic records can be retrieved by browsing through subfolders, as is the case in paper filing installations. Alternatively, most RMA software allows folders, subfolders, and files to be indexed by user-defined fields. As an example, master contract folders may be labeled with project names and indexed by contract number, the name of the contractor, and other parameters. Similarly, a subfolder label may identify the contents as "addenda," with individual files being indexed by the date, the type of addendum, or other descriptors. Some RMA programs also support full-text indexing of word processing files, e-mail messages, and other character-coded documents. RMA software also provides a conclusive method of identifying successive versions of electronic records subject to revision.

Retrieved records are displayed by launching their originating applications where available. Alternatively, most RMA software incorporates viewing modules that can display electronic records in a variety of file formats, including text, image, and CAD formats. Depending on RMA software capabilities and user privileges, retrieved records may be printed, copied, annotated, attached to e-mail messages, or transferred to other applications. RMA software provides an audit trail for importing, retrieval, printing, exporting, copying, and other activity involving specific electronic records, including unsuccessful retrieval attempts as well as completed operations. The audit trail indicates the date the activity occurred, the type of activity, and the identity of the user who initiated the activity.

As noted previously, retention functionality is RMA software's distinctive characteristic. Authorized users can specify retention periods for electronic records in conformity with an organization's approved retention policies and schedules. Retention periods may be specified at the folder, subfolder, or individual file level. Retention periods may be based on elapsed time or events. In the former case, electronic records are eligible for destruction after a fixed period of time. In the latter case, electronic records are eligible for destruction after a designated event, such as termination of contract or completion of a project, plus a specified number of years. To address evidentiary requirements, RMA software allows authorized users to suspend destruction of or extend retention periods for specific electronic records or groups of records relevant for litigation, government investigations, audits, or other purposes.

Destruction of electronic records is not automatic: RMA programs generate lists of electronic records eligible for destruction on a specified date. The list is submitted to designated persons for approval before destruction is executed. RMA software provides safeguards against the unauthorized destruction of electronic records by issuing a warning to the user when such destruction is attempted. RMA programs can print lists, certificates of destruction, or other documentation for electronic records destroyed in conformity with an organization's retention policies and schedules.

Media Filing Equipment

By definition, removable electronic recording media are stored offline when not in use. The selection of appropriate filing equipment for removable electronic media is an important component of any program for the systematic management of active electronic records. As with paper documents, records managers may be expected to advise and assist individual program units in planning filing installations for electronic media, identifying procurement sources, and evaluating specific filing products for computer, video, and audio media. Media filing installations were once exclusively encountered in centralized computer, video, and audio facilities, but they are now commonplace in office areas. As desktop computers, network servers, camcorders, and other electronic recording devices proliferate, storage equipment is required for the removable media they generate.

In some organizations, records managers may develop written specifications and lists of approved products and suppliers to guide program units. Such an approach is usually acceptable in straightforward installations that involve the selection of a few cabinets for a relatively small quantity of media. In large, complex installations, however, media filing requirements must be carefully studied and various products analyzed on an application-by-application basis.

> *The size and type of filing equipment selected for a given situation must be well suited to and compatible with various installation and application characteristics, including the number and types of electronic media to be stored, the amount of available floor space and its floor-loading characteristics, the users' reference requirements, and the surrounding decor.*

Regardless of the selection methodology employed, the purpose of filing equipment is to make electronic media accessible when required for reference and to provide an appropriate repository for such media when not in use. The size and type of filing equipment selected for a given situation must be well suited to and compatible with various installation and application characteristics, including the number and types of electronic media to be stored, the amount of available floor space and its floor-loading characteristics, the users' reference requirements, and the surrounding decor. To knowledgeably advise program units, records managers must be familiar with the available types of media filing products and understand the situations in which they can be most effectively utilized.

Where high storage capacity is required, media filing installations have historically relied on shelf- or rack-type cabinets. Such products have been used for decades by centralized magnetic tape libraries in mainframe and minicomputer installations. As their name suggests, shelf-type filing cabinets resemble bookcases. Depending on cabinet design, magnetic tape reels may rest on shelves separated by wire racks that maintain the reels in an upright position. Alternatively, tape reels may be suspended from clips inserted into a specially designed hanger bar. Tape reels measuring 10.5 inches or less in diameter can be accommodated. In most cases, reels of different sizes can be intermixed within shelves.

Shelf-type filing cabinets are particularly well suited to large, active filing areas where they cost less than drawer-type equipment. They provide faster, more convenient access to electronic media and make more efficient use of available floor space. Compared to drawer-type equipment, shelf-type filing cabinets require considerably narrower aisles, an important consideration in climate-controlled vaults and other expensive storage areas, where space is often limited. In very active filing areas, shelf-type cabinets permit convenient, simultaneous access to magnetic tapes by multiple workers. Because drawers need not be opened and closed, media filing and refiling time and labor will be reduced.

Shelf widths range from two feet to more than four feet. A three-foot shelf can hold about 35 reels of magnetic tape wrapped in tape-seal belts and suspended from clips. Shelf capacities are reduced when wire racks are used. A typical cabinet contains five or six shelves, the latter configuration approaching a height of seven feet. Most shelf-type cabinets for magnetic tapes are available in single- or double-sided models. When configured with six 50-inch shelves, a double-sided unit can store up to 600 magnetic tape reels in less than 10 square feet of floor space. Individual cabinets can be fastened together side-by-side, front-to-back, or—if ceiling height permits—on top of one another. The simplest and least expensive models are open-faced units, but some shelf-type cabinets are equipped with retractable front panels or lockable tambour-style doors that can be closed over the shelves. Closed doors offer improved appearance, protection against dust, and greater security, although shelf-type cabinets can be considered truly secure only when installed into a vault area. As a potential limitation, retractable front panels consume some interior space and may be incompatible with adjustable shelves. With some units, shelves may slide forward in the manner of lateral-style, drawer-type filing cabinets.

Similar high capacity, shelf-type cabinets are available for half-inch data cartridges, including DLT and LTO cartridges. A two-foot shelf can hold about 25 cartridges stored in compartments demarcated by metal or plastic dividers. When compared to magnetic tape reels, as discussed in Chapter 2, half-inch data cartridges offer more compact storage, both in terms of media recording capacity and physical cartridge dimensions. A double-sided cabinet with 50-inch shelves can store about 1,200 cartridges in less than eight square feet of floor space. Some cabinet manufacturers offer kits to convert conventional magnetic tape shelving for half-inch data cartridges.

For maximum versatility, several manufacturers offer mixed-media storage units that use interchangeable shelves and racks to accommodate different sizes and types of electronic media within the same cabinet. Such a cabinet might, for example, contain one or more hanging bars for magnetic tape reels, several racks for half-inch data cartridges, and additional shelves for optical disks. If desired, shelves and hanging frames can be included for binders, computer printouts, file folders, microfilm, and microfiche trays, thereby permitting storage of electronic media and related human-readable documentation in the same cabinet.

Drawer-type vertical and lateral filing cabinets, the historical mainstays of paper document storage in office installations, are available for magnetic tape cartridges; videocassettes; audio cassettes; floppy disks; and optical disks. A typical 10-drawer unit measures approximately 26 inches wide by 30 inches deep by 60 inches high. Using dividers to partition drawers into multiple rows for media filing, such a cabinet can store approximately 1,250 half-inch data cartridges, 1,300 quarter-inch data cartridges, 2,300 quarter-inch minicartridges, 650 videocassettes, 2,700 audiocassettes, or 12,000 floppy disks.

Regardless of the media for which they are intended, drawer-type cabinets are typically manufactured of steel with selected aluminum and plastic parts. Key-controlled locks may be included, but they are seldom adequate for electronic records that require special security. Safe-type files, with drawers controlled by combination locks, are available for installations that require them. As discussed in Chapter 6, insulated, fire-resistant models are also available. As with paper files, guides and dividers can be used to separate media into categories. Out guides are also available to mark the locations of media that have been removed from files.

As a group, drawer-type filing cabinets are poorly suited to very active, high volume records management applications. Time and effort are required to pull out and replace drawers each time media are retrieved, and only one person at a time can conveniently access a given cabinet. In addition, drawer-type cabinets make inefficient use of available floor space. In particular, limitations on cabinet height result in a significant amount of wasted space between the top of the cabinet and the ceiling of the room where the cabinets are installed. Often, the tops of cabinets contain piles of media or documentation that are waiting to be filed or that the cabinet cannot conveniently accommodate. A variant, sometimes convenient approach to drawer-type filing consists of a computer workstation with one or two drawers for media storage.

Other media filing equipment is intended for applications where accessibility is more important than high storage capacity. CDs and DVDs, for example, can be stored in vinyl sleeves that are edge-punched for enclosure in ring binders. The binders can be stored on shelves, in drawer-type filing cabinets, or on work surfaces. Wheeled carts and desktop storage racks for magnetic tape cartridges are principally intended for centralized computing facilities. Such devices make the most active media conveniently available. They also provide a staging area for tapes that are waiting for processing or reshelving.

A wide variety of computer storage products, ranging from racks to covered trays, are commonly utilized to store optical disks, floppy disks, and other media encountered in desktop computer and LAN server installations. Similar products are available for video and audio recording media. Such storage units are usually constructed of plastic or metal. They are typically positioned near the computers on which the filed media will be processed. Capacities range from less than a dozen to more than a hundred pieces of media.

Tub files house frequently referenced media in an open cabinet accessed from the top. Often mounted on casters, tub files can store magnetic tape cartridges, optical disks, videocassettes, and audiocassettes. A tub desk, as its name suggests, combines a tub file with a work surface. Carousel files consist of storage racks or bins mounted on turntables that can be manually rotated.

Autochangers and Hierarchical Storage Management

Whether manual or motorized, the filing devices discussed to this point are designed for offline storage of electronic records. They require operator handling of removable media. When a given tape or disk is required for reference purposes, it must be located, removed from its cabinet or other container, and mounted in an appropriate drive for processing. When work is completed, the medium must be returned to its offline storage location.

As their name suggests, autochangers automate this process. Also known as *jukeboxes* or *library units*, **autochangers** are mass storage peripherals that provide unattended access to large quantities of computer-processible information. Available for most optical disks and many magnetic tape formats, autochangers store electronic media in stacks, bins, or other receptacles. Acting on instructions from an external computer, an autochanger selects a specified optical disk drive or magnetic tape cartridge and mounts it into a drive for recording or playback of information. Depending on the device, an autochanger may incorporate one or more optical disk drives or magnetic tape units. When processing is completed, the autochanger removes the medium from its drive and returns it to the appropriate stack or bin.

Autochangers operate as online peripherals, but specific optical disks or magnetic tapes are not brought online until they are requested and mounted. Consequently, autochangers are said to provide "nearline" access to the media they contain. Media loading times range from less than 15 seconds to more than one minute, depending on the device. A full interchange cycle, however, includes the time required to locate desired information once an optical disk or magnetic tape is mounted and to unload and reshelve any previously mounted media.

Optical disk autochangers have been used in document imaging and data storage implementations since the mid-1980s. Multifunctional models can accommodate 5.25-inch magneto-optical disks in write-once and rewritable formats. CD and DVD autochangers can accommodate read-only and recordable media. Magnetic tape autochangers are available for most data cartridge formats. They permit unattended backup in mainframe, minicomputer, and network server implementations.

Optical disk and magnetic tape autochangers can also be incorporated into **hierarchical storage management (HSM)** configurations. Few, if any, computer systems employ a single storage technology for electronic records. Mainframe and midrange computer installations invariably include hard drives and magnetic tape peripherals. Most desktop and notebook computers are configured with hard drives, plus some combination of floppy disk drives, CD drives, and DVD drives. Hierarchical storage management concepts categorize and rank computer storage devices and media by their responsiveness, capacities, and costs. A typical computer storage hierarchy can be depicted as a multilevel pyramid:

- **Apex.** A computer's main memory encompasses random-access memory (RAM) and read-only memory (ROM) circuits at the apex of the pyramid. Composed of semiconductor materials, main memory is fast but expensive and limited in capacity. It is reserved for computer programs and recorded information that are under immediate execution by a central processor. Because random-access memory requires an uninterrupted power supply to retain its contents, it is unsuitable for long-term storage. RAM circuits provide working storage. To prevent loss of information, the contents of random-access memory should be saved to nonvolatile media at frequent intervals. Read-only memory circuits, which have prerecorded contents, do not permit direct recording of information by computer users.

- **Second level.** Hard drives are the principal online storage peripherals in most computer installations. They are used for information that must be immediately and continuously available for display, editing, printing, or other purposes. As previously discussed, hard drives are the storage devices of choice for frequently referenced electronic records.

- **Third level.** Autochangers for optical disks and magnetic tape cartridges provide high-capacity nearline storage for information that may be referenced at any time, but that is less likely to be retrieved than information recorded on hard drives. Such information must be available conveniently, but a delay of several seconds or even several minutes is tolerable. Optical disk and magnetic tape autochangers sacrifice some responsiveness to obtain higher storage capacity than most hard drive configurations can provide. In some cases, autochangers offer lower storage costs than hard drives for very large quantities of information.

- **Base level.** Removable computer media, stored offline until needed, form the base of the hierarchical storage pyramid. Such media are used for backup operations and archiving of inactive electronic records. Those applications are characterized by infrequent reference. In the fourth level of the storage hierarchy, rapid access is less important than high capacity and low cost. Removable media may be stored in office areas or computer rooms. Backup copies are often stored offsite for vital records protection. Retrieval of information is subject to significant, but anticipated and presumably tolerable, delays. Access times for information recorded onto offline media may range from one hour to one day or longer, depending on the storage location.

When different magnetic and optical devices are combined in a computer configuration, a system manager or authorized users can employ operating system commands or utility programs to transfer electronic records from one level of the storage hierarchy to another, as reference activity or other considerations warrant.

Hierarchical storage concepts are implicitly implemented in any computer configuration that incorporates two or more storage technologies. When different magnetic and optical devices are combined in a computer configuration, a system manager or authorized users can employ operating system commands or utility programs to transfer electronic records from one level of the storage hierarchy to another, as reference activity or other considerations warrant. In mainframe, midrange computer, and network server installations, for example, inactive data files are routinely transferred from hard drives to magnetic tapes for offline storage. Similarly, document images may reside on hard drives for a relatively brief period of intense reference activity, then be transferred to an optical disk autochanger for additional months or years; ultimately, the optical disks may be removed from the autochanger for offline storage.

These operations require manual intervention, however; the system manager or user must determine when the transfer of electronic records should occur, keep track of storage locations of particular information, and initiate retrieval operations if transferred records must be restored to higher hierarchical levels for reference or other purposes. As a fully automated alternative, hierarchical storage management software can migrate computer files between storage components based on reference activity. Files are stored on hard drives, near the top of the storage hierarchy, when they are frequently referenced. As they become less active, they are moved to lower levels in the hierarchy: from online to nearline storage, where present, and eventually to offline storage when reference activity falls below a predetermined level. From the user's perspective, however, all information appears to reside on hard drives. When previously migrated files are requested, hierarchical storage management software automatically restores them to hard drives from lower hierarchical levels. Migration is typically based on a file's reference history, but additional factors, such as the need to free hard disk space for other purposes, may also be considered. Alternatively, file migration patterns may be based on the ages of electronic records, which are typically related to frequency of reference. As previously discussed, reference activity for most electronic records decreases with age.

Media Management

As discussed elsewhere in this book, computer, video, and audio records stored on magnetic and optical media are vulnerable to damage from inherent media instabilities, as well as from various external conditions and events such as inappropriate storage environments, careless handling, and improperly adjusted equipment. To protect their electronic records, organizations must develop formal guidelines for the storage, care, and handling of magnetic and optical media. When systematically implemented, such guidelines will minimize the potential for media damage, thereby increasing the likelihood that electronic records will remain useful for their intended purposes. The following discussion presents recommendations for the management of magnetic and optical media in the following areas:

1. Selecting blank media for electronic recordkeeping

2. Maintaining appropriate environments for media storage

3. Developing handling procedures and precautions to minimize the potential for physical damage to magnetic and optical media

> *...systematic care and handling guidelines will not lengthen the limited life spans of electronic media relative to paper and microfilm. Those life spans are defined by scientific facts not business practices.*

The following discussion is limited to removable electronic media—magnetic tapes, floppy disks, and optical media—suitable for offline storage of electronic records. Hard disks, as previously defined, are fixed storage media. Hard disk cartridges, while removable, are subject to damage from head crashes and other equipment malfunctions. They are intended for actively referenced information rather than offline storage. As a cautionary note, systematic care and handling guidelines will not lengthen the limited life spans of electronic media relative to paper and microfilm. Those life spans are defined by scientific facts not business practices. But the procedures and precautions discussed next will increase the likelihood that a given magnetic or optical medium will remain useful throughout its anticipated life span, whatever that may be.

Selecting Blank Media

A systematic approach to the management of magnetic and optical media for computer, video, or audio recording begins with the selection of appropriate blank media. Certain characteristics of magnetic and optical recording media can have a significant impact on their suitability for specific applications. Businesses, government agencies, and other organizations should purchase high-quality computer, video, and audio recording media from known manufacturers. Media of uncertain origin and potentially marginal quality should be avoided. Brand-name magnetic and optical media are preferable to off-brand products. Brand-name media are typically subjected to tightly controlled manufacturing processes and strict quality control procedures. Produced from high-quality materials, they are thoroughly tested prior to sale and have low error rates. While off-brand magnetic tapes and diskettes are often attractively priced, they may be poorly constructed. Off-brand magnetic media are particularly vulnerable to particle shedding, which can lead to equipment damage as well as loss of recorded information.

Similar procurement practices are advisable for optical disks. Through the late 1980s, optical disk users had little choice but to purchase blank media from manufacturers of optical disk drives. At that time, many optical disks were proprietary products, and drive manufacturers were the sole sources for procurement of compatible media. With the adoption of standards for certain optical disk formats, however, alternative procurement sources have become available. Recordable CDs, recordable DVDs, and 5.25-inch magneto-optical disks are sold by multiple suppliers, including mail-order companies that offer substantial discounts. For best results, optical recording media, like their magnetic counterparts, must be selected for quality rather than price.

Where applicable, blank magnetic and optical media should conform to specifications published by national and international standard-setting organizations.

Further, magnetic and optical media should comply fully with specifications established by the manufacturer of the equipment on which the media will be recorded or read. Fully compliant media are sometimes described as "qualified" or "certified" for use in a given drive.

Large quantities of magnetic or optical media should not be purchased far in advance of their anticipated recording dates—a portion of their estimated life spans will have elapsed before they are used.

Magnetic and optical media intended for long-term storage of electronic records should be recently manufactured and used as soon as possible after purchase. Lifetime estimates for magnetic and optical media begin with their manufacturing dates, not the date when information was recorded. Large quantities of magnetic or optical media should not be purchased far in advance of their anticipated recording dates—a portion of their estimated life spans will have elapsed before they are used. New media should be used for storage copies of important information. Recycled media—that is, magnetic tapes, diskettes, or rewritable optical disks that were previously used for data, video, or audio recording—are unacceptable for that purpose.

Prior to use, magnetic and optical media should be stored in environmental conditions specified by their manufacturers. Such specifications are rarely restrictive. Typically, the temperature in the storage area should range from 40 to 120 degrees Fahrenheit (5 to 48 degrees Celsius), with a relative humidity of 20 to 80 percent and a maximum wet bulb temperature of 80 degrees Fahrenheit (26 degrees Celsius). In some geographic locations, humidity limits may pose problems if blank media are kept in warehouses or other storage areas that lack air-conditioning. If possible, records managers should determine whether unrecorded magnetic media were previously stored under conditions of high temperature or high humidity. Such conditions promote media degradation through **hydrolysis**, a process in which absorbed moisture interacts with and damages magnetic storage media. If hydrolysis is suspected, a period of low-humidity storage is recommended to reverse media degradation. In any case, new electronic media should be acclimated to their environments for a period of at least 24 hours prior to recording.

For very important electronic records intended for long-term retention, two or more storage copies should be created. To provide the greatest protection against the possibility of defective media, magnetic tapes, diskettes, or optical disks of the same type but from different manufacturing lots should be utilized for each storage copy.

Some manufacturers offer several grades of magnetic or optical media with varying performance and price characteristics. Standard-grade magnetic tapes, diskettes, and optical disks—the least expensive variety—are often acceptable for routine information processing. Media of the highest available quality are preferred, however, for storage copies of important information. A manufacturer's most expensive recording media are sometimes describes as "super premium" products. Compared to standard-grade media, they provide greater protection against signal dropouts that cause permanent read/write errors. Super premium magnetic tapes and diskettes are more likely to produce error-free recordings and preserve high signal levels in storage. They are manufactured to higher tolerances than most equipment requires.

Similar gradations of product quality are encountered with video and audio recording media. Super premium video tapes feature very small magnetic particles for superior image quality, while super premium audio tapes can record a broader range of frequencies than their conventional counterparts. Among optical disks, gold CD-R media, also described as "gold and gold" disks, offer superior longevity and performance when compared to green CD-R media, which is described as "green and gold." Super-premium magnetic and optical media often carry a lifetime warranty against manufacturing defects. Less expensive media, by contrast, are warranted for specific time periods, usually one to three years. It should be noted, however, that manufacturers' warranties customarily provide replacement media as the sole remedy for defective products. Liability for damage to recorded information is specifically disavowed.

Super premium magnetic and optical media often incorporate additional features that their conventional counterparts lack. As an example, some manufacturers apply a proprietary coating to the reverse side of super premium magnetic tapes. Such backcoating reduces tape slippage and friction, improves scratch resistance, and minimizes the generation of debris that can produce signal dropouts. Some manufacturers combine backcoating with a conductive substrate to reduce static electricity, which can attract airborne debris. As an additional advantage, super premium tapes and disks typically have high-precision housings that minimize vibrations and otherwise enhance recording and playback. Although too often ignored in product selection, properly designed housings can have a significant impact on media performance and reliability. Over time, poorly constructed reels, cartridges, and cassettes can experience dimensional changes that may impede media loading, increase friction, and promote tape stretching. Poorly constructed housings can also damage read/write heads and drive mechanisms.

The stability of magnetic and optical media is not defined by published national or international standards, but accelerated aging tests conducted by media manufacturers and independent researchers provide lifetime estimates for some magnetic and optical recording materials. These tests suggest that certain media, such as metal particle tapes and gold Compact Discs, enjoy stability advantages over other types. Manufacturers of metal particle tapes claim life spans of at least 30 years for their products, and some research studies suggest that longer lifetimes are likely. Magnetic tape formats that employ metal particle recording materials include digital linear tape, eight-millimeter data cartridges and videocassettes, and digital audio tape. With CDs, gold resists oxidation, thereby enhancing stability. Where media longevity is more important than storage capacity or fast retrieval responsiveness, records managers may prefer recordable CDs and DVDs to magneto-optical disks. Although their drives are slower and provide less online capacity than magneto-optical products, recordable CDs and DVDs have longer life spans than magneto-optical disks.

Based on manufacturers' claims, lifetime estimates for CD-R range from 75 to 200 years, as compared with 30 years for magneto-optical disks. In the past, some 5.25-inch magneto-optical disk manufacturers offered a choice of glass or plastic substrates. Glass substrates are typically more stable than their plastic counterparts, which tend to absorb moisture. The newest magneto-optical drives, however, support plastic media exclusively.

Because it is closely packed, information recorded at high densities is particularly vulnerable to damage associated with debris. Submicron particles that pose no significant threat at lower recording densities can eradicate information from media recorded at higher densities. Lower recording densities may consequently prove safer for magnetic media that contain important information destined for long-term storage. This recommendation is most meaningful for video recording media. Video tapes intended for long-term storage should be recorded at the fastest speed, which equates to the lowest recording density. As an added advantage, the fastest recording speed also provides the highest image quality. In computer applications, high recording densities—which are associated with the newest products—may be required to satisfy capacity requirements. Further, the highest-density computer media have different chemical compositions and longer lifetime estimates than older, low-density formats.

To decrease the likelihood of print-through in magnetic recording, thin tapes should be avoided. Examples of thin tapes include C-120 audio cassettes, which provide two hours of recording time at 60 minutes per side; T-160 and T-180 VHS-type videocassettes, which can provide more than eight hours of recording time in the EP mode; and extra-length computer tapes. Several manufacturers offer low-print audio tapes specifically designed to minimize print-through.

Storage Copies

> *Their [storage copies] use is typically restricted to the creation of additional working copies in the event existing working copies are damaged.*

For effective management of magnetic and optical media, storage copies must be differentiated from working copies. The latter, as their name suggests, are intended for ongoing information processing and reference requirements; storage copies, in contrast, are created to satisfy retention requirements or for backup protection. Storage copies are invariably recorded on removable magnetic or optical media. They often contain inactive records transferred from hard drives. Regardless of content, storage copies are seldom referenced. Their use is typically restricted to the creation of additional working copies in the event existing working copies are damaged. They also permit recovery of information in the event of a system failure or other disaster.

Storage conditions can have a significant impact on the life spans of magnetic and optical media. The following discussion presents recommendations for facilities and procedures for storage copies of magnetic and optical media that contain important electronic records. Such storage copies are sometimes described as *master copies* to distinguish them from working copies. The recommended storage environment combines temperature and humidity controls with minimization of contaminants. It is designed to preserve the utility of information recorded onto magnetic and optical media for their estimated life spans. To the extent that an organization's storage conditions deviate from those discussed next, media life will be shortened.

High temperatures and high relative humidity accelerate the deteriorative aging of magnetic tapes and diskettes. In particular, a hot, humid storage environment promotes hydrolytic degradation of binder materials, which can have a devastating impact on the chemical composition and longevity of magnetic media. These effects are well documented in scientific literature. Prevention of binder hydrolysis is consequently the principal purpose of temperature and humidity control.

All publications on this subject affirm the advantages of a cool, dry storage environment for recorded magnetic media. Since the 1960s, however, journal articles, conference papers, and manufacturers' product literature have presented different, sometimes conflicting, temperature and humidity recommendations. Intended as an authoritative source, ISO 18923:2000, *Imaging Materials—Polyester-Base Magnetic Tape—Storage Practices* has replaced ANSI/NAPM IT9.23, which was published in 1996 as the first American national standard for storage of computer media. (Similar standards for storage of photographic media, including microfilm, have been available for decades and are well known to records managers.) As its title indicates, ISO 18923 pertains to storage copies of magnetic tapes with polyester base materials only; it does not cover diskettes or older magnetic tapes with acetate base materials. The standard specifies medium-term storage conditions, which are suitable for the preservation of recorded information for a minimum of 10 years, and extended-term storage conditions, which are suitable for the preservation of recorded information of permanent value. The standard does not state or imply, however, that magnetic tapes have permanent keeping properties.

For medium-term storage of magnetic tapes, ISO 18923 specifies a maximum temperature of 74 degrees Fahrenheit (23 degrees Celsius) with a relative humidity of 15 to 50 percent. Temperature variations in the storage area must not exceed 4 degrees Fahrenheit (2 degrees Celsius) over a 24-hour period. Humidity variations must not exceed 10 percent over a 24-hour period. Rapid cycling of temperature and humidity can damage binder materials and media substrates. For extended-term storage of magnetic tapes, ISO 18923 specifies the following combinations of temperature and relative humidity:

- A maximum temperature of 74 degrees Fahrenheit (23 degrees Celsius) with relative humidity ranging from 15 to 20 percent;
- A maximum temperature of 63 degrees Fahrenheit (17 degrees Celsius) with relative humidity ranging from 15 to 30 percent; or
- A maximum temperature of 52 degrees Fahrenheit (11 degrees Celsius) with relative humidity ranging from 15 to 50 percent.

As the temperature in the storage area rises, relative humidity must be more tightly controlled. Protection against environmental damage is enhanced when magnetic tapes are stored at a low temperature and low relative humidity, but very low temperatures can lead to separation of tape lubricants from binder materials. The minimum acceptable storage temperature is 46 degrees Fahrenheit (8 degrees Celsius). Temperature variations in the storage area must not exceed 4 degrees Fahrenheit (2 degrees Celsius) over a 24-hour period, as previously noted. Humidity variations for extended-term storage must not exceed 5 percent over a 24-hour period. These temperature and humidity recommendations are similar to specifications for microfilm storage presented in ISO 18911:2000, *Imaging Materials—Processed Safety Photographic Films—Storage Practices.*

For both medium-term and extended-term storage, an air-conditioned facility is usually required to maintain temperature and humidity within approved limits. Specialized air-conditioning equipment may be necessary to maintain low temperatures within the specified humidity ranges. Where air conditioning is not practical or required, as in underground storage areas with naturally low temperatures, dehumidification will usually be necessary.

Temperature and humidity ranges specified in ISO 18923 differ from storage recommendations previously presented by other authorities. Based on a survey of published scientific studies and manufacturers' specifications for extended storage of computer tapes, the first edition of this book recommended an air-conditioned facility with a temperature of 63 to 68 degrees Fahrenheit (17 to 20 degrees Celsius) with relative humidity ranging from 35 to 45 percent. A 1990 recommendation from the U.S. National Archives and Records Administration similarly specified a temperature of 62 to 68 degrees Fahrenheit (16 to 20 degrees Celsius) with relative humidity of 35 to 45 percent. Those recommendations do not conform to specifications presented in ISO 18923; at 62 to 68 degrees Fahrenheit, relative humidity in the tape storage area should not exceed 30 percent. SMPTE RP-103, *Recommended Practice*, published by the Society of Motion Picture and Television Engineers in 1982, specified a temperature of 67 to 74 degrees Fahrenheit (19 to 23 degrees Celsius) with a relative humidity of 30 to 70 percent as an acceptable range that minimizes the risk of media degradation while still permitting some flexibility in facility design. That specification is clearly out of compliance with ISO 18923. Storage recommendations by manufacturers of magnetic media are often less restrictive than those presented in ISO 18923 and other published authorities.

ISO 18923, as previously noted, is limited to magnetic tape. According to ISO 18925, *Imaging Materials—Optical Disk Media—Storage Practices*, the recommended environment for long-term storage of CDs is a maximum temperature of 74 degrees Fahrenheit (23 degrees Celsius) with relative humidity ranging from 20 to 50 percent.

Optical and magnetic media should never be stored in direct sunlight, placed near radiators, or otherwise exposed to intense heat sources. CD-R media, which are not housed in protective cartridges, may be damaged by exposure to light. Their dye layers can fade, with a resulting reduction of contrast that will impede retrieval of recorded information. CD-R media should be stored in jewel boxes or other containers when not in use, and the containers should be kept in closed cabinets. Light stability is not an issue with other optical disks.

Some magnetic and optical media are encapsulated in protective cartridges; however, they are not hermetically sealed. Dust and other contaminants can infiltrate media housings, rendering portions of recorded information unreadable. Very small dust particles can damage information recorded on high-density media. Although cleaning equipment and supplies are available for specific media, a clean, dust-free storage environment affords the best protection against contaminants. Air conditioning is usually necessary, both for temperature and humidity control and to remove pollutants. Most air-conditioner filters will capture dust particles measuring 10 microns or larger, but smaller particles can damage high-density magnetic recordings. Electronic air filters are typically necessary to trap such particles. ISO 18923 cautions against gaseous impurities such as ammonia, chlorine, peroxides, smoke, sulfides, and oxides of nitrogen.

Media storage areas must be cleaned regularly. To minimize scattering of dust particles and other potentially harmful contaminants, proper housekeeping habits must be observed. Some authorities recommend double-bagged or water-filtered vacuum cleaners as the preferred cleaning instruments. A vacuum system with an exhaust pipe is recommended to evacuate dust from the storage area. Static-free, chemically inert wipes are recommended for cleaning shelves and media containers. Ordinary dust rags, steel wool, abrasive cleaning materials, or chemical cleaning solutions should not be used. Floors should be dry-mopped or cleaned with a minimum amount of water followed by dry mopping. Floor wax and buffing machines can generate debris from abrasions caused by foot traffic.

To minimize the likelihood of cinching, magnetic tapes should undergo a slow unwind/rewind cycle to obtain a smooth, evenly tensioned pack prior to storage. **Cinching** occurs when the tape wrinkles or folds back onto itself. Until recently, many records professionals assumed that magnetic tapes in storage had to be unwound and rewound at regular intervals to alleviate accumulated stress or to tighten up loose tapes. Such rewinding is described as "exercising" or "retensioning" a tape. Some published sources recommend annual rewinding of magnetic tapes, which creates an enormous burden of time and labor costs in large media collections. Others report that rewind intervals as long as 3.5 years are acceptable for tapes stored in a controlled environment. Current thinking suggests, however, that periodic rewinding of magnetic tapes is not necessary. ISO 18923 is notably silent on this issue; periodic rewinding is not mentioned in its discussion of tape tensioning. Some media manufacturers advise against periodic rewinding of magnetic tapes, although they do recommend a full unwinding and rewinding to exercise stored tapes just prior to use.

> *ISO 18923 recommends inspection of magnetic tapes at five-year intervals, with more frequent inspections if temperature and humidity deviations have occurred.*

For early detection of dangers to recorded information, storage copies of magnetic and optical media should be inspected regularly. ISO 18923 recommends inspection of magnetic tapes at five-year intervals, with more frequent inspections if temperature and humidity deviations have occurred. Earlier publications recommended annual inspection of stored media. Frequency aside, inspection should involve a visual examination of the medium and its housing, followed by the retrieval or playback of recorded information. In a large collection of magnetic or optical media, individual examination of magnetic tapes, diskettes, or optical disks can prove prohibitively time-consuming. In such situations, a portion of the collection should be sampled. Alternatively, one or more control media containing test signals can be created for inspection purposes. Such control media should be created on the same system, with the same recording materials, and with the same recording characteristics as media that contain data, video images, or audio signals. The control media should be inspected on a regular basis for recording errors and physical damage. If permanent errors are detected in the control media, the entire media collection must be examined.

To provide additional protection against permanent error conditions that can render information unretrievable, the contents of magnetic tapes, diskettes, and optical disks can be copied onto new media at regular intervals. Such periodic copying is described as "renewing" magnetic or optical media. If new media are used, periodic copying can extend the life of recorded information indefinitely, thereby effectively overcoming problems associated with the nonarchival nature of electronic media. Copying can also be used to transfer information from deteriorating or obsolete media. Digitally-coded information can be copied an indefinite number of times without degradation. In the case of video and audio recording based on analog signals, however, a loss of image and/or sound quality from one generation of copy to the next inevitably occurs. This loss imposes limits on the number of times such information transfers can be performed. The extent of generation loss will vary with the quality of the original recording and the characteristics of equipment and media utilized for copy production. To minimize the adverse effects of temperature and humidity variations, media copying should be performed in the long-term storage environment itself.

Magnetic and optical media removed from an environmentally-controlled storage facility and taken to a work area with different environmental characteristics should be acclimated to the new environment before use to prevent moisture condensation. Such acclimatization is especially important for densely recorded digital media with narrow track widths. According to ISO 18923, temperature acclimatization for magnetic tapes can take 30 minutes to four hours, depending on the type of medium. Humidity acclimatization is a slower process, requiring one day to several weeks or longer. Wider tapes require longer acclimatization times than their thinner counterparts. The acclimatization process can be accelerated by unwinding and rewinding a magnetic tape several times, thereby exposing more of the tape surface to the new environment. Exposed media will achieve thermal equilibrium in seconds and moisture equilibrium in minutes. Magnetic media intended for long-term storage should be returned to an environmentally controlled facility immediately after use.

Computer tape cartridges, videocassettes, audiocassettes, diskettes, and optical disks should be stored in containers when not in use. To prevent the accumulation of dust and other contaminants, containers should be closed at all times, even when they are empty. To prevent accidental overwriting of information intended for long-term storage, write-enable rings should be removed from magnetic tape reels. With diskettes, magnetic tape cartridges and cassettes, and rewritable optical disks, write-protect tabs or other recording inhibitors should be activated.

To prevent accidental erasure of electronic records, permanent magnets and any other objects that generate magnetic fields are prohibited in storage areas for magnetic media. Most optical media are unaffected by magnetic fields, but magneto-optical disks are a notable exception. Their contents are subject to accidental erasure through inadvertent exposure to magnetic fields of sufficient strength. Combustible materials are likewise forbidden in media storage areas. Carbon dioxide or other dry fire protection methods should be employed. The method selected must not produce potentially harmful residues.

For magnetic and optical media that contain vital electronic records, as defined in Chapter 6, additional copies should be created for storage at a secondary site. The environmental controls and storage precautions outlined above should be implemented at the duplicate site.

Media Handling

All information storage media are imperiled by use. Improper handling is a common cause of physical damage to information recorded onto magnetic and optical media. Although certain magnetic tapes, diskettes, and optical disks are encapsulated in protective cartridges, they are not impervious to harm. Computer room personnel, administrative workers, or other employees may handle media in a careless manner. Magnetic tapes, diskettes, or optical disks may be damaged in transit or by improperly adjusted equipment. Media surfaces can be scratched or otherwise defaced, with resulting eradication of recorded information. Media handling and label preparation recommendations are provided in Figure 7.1.

The potential for media damage can be minimized or eliminated by strict adherence to proper handling procedures and precautions. The following discussion is based on recommendations presented in various published sources and in manufacturers' product literature. Care and handling of magnetic tapes is covered by ISO 18933, *Imaging Materials—Magnetic Tape—Care and Handling Practices for Extended Usage*, and ISO 18938, *Imaging Materials—Optical Discs—Care and Handling Practices for Extended Storage*. The recommendations presented here apply equally to working copies and storage copies, although the latter should be handled as little as possible. If frequent reference to storage copies is anticipated, one or more working copies should be made.

Contact with magnetic and optical media should be limited to protective housings. To guard against the damaging effects of skin oils and fingerprints, recording surfaces should never be touched. Portions of magnetic media routinely exposed require special handling precautions. With 5.25-inch diskettes, for example, recording surfaces are exposed in both the oval slot and hub ring. Magnetic tapes are likewise exposed along one edge of audiocassettes and data cassettes. When handling

Media Handling
and Label
Preparation
Recommendations

Figure 7.1

Media Handling Recommendations

- Magnetic and optical media must be handled gently at all times.
- Nine-track reels, for example, should be carried by their hubs to avoid damage to protruding tape edges.
- Magnetic tape cartridges and cassettes, diskettes, and optical disks should be handled by their edges.
- Magnetic and optical media should never be squeezed, placed under heavy objects, or otherwise subjected to pressure.
- Magnetic and optical media should be shelved in an upright, vertical position to prevent warping of containers.
- Magnetic and optical media should never be stacked horizontally—storage containers should not support the weight of other containers.
- All magnetic and optical media should be kept in protective containers when not in use.
- Storage copies of magnetic tape reels should always be enclosed in wraparounds, which should not be removed until a given tape is about to be used. Wraparounds should be replaced immediately after a tape is used.

Label Preparation Recommendations

- Adhesive labels should be used to identify media contents.
- Contents should be written on labels before attaching them to magnetic or optical media to avoid applying pressure to media.
- Erasers should not be used to modify media labels because they exert pressure and generate potentially troublesome debris.
- Outdated or otherwise incorrect labels should be removed and replaced with correct ones.
- Graphite pencils can likewise generate debris. They should not be used for label preparation.
- Adhesive labels should never be attached to the unrecorded sides of CDs or DVDs. Such labels may contain solvents that can damage a disk's protective coating and reflective metal layer.
- Permanent markers should not be used to label CDs or DVDs because they may contain solvents that can damage a disk's protective coating and reflective metal layer. Markers with water-soluble ink are acceptable, however.
- Some recordable CDs and DVDs are designed for use with ink jet or thermal transfer labels, but an improperly aligned label can put a CD or DVD out of balance when it is spinning at high speed.
- Removal of an adhesive label can damage a medium's protective coating, as can ballpoint pens or other writing instruments with sharp points.

---

such media, care must be taken to avoid contact with the exposed recording surfaces. Cartridge shutters, which expose certain magnetic and optical media when mounted into appropriate drives, should never be retracted manually.

High humidity is the leading cause of chemical damage to magnetic and optical media. When combined with high temperature, it can also promote the evaporation of lubricants and growth of fungus on magnetic tapes and diskettes.

Environmental conditions for working copies are less restrictive than those required for storage copies. For magnetic media, published sources and manufacturers' recommendations specify temperatures of 60 to 90 degrees Fahrenheit (16 to 32 degrees Celsius) with a relative humidity of 20 to 80 percent. Manufacturers' recommendations for optical disks, as previously noted, are even less stringent. High humidity is the leading cause of chemical damage to magnetic and optical media. When combined with high temperature, it can also promote the evaporation of lubricants and growth of fungus on magnetic tapes and diskettes. Very low humidity, on the other hand, increases static electricity, which attracts airborne debris and creates head/media interfaces problems. With magnetic tapes, low temperatures encourage loose tape windings, promote loss of lubricants, and increase the likelihood of cinching. A work area characterized by both high temperature and high humidity poses the greatest threat to magnetic and optical media. Combinations of low temperature and low humidity, while still potentially troublesome, pose fewer risks.

Work areas must be cleaned regularly:

- Dust should be cleared from containers prior to removing magnetic or optical media.
- Dust should be cleared from nine-track reels prior to removing wraparounds.
- Eating, drinking, and smoking should be prohibited in all areas where magnetic and optical media are used or stored.
  - Food and beverages may be accidentally spilled onto media.
  - Smoke particles are potentially destructive contaminants that can infiltrate media housings and storage devices.
- Coffee makers and other devices that create water vapors should not be operated in close proximity to magnetic and optical media because they increase the relative humidity in localized areas.
- Media should not be exposed to radiators, direct sunlight, or other sources of heat. Placing magnetic and optical media on top of tape or disk drives exposes them to both heat and dust.
- Some computer peripherals, such as printers, generate debris. Media and their associated storage equipment should be located as far away from such devices as is practical.

Although the dangers of accidental erasure, as discussed elsewhere in this book, are less significant than other threats to media stability, magnets must be prohibited in all offices or other work areas where magnetic or magneto-optical media are utilized. To avoid inadvertent exposure to magnetic fields in transit, a distance of three inches should be maintained between magnetic or magneto-optical recording media and the sides of transport containers. Specially designed transit cases are available for that purpose.

Magnetic and optical media should not be loaded into recording or playback equipment until the information they contain is ready to be processed. Media should be removed from equipment immediately after use and should never remain in equipment when not in use. Equipment operators and others responsible for the care and handling of magnetic media should visually inspect a given medium each time it is used. Unusual conditions should be reported for corrective action. Examples of such conditions include scratches, cracks, or other damage to media or protective casings; tape rubbing against the side flanges of a reel or cartridge; folded tape layers; buckling or cinching; excessive accumulations of dust or other contaminants on media or containers; and particle shedding. Suspect media should be tested immediately for usability. A new copy should be made of any medium that appears to be physically or chemically damaged.

Readability problems can often be resolved by cleaning CDs and DVDs prior to use. Dust can be removed from such media with a soft, lint-free cloth by wiping them in a circular motion from the center to the outer edges. Conventional household cleaners should never be used with read-only optical disks; they contain solvents that can damage a disk's protective overcoat. With magnetic tape and optical disks, temporary errors can usually be corrected by cleaning the media in a manner specified by the manufacturer. Several manufacturers offer cleaning devices and supplies for magnetic and optical media. Such kits should always be used in strict conformity with their manufacturers' directions. Repeated occurrences of temporary errors indicate media deterioration. Such tapes should be recopied as soon as possible.

Magnetic and optical media are affected by the storage peripherals in which they are read or recorded. Increased operating speeds and recording densities make the condition of storage equipment an important consideration in a systematic program for care and handling of magnetic media. Recommendations for the use of storage peripherals include:

- All storage peripherals must be in proper operating condition. Defective devices can damage magnetic and optical media. They should be taken out of service and not used until repaired.

- Preventive maintenance procedures recommended by equipment manufacturers should be enforced.

- Machine components that come into contact with magnetic and optical media should be cleaned regularly in a manner specified by the equipment manufacturer because dust, oxide particles, and other contaminants can affect recording and playback. Examples of such components include read/write heads, guides, and rollers.

- Tape drives in minicomputer and mainframe installations should be cleaned once per shift and whenever permanent errors are encountered. Read/write heads and tape cleaner blades should be cleaned twice per shift and immediately before any critical operation. Tape-drive guides must be properly adjusted to prevent edge damage.

Summary

Within computer storage media, electronic records are organized into files that are grouped into directories and, in the case of high-capacity media, subdirectories. These entities are sometimes equated with the familiar components of paper-based filing systems. Although such comparisons are somewhat forced, electronic storage media can be viewed as the computer-based counterparts of file cabinets, while directories and subdirectories are compared to drawers or portions of drawers. In graphical computing environments, directories and subdirectories are typically represented by folders, while files are represented by icons. The term "file" is seldom applied to audio and video recordings, but parallels can be drawn with individual audio selections and video programs contained on a given tape or disk.

Systematic file grouping and labeling practices are prerequisites for effective management of electronic records. Clear, informative labeling is essential for identification of removable computer, audio, and video media. In computer applications, internal volume labels should also be assigned. Unrelated files should not be intermixed within media, directories, or subdirectories. Meaningful file and directory names are critical for accurate identification. Such names should reflect the purpose and contents of specific directories and files. Increasingly, computer operating systems permit long file and directory names. Even where constraints are imposed by the operating system, mnemonic names that reflect file content can usually be devised, and file extensions can be effectively utilized to designate particular file types. Despite proper naming practices, files may become "lost" within high-capacity storage media. Addressing this problem, utility programs are available that will search all or part of a designated medium for files containing specified character strings.

Content management products and records management application (RMA) software are designed to categorize, store, and control electronic records throughout their life cycles. Available products can import electronic records in various formats from their originating applications and index them for retrieval when needed. Useful features include flexible retrieval capabilities, version control functionality, audit trails for reference activity, and automatic deletion of electronic records when their retention periods have elapsed.

A wide variety of filing equipment is available for removable electronic media. In large, active filing areas, shelf- or rack-type cabinets have historically been preferred for their high media capacities. Models are available for various combinations of disks and tapes. Mixed-media units can accommodate different sizes and types of media on interchangeable shelves and racks. Drawer-type cabinets are suitable for smaller electronic media, including magnetic tape cartridges, diskettes, certain optical disks, audiocassettes, and videocassettes. Other filing configurations include desktop trays, binders, and tub files. Autochangers, also known as *jukeboxes* and *library units*, are available for optical disks and magnetic tapes. They provide unattended, nearline access to large quantities of electronic records. Optical disk autochangers have been widely implemented in document imaging implementations. Magnetic tape autochangers permit unattended backup of hard drives in mainframe, midrange computer, and network server installations. Autochangers also play an important role in hierarchical storage management (HSM) configurations.

Formalized guidelines for the storage, care, and handling of magnetic and optical media can minimize the potential for damage to electronic records, thereby increasing the likelihood that such records will remain useful for their intended purposes. Such guidelines must cover the selection of blank recording media, storage environments, and media handling procedures and precautions. Organizations should purchase high-quality blank magnetic and optical media from known manufacturers. Such media should fully comply with the requirements of the equipment in which they will be recorded or read, and they should be used only for their intended purposes. New rather than recycled media should be utilized for important electronic records intended for long retention. Prior to use, unrecorded media should be stored under conditions recommended by their manufacturers.

Working copies of magnetic and optical media are designed to satisfy ongoing information processing and reference requirements. Storage copies, in contrast, are created for retention or backup purposes. Strict environmental controls, minimization of contaminants, and proper handling procedures are essential if storage copies are to remain useful for the maximum possible time. To provide the greatest protection for very important electronic records, two or more storage copies should be created. A clean storage area with tightly controlled temperature and relative humidity must be provided. Storage copies of magnetic and optical media should be inspected at regular intervals. To avoid damage from careless handling or improperly adjusted equipment, storage copies should be referenced as infrequently as possible. Careless handling is a common cause of physical damage to working copies of electronic media. Proper handling procedures must be strictly enforced. Equipment that creates and retrieves electronic records must be properly maintained.

Suggestions for Further Study and Research

Since the early 1980s, electronic records have been discussed in a large and rapidly growing body of books, articles, conference papers, and other publications that contain more detailed or otherwise different treatments of topics covered in this book. Library databases, which are widely searchable at library Web sites, are the best resources for citations to books and monographs about electronic records. Large national and academic libraries are likely to have the most complete holdings. For a directory of online library catalogs, see www.libraryspot.com. The online catalog of the Library of Congress (www.loc.gov) is a good starting point. "Electronic Records" is a Library of Congress subject heading, as are "Electronic Public Records," "Computer Storage Devices," "Data Recovery (Computer Science)," "Data Protection," "Data Warehousing," "File Organization (Computer Science)," "Magnetic Recorders and Recording," "Magnetic Memory (Computers)," "Magnetic Disks," "Magnetic Tapes," "Optical Disks," and "Optical Storage Devices."

Various business indexes and databases contain citations to articles about electronic records in professional journals, popular periodicals, and newspapers. Examples of online databases likely to be available in many medium-size and larger academic and public libraries include ABI Inform, Business and Management Practices (BaMP), Business and Industry Database, Business Dateline, Globalbase, Management Contents, Newsletter Database, PROMT, Trade and Industry Database, and Wilson Business Abstracts. Articles indexed in these databases range from brief overviews of electronic recordkeeping issues and concerns to detailed case studies that describe records management practices in specific companies or government agencies.

Scientific and technical databases index articles, reports, conference papers, and other publications that deal with trends and innovations in information storage and retrieval, as well as the capacities, performance attributes, life spans, and other characteristics of specific magnetic and optical media. Examples of such databases include Abstracts in New Technology and Engineering (ANTE), Computer Database, Ei COMPENDEX (Engineering Index), Information Science Abstracts, INSPEC, SciSearch (Science Citation Index), and Wilson Applied Science and Technology Abstracts.

The legal status of electronic records, particularly their role in evidence, is examined in hundreds of articles in law reviews and other legal publications. The well-known Lexis and Westlaw online services provide the most comprehensive indexing of these legal information sources. Other useful legal databases include the cases and codes section of Findlaw (www.findlaw.com/casecode/), the Legal Resource Index and the Wilson Index to Legal Periodicals and Books. The Law Library of Congress, the world's largest collection of law books and legal resources, provides an excellent online guide to U.S. and international legal resources. The Code of Federal Regulations can be accessed through several Web sites, including www.gpoaccess.gov. Other Web sites provide online access to state and local regulations.

Google and other Web search engines are obvious starting points to locate pertinent Web sites about electronic recordkeeping topics, but the voluminous results they deliver can require time-consuming browsing. At the time of this writing, for example, a Google search for Web pages containing the phrase "electronic records" retrieved over 3.11 million items covering policies, procedures, practices, projects, and problems in varying levels of detail and with varying degrees of reliability and usefulness. When searches are narrowed to focus on specific topics, fewer items are retrieved, but the results are still unwieldy. For example, a Google search for "electronic records" and "vital records" retrieved over 17,000 items, and a search for "electronic records" and "file formats" retrieved over 11,000.

The Web sites of national, state, and provincial archival agencies contain much useful information about electronic records, including policies, procedures, regulations, and position papers. Examples include the Web sites of the U.S. National Archives (www.archives.gov), National Archives of Canada (www.archives.ca), National Archives of Australia (www.naa.gov.au), and British Public Records Office (www.pro.gov.uk). Readers are cautioned that Web addresses and site contents are subject to change. Vendor Web sites are good starting points for technical specifications, case studies, white papers, and other information about computer storage media, electronic content management software, records management application software, and other product groups discussed in Chapters 2 and 7.

Previous editions of this book included photos of computer storage devices and media. Those photos played an informative role when computer storage products were new and unfamiliar to many records managers, but that is no longer the case. Photos were consequently omitted from this edition. Readers who want to see examples of specific products can consult the Web sites of storage equipment and media manufacturers and resellers. Examples include: www.westerndigital.com, www.maxell.com, www.emc.com, www.maxtor.com, www.hp.com, www.ibm.com, www.imation.com, www.lacie.com, www.verbatim.com, www.plasmon.com, www.sony.com, www.quantum.com, www.tandbergdata.com, www.seagate.com, www.fujifilm.com, and www.tdk.com. Readers are cautioned that the Web addresses of computer storage companies may be affected by mergers, acquisitions, or other corporate events.

Glossary

The following listing provides brief definitions of selected terms and acronyms pertaining to electronic records as they are used in this book. For fuller explanations of specific terms, relevant portions of individual chapters should be consulted.

A

AAC. Advanced audio coding, a format for digital audio.

AIFC. A compressed implementation of the audio interchange file format (AIFF); a compression method for digitized audio information.

AIT. Advanced intelligent tape, an 8mm tape cartridge format developed by Sony.

Alloy. A combination of two or more metals. Many magnetic and optical recording materials consist of alloys.

analog coding. A coding scheme in which information is represented by continuously varying signals. Electronic records created by many audio and video systems employ analog coding.

ASCII. The American Standard Code for Information Interchange, a widely utilized coding scheme that specifies bit patterns for computer-processible information.

ASCII text file. A file that contains characters represented by the American Standard Code for Information Interchange. ASCII text files, which can be produced by many word processors and other computer programs, are typically devoid of formatting information.

autochanger. A robotic retrieval unit that provides unattended access to information recorded on optical disks or magnetic tapes; also known as a *jukebox* or *library unit*.

B

backup. The process of duplicating information, primarily for protection against damage or loss.

Beta format. A half-inch video tape cassette format introduced by Sony Corporation in 1975.

bit-mapped image files. Computer-processible files that encode images as patterns of dots, each represented by one or more bits that define the tonal values of a given area within an image.

bits per inch (bpi). The most common measure of linear recording density in computer systems.

Blue-ray. A high-capacity DVD format developed for high-definition video and subsequently adapted for computer storage.

bpi. See *bits per inch.*

C

camcorder. A video camera that incorporates a videocassette recorder.

CD. See *compact disc.*

CD-R. Compact disc-recordable, a write-once optical disk in the compact disc format.

CD-ROM. Compact disc-read only memory, a read-only optical disk format for computer-processible information.

CD-RW. Compact disc—rewritable, an erasable optical disk in the compact disc format.

CFR. Code of Federal Regulations.

CGM. Computer graphics metafile, a format for computer-processible images.

coercivity. The amount of force, usually measured in oersteds, required to orient magnetic particles.

cinching. The wrinkling or folding of magnetic tape back onto itself.

cold site. An unfurnished space suitable for the installation of computer and communications equipment.

compact disc (CD). Designation for a group of optical disk products that are based on specifications developed jointly by Sony and Philips. Compact disc formats are available for audio signals, computer data, and other information. Each format is identified by its own acronym.

computer graphics metafile format (CGM). An image file format supported by many computer programs.

CSV. Comma separated values, a computer file format for importing and exporting spreadsheets and databases.

C-type cassette. A four-millimeter magnetic tape format used for audio recording and, occasionally, data storage; also known as a *Philips-type cassette.*

Curie point. The temperature at which a given recording material loses magnetization.

D

DASD. Direct access storage device, an acronym applied to hard disk drives in large computer installations.

DAT. See *digital audio tape.*

data archiving. The process of transferring electronic records from online storage devices, such as hard drives, to removable recording media, such as magnetic tape or optical disks, for offline storage. In most cases, the archived data is relatively inactive and does not need to be accessible online.

database. A file containing records organized into one or more data elements, called *fields*, which store particular categories of information.

data compression. Techniques, implemented through computer programs, that reduce the amount of storage space required for a given quantity of information. Data compression is encountered in computer, audio, and video systems.

data interchange format (DIF). The first spreadsheet program developed for microcomputers.

data migration. (1) The process of moving data from one information system or storage medium to another. (2) The process of converting electronic records to new file formats or storage media to maintain their usability over time.

data warehouse. A large database structured to support decision-making.

digital audio tape (DAT). A four-millimeter magnetic tape format utilized for audio or data recording.

digital coding. A coding scheme that represents information by predetermined sequences of bits. Electronic records created by computer systems employ digital coding, as do certain audio and video records.

Digital Data Storage (DDS) Manufacturers Group. An organization that defines specifications and data recording formats for digital audio tape.

digital document images. Images that are true copies of the documents from which they were made. A true copy is one that accurately reproduces an original document.

digital document imaging systems. Bit-mapped image representation systems that can complement, supplement, or replace paper filing systems and microfilm.

digital linear tape (DLT). A high-capacity recording media that uses half-inch magnetic tape enclosed in a plastic cartridge.

directory. A table of contents for an electronic storage medium.

diskettes. Platter-shaped magnetic recording media with flexible substrates; also known as *floppy disks.*

drawing interchange format (dxf). A file format used by computer-aided design programs.

DV cassette. A magnetic tape format for digital video recording.

DVD. Digital versatile tape, an optical disk format intended as a successor to compact discs. DVD formats include read-only, recordable, and rewritable varieties, each identified by its own acronym; also known as *digital video disc.*

DXF. Drawing interchange format, a popular format for CAD files.

E

EBCDIC. The Extended Binary Coded Decimal Interchange Code, a coding scheme that specifies bit patterns for computer-processable information.

ECM. Electronic content management, document content management software that has been broadened to accommodate a wider variety of digital content, including Web pages, blogs, wikis, video clips, and audio clips.

EDI. Electronic data interchange. The transmission of computer-processable purchase orders, invoices, and other transaction-oriented information between organizations.

e-discovery. Discovery-related activities conducted during litigation that involve electronic records.

eight-millimeter tape. A magnetic tape format for data and video recording.

electronic record. A record that contains machine-readable, as opposed to human-readable, information.

electronic signature. Any electronic method of signing a computer-processable record.

EPS. Encapsulated PostScript, a vector-based image file format based on the PostScript page description language.

extension. An optional addition to a file name used with certain computer operating systems. It typically indicates the type of information that the file contains.

F

federated searching. Simultaneous searching of multiple information resources.

ferromagnetic. A type of recording material that can be easily magnetized and will retain magnetization in the absence of a magnetic field.

field. A data element within a database record.

file. A general term that denotes a collection of records. In most cases, the term is modified by one or more adjectives that indicate the type of information a file contains, the applications it serves, or its relationship to other files.

fixed magnetic disk drive. A magnetic disk drive with nonremovable, rigid platters. It is the most common type of hard disk drive.

flash memory. Computer storage media that utilize solid-state technology.

floppy disk. A platter-shaped magnetic recording medium with a flexible substrate; also known as a *diskette.*

FRCP. Federal Rules of Civil Procedure.

FRE. Federal Rules of Evidence.

G

gamma ferric oxide. A material widely-utilized for magnetic recording. It consists of small iron particles that are dispersed in a binder compound on disk or tape substrates.

GIF. Graphics image file format, a widely utilized format for computer images in Internet, intranet, and extranet implementations. It generates low-resolution images that are gradually improved as more detailed information arrives.

Group 3. A file compression method employed in electronic document imaging and facsimile installations.

Group 4. A file compression method employed in electronic document imaging and facsimile installations.

H

half-inch data cartridges. Magnetic tape formats developed by IBM and subsequently adopted by other manufacturers. Examples include the 3480, 3490, 3490E, and 3590 magnetic tape formats.

hard disk. A type of magnetic disk that has a rigid aluminum substrate. Hard disks are the storage media of choice in high performance computing applications. They may be fixed or removable.

hard disk array. A group of hard drives that are treated by a computer as a single logical drive for recording and retrieval purposes.

hard disk cartridge. A rigid magnetic disk enclosed in a removable plastic cartridge.

hard drive. A magnetic disk drive with a nonremovable hard disk.

HDTV. High-definition television, a technology that increases the amount of detail visible in television images.

helical scan recording. A method of magnetic tape recording that uses two or more read/write heads to record data in narrow diagonal tracks.

hot site. A fully-equipped, standby computing facility available to subscribers for emergency use on short notice.

HSM. Hierarchical storage management. HSM concepts categorize and rank computer storage devices and media by their responsiveness, capacities, and costs.

HTML. Hypertext markup language, a mark-up language used for information on the Internet and in intranets and extranets.

hydrolysis. A process in which absorbed moisture interacts with and damages magnetic storage media.

I

IEC. International Electrotechnical Commission, the group that standardized designations for magnetic materials employed in audio tape recording.

image file. A file that contains computer-processable images.

information life cycle. The distinct phases of the existence of information, from creation to final disposition.

inter-record gaps. Blank spaces left between groups of records on nine-track magnetic tapes. Also known as *inter-block gaps*, they can significantly reduce the data storage capacity of a given tape.

J

JBIG. An image compression method developed by the Joint Bi-level Experts Group.

JPEG. An image compression method developed by the Joint Photographic Experts Group for use with photographs. It is an interrelated group of algorithms that supports various combinations of image quality and compression.

JPEG file interchange format (JFIF). The file format associated with JPEG compression algorithms, which were developed by the Joint Photographic Experts Group.

jukebox. A robotic retrieval unit that provides unattended access to information recorded on optical disks or magnetic tapes; also known as an *autochanger*.

K-L

key field. A field selected for indexing within records contained in a database.

longitudinal recording. A form of magnetic recording in which magnetizable particles are oriented horizontally within tracks on a disk or tape.

lossless compression algorithms. Algorithms that achieve compression without omitting any information from computer files.

lossy compression algorithms. Algorithms that reduce storage requirements by omitting information from computer files.

LTO. Linear tape-open, a magnetic tape technology for computer data.

M

machine-readable information. A coded form of information suitable for processing by computers or other machines such as audio or video devices. Electronic records, by definition, contain information in machine-readable form.

magnetic card. An obsolete, rectangular medium coated with a magnetizable recording material.

magnetic disk. A platter-shaped substrate coated with a magnetizable recording material.

magnetic tape. A thin ribbon or strip of polyester coated with a magnetizable recording material. It may be wound onto a reel or packaged in a cartridge or cassette.

magneto-optical disk. A rewritable optical disk that uses lasers to record information on a magnetizable material.

metadata. Information that defines and describes an electronic record but is not part of the record.

metafile format. A computer file format that transcends specific programs.

microcassette. An audio tape recording format utilized in voice dictation systems.

microfloppy disk. A 3.5-inch diskette.

minicassette. An obsolete audio tape recording format utilized in voice dictation systems.

mini-DV cassette. A digital video tape recording medium intended for use in camcorders.

minifloppy disk. A 5.25-inch diskette.

MPEG-2. A compression method developed by the Motion Picture Experts Group for such applications as digitized video images and computer animation.

MP3. A compressed file format for digital audio information.

N

nearline storage. An autochanger that provides unattended access to information recorded on optical disks or magnetic tape.

nine-track tape. A magnetic tape that contains information recorded in nine parallel tracks running down the length of the tape. Nine-track tape measures one-half inch wide and is wound around a reel.

NTSC. A television standard developed by the National Television Systems Committee.

O

ODF. Open document format, a file format developed by the Organization for the Advancement of Structured Information Standards.

oersted. A measure of coercivity in magnetic recording systems.

offline information. Information stored apart from the device on which it will be retrieved or played back.

online information. Information immediately and continuously available to a computer.

optical cards. Wallet-size media coated with an optical recording material; also known as *optical memory cards*.

optical disk. A platter-shaped medium on which information is recorded by altering the light reflectance properties of selected areas.

optical tape. A ribbon or strip of polyester coated with an optical recording material.

P

PAL. The Phase Alternation Line standard for television images.

paper tape. An obsolete computer format that stored digitally-coded information as predetermined patterns of holes punched into a paper ribbon.

PDF. Portable document format, a file format developed by Adobe for machine-readable documents with complex formatting characteristics

PDF-A. A version of the PDF format developed for archival applications.

PET. Polyethylene terephthalate, a material used for magnetic tape substrates.

phase-change recording. A type of optical recording that employs materials capable of changing from a crystalline to an amorphous state, or vice versa.

Philips-type cassette. A magnetic tape format utilized for audio recording and, occasionally, data storage; also known as a *C-type cassette.*

playback stability. The ability to retrieve previously recorded information.

portable network graphics (PNG). An image format developed as a replacement for GIF for use on the World Wide Web.

proprietary file format. A computer file format associated with specific computer software.

punched cards. Paper cards that contain characters represented by predetermined patterns of holes punched in designated columns.

Q

QIC formats. A group of standard recording formats for quarter-inch magnetic tape cartridges.

quadraplex recorder. An older type of video recorder that utilized two-inch tape.

R

RAID. Redundant array of inexpensive disks; alternatively, redundant array of independent disks. RAID devices are hard drive arrays with fault-tolerant attributes.

rare-earths. A type of recording materials employed by magneto-optical disks.

read-only optical disk. A type of optical disk that contains prerecorded information. Produced by a mastering and replication process, such disks have no recordable properties.

read/write optical disk. A type of optical disk that permits direct recording.

real-time backup. A disaster recovery method that employs simultaneous or nearly simultaneous recording of information by multiple computers.

recording stability. The period of time that a given magnetic or optical storage medium permits reliable recording of new information.

records inventory. A detailed listing that includes the types, locations, dates, volumes, equipment, classification systems, and usage date of an organization's records in order to evaluate, appraise, and organize the information. It is a fact-finding survey that identifies and describes the characteristics of records created, received, and maintained by all or part of a corporation, government agency, educational institution, professional services firm, not-for-profit entity, or other organization.

records retention schedule. A list of records series maintained by all or part of an organization, together with the period of time that each series is to be kept.

records series. A group of logically-related records that supports a specific business or administrative operation.

reference activity. The frequency with which a given records series is consulted for operational or other purposes.

remanence. The magnetism that remains in magnetic recording material when an external magnetic field is removed.

removable disk systems. Magnetic or optical disk systems that permit removal of platter-shaped media from drives on which they are recorded or read. The removable disks may feature rigid or plastic substrates. They are often encapsulated in protective cartridges to facilitate handling.

rewritable optical disk. A type of optical disk that permits erasure and overwriting of previously recorded information.

risk analysis. An analysis to determine and evaluate risks; also known as *risk assessment.*

RMA. Records management application, a type of software.

RTF. Rich text format, a file format developed by Microsoft for cross-platform exchange of documents.

S

SDLT. Super digital linear tape, a high-capacity version of DLT technology.

SECAM. The sequential couleur a memoire format for television images. French for "Sequential Color with Memory".

security copies. Additional record copies created as protective measure; also known as *backup copies.*

serpentine recording. A recording format that features two or more groups of parallel tracks that run from the beginning to the end of a magnetic tape and back again.

SGML. Standard generalized markup language. A mark-up language used on Internet sites.

solid-state media. Computer storage media, such as flash memory cards and USB flash drives, that utilize semiconductor materials.

source documents. Paper documents that contain information to be converted to electronic records.

structured electronic records. The contents of computer databases that have a prescribed, repetitive format.

substrate. The base material, as applied to electronic storage media, on which a recording layer is coated. Substrates may be rigid or flexible. They are usually platter-shaped or ribbon-shaped.

SAIT. Super AIT, a high-capacity version of Sony's advanced intelligent tape format.

SuperDisk. A high-capacity floppy disk format; also known as *LS-120*.

Super-VHS. A variant of the VHS video tape recording format that yields high-quality images.

SYLK. Symbolic link format, a file format developed by Microsoft for the interchange of information among computer programs.

T

tagged image file format (tif). An industry standard format supported by many imaging programs.

TCO. Total cost of ownership, a concept that relates to the true cost of acquiring and using information technology.

tellurium. Recording material employed by some optical disks.

text file. A computer file that contains character-coded representations of letters of the alphabet, numeric digits, punctuation marks, and other symbols encountered in typewritten documents. Text files may be created by word processing programs, electronic mail programs, or other computer software.

TIF. Tagged image file format, a file format for computer-generated images.

transition metals. Recording materials employed by magneto-optical disks.

Type I magnetic tape. Audio recording tape coated with gamma ferric oxide.

Type II magnetic tape. Audio recording tape coated with chromium dioxide.

Type IV magnetic tape. Audio recording tape coated with iron particles.

U

UBREA. Uniform Business Records as Evidence Act.

UDO. Ultra density optical, a high-capacity optical disk format.

UL. Underwriters Laboratories.

U-matic. An obsolete video recording format that utilized three-quarter-inch tape enclosed in cassettes.

Unicode. A computer coding scheme that can represent many different characters in multiple alphabets.

unstructured electronic records. Electronic records, such as word processing files and e-mail messages, that have no prescribed organization or format.

URE. Uniform Rules of Evidence.

V

vector-based image format. A method of defining computer-processible images as geometrical shapes; also known as *object-oriented* or *shape-defined images.*

VHS. A half-inch video tape cassette format.

VHS-C. VHS-compact, a variation of the VHS format designed for use with camcorders.

video disk. A platter-shaped medium that stores video images accompanied by audio signals. Most video disks are read-only media.

virus. A computer program that can insert a copy of itself into another program.

vital record. A record that is essential to an organization's mission.

vital records program. A set of policies and procedures for the systematic, comprehensive, and economical control of losses associated with vital records.

volume. A logical subdivision created when a physical storage medium, such as a magnetic disk, is partitioned into segments.

VXA. A magnetic tape system that uses packet technology for high reliability and error-free data recovery.

W

WAV. Waveform audio file, a format for digital audio information.

write-once optical disk. A nonerasable type of read/write optical disk; also known as a *WORM disk.*

Index

About the Author

William Saffady is a Professor at the Palmer School of Library and Information Science, Long Island University in New York City, where he teaches courses on information management topics. He previously held similar faculty positions at the State University of New York at Albany, Vanderbilt University in Nashville, TN, and Pratt Institute in New York City.

Dr. Saffady is the author of over three dozen books and many articles on records management, document imaging, information storage technologies, office automation, and library automation. Books published by ARMA International include *Digital Document Management; Records and Information Management: Fundamentals of Professional Practice; Electronic Document Imaging: Technology, Applications, Implementation; Managing Electronic Records,* Fourth Edition; *Micrographics: Technology for the 21st Century; Cost Analysis Concepts and Methods for Records Management Programs; Knowledge Management: A Manager's Briefing;* and *Records and Information Management: A Benchmarking Study of Large U.S. Industrial Companies.*

In addition to teaching and writing, Dr. Saffady serves as an information management consultant, providing training and analytical services to corporations, government agencies, and other organizations.

About the Association

ARMA International is the leading professional organization for persons in the expanding field of records and information management.

As of February 2009, ARMA has about 10,000 members in the United States, Canada, and 37 other countries around the world. Within the United States, Canada, New Zealand, Japan, Jamaica, and Singapore, ARMA has nearly 150 local chapters that provide networking and leadership opportunities through monthly meetings and special seminars.

ARMA's mission is to provide education, research, and networking opportunities to information professionals, to enable them to use their skills and experience to leverage the value of records, information, and knowledge as corporate assets and as contributors to organizational success.

The ARMA International headquarters office is located in Lenexa, Kansas, in the Kansas City metropolitan area. Office hours are 8:30 A.M. to 5:00 P.M., Central Time, Monday through Friday.

ARMA International
13725 W. 109th St., Ste 101
Lenexa, Kansas 66215
913.341.3808
800.422.2762
Fax: 913.341.3742
hq@arma.org
www.arma.org